IN SEARCH OF THE

MAGIC OF

FINDHORN

IN SEARCH OF THE
MAGIC OF
FINDHORN

KARIN BOGLIOLO
& CARLY NEWFELD

FINDHORN
Press

First published by Findhorn Press 2002

ISBN 1 899171 69 X

British Library Cataloguing-in-Publication Data.
A catalogue record for this book is available from
the British Library.

Edited by Tony Mitton
Illustrations © Marko Pogačnik 2002
Front cover by Dale Vermeer Design
Back cover design by Thierry Bogliolo
Layout by Thierry Bogliolo

Printed and bound by WS Bookwell, Finland

Published by
Findhorn Press
305a The Park, Findhorn
Forres IV36 3TE
Scotland, UK

tel 01309 690582
fax 01309 690036
e-mail: info@findhornpress.com

findhornpress.com

CONTENTS

TO THE GLOBAL FINDHORN
FAMILY—PAST, PRESENT
AND FUTURE.

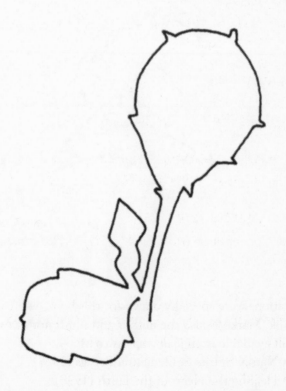

All the illustrations were specially drawn for this book by Slovenian artist Marko Pogačnik. Marko is also the author and illustrator of five Findhorn Press books (all available from *findhornpress.com*):

- Nature Spirits & Elemental Beings (1997)
- Healing the Heart of the Earth (1998)
- Christ Power and the Earth Goddess (1999)
- Earth Changes, Human Destiny (2000)
- The Daughter of Gaia (2001)

INTRODUCTION

27 years ago the magic of Findhorn came looking for me and found me living in southern Spain.

After 5 years of running a restaurant and diving centre in Marbella, Spain with my first husband Peter, I had broken out of my conservative lifestyle and spent 3 months at a centre for Humanistic Psychology. I hardly knew what the words meant. When someone told me I should I read *Siddhartha* to help me understand what I was getting into, I went to the book store and asked for a book called *Sid Arthur*! Yet the pull for change was so great that I left my child, my husband and my business in order to spend three months looking inside myself, to understand who I was and how I fitted into the universe.

Three months of learning to meditate, engaging in bioenergetics, yoga, enlightenment intensives, encounter groups and workshops, left me completely changed, open to the new, willing to take risks. I decided to leave my husband and live with Tony Mitton (one of the other participants on our course), bringing my 8 year old daughter Tamsin with me. Tony had also left his wife and was agonising about his four children, and for a while the new situation was hell for everybody.

The following summer I found I was pregnant, in spite of taking the pill. I had forgotten to take it for just one day, June 18th 1975. I know the exact date because it was the birthday of Tony's eldest son. So here I was, trying to decide what to do next. Using my new-found skill of meditation, I asked what I should do. The answer I heard inside myself was "Findhorn."

Hearing anything 'inside myself' was a shock, but hearing a word I did not recognise at all was even stranger. I had no idea what "Findhorn" was, although Tony thought it was a place somewhere in the UK. Over the next few months "Findhorn" came into my consciousness several times, and we asked others what or where it was. Then came the day when Tóny found it, in the last chapter of the book *The Secret Life of Plants*. We learned that Findhorn was a community in the North of Scotland where people lived together in love and harmony (what on Earth did that mean?) and grew giant cabbages. Cabbage is not my favourite vegetable, so I would have to find a better reason to go there!

The pull to go to Findhorn was stronger than my aversion to cabbage, and shortly afterwards Tony, Tamsin and I found ourselves driving from the

south of Spain to the north of Scotland in a motorhome lent by his mother. By now I was six months pregnant with my son Michael (yes, my inner 'voice' or 'knowing' was at it again, telling me my child wanted to be born in Findhorn and that his name was Michael—with that name I hoped it would be a boy!).

On December 5th 1975 we arrived at the Findhorn Community (here I need to make a distinction between the ancient village of Findhorn and the Findhorn Community, which is very recent, having only got started in 1962, but for the sake of simplicity I will mostly use just the word Findhorn from now on). My shock and dismay was enormous. Arriving on a cold, grey December day, we found a caravan park full of old trailers and some small wooden houses. Where was the beautiful community I had imagined? I spoke some very strong words to whoever had sent me there and told them they had made a big mistake!

It took exactly 24 hours for the magic to happen for me. It was not my first vegetarian meal in the community centre; it was certainly not my first night sleeping in a tiny caravan where everything shook when we walked.

It was not even the warm welcome from the friendly community members, or finding myself part of an "Experience Week" with interesting people from around the world who had also found themselves drawn to this place. My first magic moment happened sitting in a tiny old theatre watching an audio visual called "Love Is." Suddenly, from where I do not know, a soft, gentle mantle of loving energy enveloped me. Wordlessly it said, "Welcome home." I experienced such a sense of love, joy and acceptance that nothing else mattered, not my ugly surroundings, not the cold weather, nor the rickety old caravan I was living in. I had come home.

This is not the place to tell you how Findhorn evolved over the next 25 years. There are other books that have told that story. In regards to my personal life, my son Michael was born the following March, and both he and my daughter grew up in the community. Tony and I separated lovingly and supportively some years later and he and his new wife are my dearest friends. I married my beloved new husband Thierry in 1992, and we have been running the Findhorn Publishing business together since then. Through all these changes I lived at Findhorn, until in 1998 we moved to the USA, lived there for three years, and in 2001 returned to Europe to live in France.

Sometime during those last few years at Findhorn I lost my original deep, loving connection with the community. Never completely, but in many situations I found myself uncomfortable, no longer feeling myself as much part of it all as I had earlier. I had, and still have, many dear friends there and I admired and was grateful for the new people arriving to bring fresh ideas and energy to our community. But I felt myself to be on the fringes of what was occurring, not particularly interested in many of the new things happening.

I am writing this introduction in my new home in Beziers, France. There is no book yet, perhaps there will not be one. In me is nothing more than an impulse to once more go in search of the magic of Findhorn, to renew my quest for "home." Will I find it? Will the Angel of Findhorn welcome me as before? Is there still magic there? I will share my adventures with you, whatever the outcome will be.

Karin Bogliolo, Beziers, October 17th 2001

THE ANGEL OF FINDHORN

My vision of the Angel of Findhorn: the movement of the hands denotes the quality of transformation, the movement of the feet shows the will to step down and to manifest.

Marko Pogačnik

GLOSSARY

ANGEL OF FINDHORN

Nine months after Dorothy, Peter and Eileen moved to Findhorn Bay Caravan Park, Dorothy perceived the embryonic presence of "The Angel of Findhorn," which she was originally only able to contact through the Deva known as The Landscape Angel. The Landscape Angel overlit the entire geographical area and was focussed on the land itself, the soil and its nutrients. It also became an "envoy" for other Angelic contacts. In 1963, Dorothy was told that the Angel of Findhorn was "still nebulous but growing phenomenally fast," and that ". . . we were in a sense part of its body." Several years later, as the community expanded, she had the first direct communication during which the Angel asked specifically, "Do not form a clear concept of me and so keep me in limitation . . . I have many parts to play and much to do, and we shall do it together . . . I am in you and you are in me . . . . I am the Spirit of a place, yet much more." To this day, many members of the greater community, staff of the Foundation, visitors, and people who consider themselves part of the global Findhorn family believe they have been touched and called by "The Angel of Findhorn" and that each person is in some way part of "the body" of that ever-changing Angel.

ATTUNEMENT

A time to bring together a group, usually in silence and holding hands, before beginning any task or experience. This can happen several times a day, before eating, before working, before a workshop session or even before a longer bus journey. Departments and work areas also hold weekly attunements which can take several hours and are a time for personal sharing and bringing a group together in a more in-depth way.

BAG END

Area at the end of Pineridge where the first ecological buildings were constructed.

BARREL HOUSES

A cluster of 5 houses in Pineridge made from recycled whisky vats.

CHRIST ENERGY

In the Western mystery tradition epitomised by the early 20th Century writings of Alice A. Bailey, The Christ energy is described as "a dawning upon the awakening consciousness of humanity, the great paralleling truth of God Immanent—divinely pervading all forms . . . expressing innate divinity." The divine love, forgiveness, and selfless service which Jesus the Christ demonstrated are considered hallmarks of the emerging Christ consciousness, and all people of goodwill who practice and intend those life principles are in some way manifesting and being touched by the Christ energy. (see *The Reappearance of The Christ* by Alice A. Bailey. www.lucistrust.org)

CLUNY HILL COLLEGE

A former hotel in the nearby town of Forres, which the community bought in 1975 and which now houses many guests and members, and where many of the educational programmes are held.

COMMUNITY CENTRE OR CC

A large wooden building that houses The Park kitchen and dining room, as well as an upstairs lounge. Members and guests take their meals here.

CORNERSTONE

Eileen Caddy's ecological house in the centre of the community.

CULLERNE GARDENS

The land around Cullerne House, where many of the organic fruits and vegetables are grown.

CULLERNE HOUSE

A large house, formerly member housing and now the centre of the Findhorn Flower Essences.

DEVA

The Sanskrit word for 'shining one'. Used at Findhorn as another word for Angels, or Life Force, or Energy.

ÒRUMÒUAN

A large house in Forres, formerly member housing and meeting space, now the home of the Moray Steiner School.

FIELÒ OF ÒREAMS

An area of 5 acres at The Park, continuation of the eco-village.

FINÒHORN COMMUNITY

The very diverse cluster of individuals and groups that have grown up around the ideas of the Findhorn Foundation. Is usually expressed in the context of people in the local area.

FINÒHORN FOUNÒATION

Established as a charitable trust, this is the legal entity that is home to Findhorn's core spiritual practice and world outreach.

FINÒHORN VILLAGE

The village about a mile from the Findhorn Community. Many community members now live in houses in the village.

FOCALISER

The person who leads any activity or work. This is rather different to a manager or leader, because it is the person who focuses the energy for the group. Often this can also be the leader, but does not necessarily have to be.

FOCALISING

As above, the act of focussing the energy that brings a group together or allows a task to be done.

FORRES

A nearby town, quite ancient and mentioned in Shakespeare's Macbeth. Cluny Hill College is on the outskirts of Forres, as is Newbold House.

GREEN ROOM CAFÉ

A coffee shop, part of the Universal Hall, serving organic food and drinks.

KINLOSS

A nearby village. The Kinloss Royal Air Force base is close to The Park and the Nimrod aircraft (used for worldwide operations in peace, crisis and war, as well as search and rescue 365 days a year) can often be seen and HEARD in the area.

KP

A weekly duty, and hopefully joy, for all community members who eat in the CC or Cluny—as part of a clean-up crew after meals (from the military expression *Kitchen Patrol*).

MANIFESTATION OR LAWS OF MANIFESTATION

The materialisation of practical things in daily life that come about by conscious intention, clarity, positive thought and release of expectations. An example might be the need for a specific item, say, a bicycle. Assuming the person wanting the bike doesn't have the ready cash or credit line to simply go out and buy it, they first get very clear that they really need the bike. Emotions such as doubt and fear are faced and superseded by clarity and faith. The person then relaxes and releases any expectation of how this will come about. The alignment of need, clarity and release opens the way for the next step. With their mind free of wondering how or when, the voice of intuition is clearer and, for instance, the person may see a bike advertised in an unexpected sale, or run into an old friend who 'just happens' to be selling their bike, or get a short-term job or assignment that seems to 'come out of the blue' and makes them exactly the amount of money needed for the bicycle they want. A deeper layer of manifestation is the unwavering belief in a benevolent and abundant universe—that "God knows your needs even before you do, trust in Him." (see *Everyday Miracles* by David Spangler, Bantam Doubleday Dell 1995).

NETWORK NEWS

The quarterly newsletter of the Findhorn Foundation (mostly addressed to the network of Stewards and Friends of the Findhorn Foundation).

NEWBOLD HOUSE

An independent sister community near Cluny Hill College, which also runs workshops and educational programmes.

PARK BUILDING

A confusingly named grey stone building at The Park, housing the Library, a Meeting Room, the Conference Office and a Sanctuary.

PHOENIX COMMUNITY STORES, OR JUST 'PHOENIX'

The community store at The Park selling organic foods, books, music and crafts.

PINERIDGE

An area of land on the edge of The Park, next to The Field of Dreams. Formerly filled mainly with caravans and mobile homes, now also houses many of the ecological new houses, the Nature Sanctuary and the Barrel Houses.

RAINBOW BRIDGE

A weekly community newspaper.

SANCTUARY

A room for meditation and prayer.

STATION HOUSE

A large house in Findhorn Village housing a number of Foundation members.

THE MEDWAY BUILDING

This wooden building houses the Accounts Department, and various administrative offices.

THE PARK

The area of around 22 acres where the original community was born. It now belongs to the Findhorn Foundation and is the home of the Holiday Caravan Park, Pineridge, the Universal Hall, the Central Area and many other buildings and activities. A virtual tour of the Park is available on the world wide web: http://www.findhorn.org/virtual_tour/park/index.html

THE PRESS BUILDING

Next to the Universal Hall, houses a printing business and Findhorn Press.

THE RUNWAY

In WW2 this was part of the Kinloss Airbase and is now the main road in The Park.

UNIVERSAL HALL, OR JUST 'HALL'

A large building built by the community, which is situated at The Park. This is where artistic performances, meetings and conferences are held. It can comfortably hold 300 people. There are also various other rooms in the Hall, including a Dance/Drama studio, a Music Room and the Green Room Café.

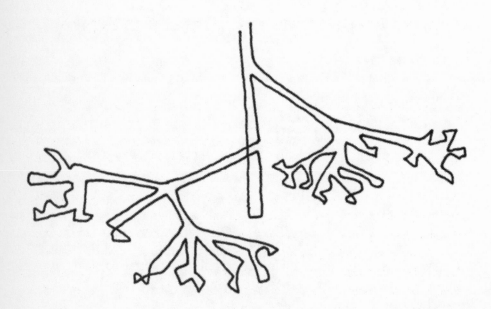

THE HISTORY AND LEGENDS OF
THE FINDHORN COMMUNITY

The woman slides quietly out of her bed, trying not to wake her sleeping husband. She checks the clock—it is 4 a.m., though she no longer has any need of an alarm clock—her inner clock wakes her every morning at the same time. She notices the delicate lines of frost on a window and quickly dresses in many layers of warm clothes, extra socks and an old pair of lined boots. Softly, she opens the door of the room that serves as both living room and bedroom and hears the gentle breathing of her three young sons, fast asleep in their bunks in the tiny room along the short hallway. She walks past the narrow family kitchen, and out into the freezing night air, catching her breath as the bitter cold hits her nostrils. She pulls her woollen scarf tighter around her face. Her footsteps make small crunching sounds on the snow as she walks away from the caravan that is her home. Glancing back for a brief moment at the darkened windows, she is sure that David, Christopher and Jonathan are still sound asleep.

Even in the dark, she easily finds her destination—a small, featureless concrete building. She enters and finds the four inner doors all wide open, and as usual, slips into the first one and closes the door behind her. There is little chance she will be disturbed at this time of the night, although later there will be a morning rush for the toilets by other residents of the caravan park. Gradually the shivering stops. She sits quietly in meditation—and waits. After a while, she reaches in her pocket for a short piece of pencil. It has been sharpened many times and must be used to the end, there is no money for new pencils. She opens the notebook she has brought with her and begins writing. Faster and faster, her hand speeds over the pages, filling them with her small, neat handwriting. Occasionally, she stops, closes her eyes and lets her hand fall into her lap. Then more and more words appear on the blank, lined pages.

At last her task is over. With a deep, deep sigh of gratitude she leaves her small space, wraps her warm coat tighter around her, slips the exercise book into the pocket and walks back to the small caravan she calls home. Quietly, she begins to cook breakfast for her family. She has no thought that the words she has written will one day inspire countless numbers of people around the world. She does not yet know that her private, morning writing—such simple words, and yet so very powerful—will bring people to this same spot to find their own connection to spirit, to follow their inner guidance just as she has done this very morning—and every morning for the past year. For now, her attention is on the porridge she is cooking, and on waking her children to go to school.

∞∞∞∞

One year earlier, on a crisp, sunny November afternoon, Eileen's husband Peter had towed their summer holiday caravan into a hollow at the northwest end of Findhorn Bay Caravan Park, hoping that the lower ground might provide some shelter from the bitter winds that blew relentlessly off the Bay.

The Caddy family and their long-time friend Dorothy Maclean had returned to Morayshire in the hope that Peter would be re-hired to manage the four-star Cluny Hill Hotel. Under his astute management, and supported by Eileen's daily guidance from God, he had restored the old Victorian spa hotel to a dignity that had made the whole town of Forres proud. The Caddys had been so successful in raising the spirit of Cluny Hill Hotel that in 1961 the hotel's owner had sent them and many of their staff to manage the ailing Trossachs Hotel in Perthshire, hoping they would work the same magic there. Despite their best efforts, The Trossachs had proved a formidable task, clothed as it was year round in damp and dreary mists. Peter was sacked as manager after their first season and the family returned north to Morayshire where they had many friends and business associates who—Peter felt sure—would help him find a good position in town.

However, as winter set in, Peter was still unemployed, and the 'friends' who a few years earlier had wined and dined at the elegant Cluny Hill Hotel had seemingly disappeared. Living on the dole (National Assistance), with no money for a house in the town of Forres or even in the nearby fishing village of Findhorn, Peter and Eileen were left with only one option—to tow the holiday caravan they had been keeping in the village to the nearby Caravan Park and make the best of it for the winter. The cheapest site available was next to an old rubbish dump. They parked there. It wouldn't be long, they knew, before they could return to Cluny Hill. God had told Eileen in no uncertain terms that they would return to Cluny, and if God said so—then they would.

∞∞∞∞

Peter was a practical man, strong, athletic, with a sharp, incisive mind. He had been a Catering Officer in the Royal Air Force and had travelled the world feeding British troops stationed in the Far East, the Indian subcontinent, and the Himalayas. On one such tour of duty he had met Eileen Combe, an elegant woman with clear spiritual principals—and married, with five children, to a senior officer in the Royal Air Force. In the course of his travels he remained friends with the Combe family, including their children, and enjoyed dinners with the family and tennis games with Eileen.

Central to Eileen's spiritual practice was the discipline of sitting still in order to receive God's guidance. For an active man like Peter, this was rarely the way in which he attuned to the will of God. His early spiritual training in 'soul science' had been through a Rosicrucian Order and it had instilled in him the need to follow his intuition moment-by-moment. Whether in the Air Force or in his personal life, Peter's practice of instantly following each small, intuitive knowing had almost always led him—step-by-step or leap-by-leap—to success.

There was, however, one significant time when Peter received 'guidance' while actually sitting still! In October 1952 he was stationed in the Middle East and took the opportunity to visit the holy sites in Jerusalem. At sunset, he was resting on a hill overlooking the city— thinking about nothing in particularly, and certainly not meditating— when out of the blue he clearly heard the words, "Eileen is your other half." He was astonished! He liked and respected Eileen very much, but had never thought about her in a romantic way. Besides, she was married with five children! He was also fairly sceptical of the idea of soul partners. "People meet their soulmates once in a blue moon," he thought, and dismissed the idea as ridiculous!

However, he could not dismiss the clarity with which he heard the voice, and decided that the next time he saw the Combes he would tell

Eileen that God had said they were soul halves—just to see what she thought! That Christmas, he was invited to dinner with the family—and perhaps this story begins to weave a first magic thread on that December evening. Finding a moment alone with Eileen, he confessed that God had said that they were to be together. As he spoke, they glanced out of the window to see a blue moon rising! Eileen's response was simply that if it was to be so, that God would take care of the details. And so it came to pass . . .

∞∞∞∞

It was almost ten years later that Peter towed the old summer caravan into the sandy hollow at the top end of Findhorn Bay Caravan Park. A few days later, in howling winds with icy sleet driving in his face, he planted a beech hedge, put up some fencing, and drove into the nearby town of Forres to sign on at the Labour Exchange and renew old business contacts. He was hopeful that one way or another he'd land a good position in town within the next few days—something that would tide him over until he was re-instated as Manager of Cluny Hill Hotel.

Days, however, dragged on into weeks, and weeks into months. It didn't make sense! Peter Caddy had lived in Forres for several years when he managed Cluny Hill. He knew everyone who was anyone in town. He had a record of extraordinary accomplishments and was familiar with success. Could the bad luck that had dogged him in the Trossachs have followed him here? The thought did cross Peter's mind but he was not one for heeding any but positive thoughts. Besides, both Eileen and Dorothy had received guidance that they were all to stay in the Caravan Park. That, too, didn't make sense, especially with three growing sons to feed, but Peter trusted their guidance, and expected that the perfect job was waiting for him—it was just a matter of timing! Not only that, but Peter and Eileen both knew, without a shadow of doubt, that they would be returning to Cluny Hill. God had told Eileen, and Peter just knew it!

Peter built a wooden annex onto the side of the caravan, just big enough for Dorothy's bed and a night stand. Dorothy had been Peter's secretary at Cluny Hill and she, too, was sure they would return there. She also could not find work—even temporary jobs—and so she spent her days repairing the little caravan—remembering to do everything with love and to 'the glory of God', as her spiritual teacher had instilled in her.

For many years, Dorothy, Peter, and later on Eileen had been trained by a wise teacher called Sheena to go within and develop their inner connection to God. Under Sheena's counsel, they had each learned to recognize, listen, trust, and follow their guidance implicitly. So, as winter damp and darkness enfolded the little caravan, they shared their guidance with one another just as they shared meals. A bright coke-burning stove provided the little caravan with heat, and the three adults and three boys read or did homework until it was time to convert the dining-room table into the base for the mattress that made up Peter and Eileen's bed. The boys slept in an even smaller room with hot water bottles and woollen blankets as their only source of warmth. Regularly, Peter went into Forres to look for work but came back empty handed.

One morning a farm truck spilled a bundle of straw, which scattered everywhere, as it turned into the caravan park entrance. Driving right behind, Peter stopped to pick up the straw, realising how useful it would be for the vegetable garden he was planning to plant as soon as he could dig a spade into the frozen ground. On another occasion Eileen and Dorothy set off to shovel horse manure and that, too, went into the garden.

Thankfully, spring came early that year, and Peter planted every kind of vegetable they could think of even though he had never planted vegetables before. Later on he planted flowers to brighten up their little plot and beautify the caravan. Yet even with the warmer weather the ground was still hard, and the sandy soil hardly seemed likely to support a thriving garden. Not to be outwitted by anything, Peter mixed together the spilled straw, the horse manure and the potato peelings that Eileen had been tossing out, and made a primitive compost heap. On his regular trips to seek work, he scavenged for other compost ingredients—fruit and veggie trimmings from the greengrocers, old grass mowings from the caravan park lawn, potash from a burned-out wood fire, even barley residues from a nearby whisky distillery! By May, the compost was 'steaming', and Eileen had received guidance that all their hard work was helping put their own radiation and vibrations into the soil.

One day, Dorothy had a suggestion to "feel into the nature forces," understanding for the first time that nature had an intelligence, and that she could learn to harmonize and co-operate with that force. That, she thought, was going to be easy because she loved nature: hiking over the sand dunes to the beach or rambling in the nearby forest at Randolph's Leap where the River Findhorn and the River Divvy meet in a gentle cascade of rocks and rapids. However, when Peter heard of Dorothy's instruction to "attune to nature," he had other ideas. Under his Rosicrucian teacher Dr. Sullivan, Peter had learned a little bit about the elemental spirits of fire, earth, air and water and had often wondered how they helped things to grow and flourish. He asked Dorothy if she thought they might be willing to offer them some practical help in their gardening endeavours, and could she please try to contact them!

However, it was not the elemental nature spirits from the Faerie Kingdom to which Dorothy attuned, it was the overlighting angelic presence of the garden pea itself! The garden pea family angel as it were, which Dorothy preferred to call a Deva after the Sanskrit word for Shining One—and to avoid the usual association of angels as being only blond and wearing flowing white robes and golden halos. Dorothy's angels were much more practical even though they were formless energy fields.

Once the garden pea Deva had made her presence felt, there was no stopping either Dorothy or Peter! Peter asked Dorothy to get answers from Devas at every turn, and soon she met a very expansive presence that she called the Landscape Angel. She learned that the Landscape Angel was a local aspect of the Planetary Angel, and through her attunement to the Landscape Angel she learned that every species of plant had its own overlighting angel—or Deva—which retained the blueprint for the pattern, shape, design, and growth of that plant species and directed its course and timing. For human understanding, Dorothy interpreted the Angel's description in terms that this was similar to the way an architect designs a building and prepares the plans to give to the building contractors—which are the nature spirits themselves—to do the next stage and then pass the process onto humans who carry out the actual work!

Many people, who are natural-born gardeners, the proverbial 'green thumbs', have an innate attunement to the Devas and nature spirits, but Peter and Dorothy, neither of whom had ever been seriously inclined to lift a spade before, had to learn all this from scratch. And so another thread of the magic was gently woven into the fabric of the Findhorn Community as the first Findhorn Garden—in the magical summer of 1963—flourished under the care of Devas and Humans—with Peter, Eileen and Dorothy representing the trinity of Light, Love and Wisdom respectively..

And, still, every morning in the quiet hours before dawn, Eileen Caddy was slipping out of bed and—so as not to disturb her sleeping family— quietly stealing out of the cosy caravan to the public loo in the middle of the caravan park, to sit quietly and receive her guidance from God.

Through Peter's hard, physical work, Eileen's steadfast faith and guidance, and Dorothy's clear attunement with the overlighting angelic presences, the Findhorn Garden grew and flourished. It had become clear that Peter must have been 'prevented' from finding work in Forres so that he could begin his 'real' work—establishing the community of Findhorn. Eileen had received guidance that their little corner of Findhorn would one day become a 'Centre of Light', and although none of them really knew what that meant, they trusted her guidance. Another family—a woman called Lena, also trained by Sheena, and Lena's three children—had a caravan nearby, and Lena, Dorothy and Eileen often spent hours together in meditation, attuning telepathically with other Centres of Light around the world. At this same time Eileen had a vision that their Centre at Findhorn was to be linked in a Triangle of Light to the tiny island of Iona in the Hebrides—the sacred seat of Christianity in Great Britain and Ireland—and to the ancient town of Glastonbury, which was the heart of Avalon in the Arthurian legends. Cluny Hill, she was told in guidance, was the actual power point that linked with the Tor in Glastonbury. Eileen, Dorothy, Lena and an American friend named Naomi began daily visualisations to strengthen the links with these ancient centres.

In 1965, Peter and Dorothy undertook a journey to Glastonbury where they met Wesley Tudor Pole, the founder of the Chalice Well Trust and a man with deep convictions about the power of the inner, unseen worlds. It was Tudor Pole who had instigated 'the silent minute' during WWII—a time of daily, national silent prayer at 9:00 p.m. each evening that was said to have contributed to Britain's victory in the war. That same year Peter also met Sir George Trevelyan—considered "the Grandfather of the New Age"—a highly renowned educator, writer and poet, steeped in the laws of esotericism. Sir George visited Findhorn as often as he could and greatly respected the work of the community. In turn, everyone who knew him dearly loved and respected his wisdom and humour.

By the small group's fourth summer, word had spread about the extraordinary garden built on sand in the middle of a caravan park in the north of Scotland, and also about the meditations and spiritual attunement that the families were practicing each day. That Easter—1966—five guests visited "the magic garden," and seventeen more came in the early summer. Two of those guests were to have an enormous though quiet impact on the families in the budding community: Joanie Hartnell Beavis had been living in Lancashire with her friend and spiritual teacher, Liebe Pugh; Robert Ogilvie Crombie—known as ROC—was a scientist, an actor, and accomplished pianist who lived in Edinburgh. The following year, Joanie moved to Findhorn, ultimately becoming Eileen's closest friend, helper and confidant. ROC always kept his flat in Edinburgh but visited the community many times each year, becoming its protector on the inner realms and the guardian of the land on which the community was being built, as well as Peter's most trusted spiritual advisor.

ROC had studied the esoteric arts for many years and a few weeks after his first visit, he had an extraordinary awakening to a realm that he believed existed but had never before encountered first hand—the faerie realm. While walking in his favourite spot in Edinburgh's Botanical Gardens, he 'met' a faun—a nature spirit who introduced himself as Kurmos—and a little later encountered the great god Pan himself. ROC's meeting with the nature spirit and with Pan heightened his awareness of that particular kingdom of nature, and he realised that the "magic garden" growing at Findhorn was alive with such Beings. As he became at ease with his new, though to others invisible, friends, ROC brought their wisdom to the community and was always enthusiastically greeted by the nature spirits there. By the summer of 1967, with the assistance of the Faerie kingdom through ROC, the Devic kingdom through Dorothy, and the Human kingdom through Peter, the garden was growing to new heights of splendour. People from all over the country wanted to come and see the vibrant flowers and magnificent vegetables—and even some of Britain's well-known gardeners and horticulturists came to visit. After the BBC brought a television crew in 1969, six hundred people wrote to the community wanting to visit!

∞∞∞∞

And so the magic unfolded. The same spiritual principles of faith and guidance and "love as work in action" spurred the founders of the Findhorn community in their daily lives. Whenever something or someone was needed, they magically turned up to selflessly give of their specific skills! When ROC and Dorothy thought that it would be a good idea to publish their guidance from the Nature Spirits and Devas, a printer named Victor came to visit, and a booklet called "The Findhorn Garden" was printed on an old Gestetner press. The wisdom spread far and wide—even to the United States of America.

One morning, Eileen had a vision of six cedar wood bungalows. A month or two later, six elegant mobile homes were delivered and then purchased by those wanting to join in the work of the fledgling community. Sometime earlier, she had had a vision of a simple Sanctuary, big enough to hold about sixty people. That, too, was built exactly as she had visualised it—the money for it came at the precise time when they needed to pay the builder and the furniture shop. Once the Sanctuary was built, Eileen no longer had to traipse to the caravan park loo in the wee hours before dawn. It also had a very efficient heating system!

When Eileen and Joanie wondered how they were going to cook for so many people out of the tiny kitchens in their caravans—not to mention how to seat the diners somewhere—Eileen 'saw' in meditation a beautiful community centre with a commercial kitchen outfitted in stainless steel, and a dining room big enough for two hundred people! Soon afterwards a donor who believed in the work they were doing paid for the building and all the equipment. A charitable foundation, the Findhorn Trust, was established to receive donations, many guests bought and donated caravans for other guests and community members to stay in, and by the summer of 1970 over thirty people—ranging from a newborn baby to an octogenarian—were living in the Findhorn Community. Each morning Eileen and Dorothy read their guidance from God to community members in the Sanctuary, and each day Peter headed the work force in building, gardening, beautifying and cleaning. "Work is Love in Action" became everyone's daily motto, and through that work the community grew and grew.

Then, in August of that same year, two people came to visit from America who were to have one of the greatest influences of all. David Spangler was a young man in his mid-twenties who had great vision and wisdom. Myrtle Glines, his companion, and many years older than he, was like a protector to him, and a trained counsellor in her own right. From 1970 to 1973 David and Myrtle lived in the community, and their presence sowed the seeds for the growing and nurturing of people, as well as flowers and vegetables. They helped to establish the education branch of the community as well as attending to the spiritual life of the many members.

When David arrived at Findhorn that August, he instantly attuned to a strong presence known as Limitless Love and Truth or the All Knowing One. Through David, Limitless Love and Truth gave extraordinary and very practical teachings for the community as a whole as well as for many individuals, and they bestowed a legacy of work that forms a strong and timeless foundation of spiritual teaching.

Built on such a foundation of strength, and with the co-operation of the kingdoms of Nature and a core of artists, visionaries, spiritual seekers and skilled and talented workers, the Findhorn Community grew to become the true Centre of Light that had been envisioned by Eileen. Now so many people were coming to participate in the courses offered by the Education Branch that space was becoming very stretched in the community buildings around the caravan park. In the summer of 1975 a special piece of God's guidance—cherished and held in faith for nearly fifteen years—came to fruition. Cluny Hill Hotel was purchased by the Findhorn Foundation. Peter and Eileen, and two hundred other people— were returning to Cluny!

GATHERING THE MAGIC

A TRANSATLANTIC CALL

"Allo, oui?"

"Hi, Karin!" I pause for a moment before introducing myself. I can literally see Karin's face and hear her thoughts as she thumbs through her memory archives, trying to place my voice. I grin as I picture her, remembering her from twenty years earlier—warm smile, roundish face, natural blond hair, always laughing, always ready to greet someone with a hug—no matter how busy she was. Karin had focalised the Findhorn community kitchen for many years, and her name and image there was synonymous with Cheese Soufflé, so cheesy and tall that my mouth waters even as I wait for my moment to announce myself. Karin and I have been e-mailing one another for several years, but today I want to call her in person.

"Karin, this is Carly—in New Mexico."

"C a r l y ! How lovely to hear from you. What a surprise!" she exclaims, reverting effortlessly to English. Karin's native tongue was originally German; she spent most of her childhood in England and now lives in the South of France. I am slightly envious of her ability to speak so many languages. I try out my very rusty French.

"Karin, comment va vous?"

I hear her laugh at the end of the phone.

"Not even close, Carly. I can't believe you're ringing me, are you here in France, perhaps?"

"No, sadly, I'm not, I'm in New Mexico and it's freezing today, but I want to tell you about a Findhorn Gathering I'm hosting in a few weeks. I know you're thinking about writing a book and I'm calling this Gathering to re-inspire magic and synchronicity in our lives, and especially relive how each person was drawn into the magical world of Findhorn. There will be quite a few of our old friends there as well as people who may have just heard about the community. And, really, I just wanted to hear your voice!"

We chat for a while, drinking cups of tea on separate continents. I want to hear Karin's own story about how she was drawn to Findhorn, and how magical happenings continued to weave their way through her life, even after she had left the community.

That, it seemed, was the thread that everyone held in common—how even difficult and challenging life experiences were touched by the hand of magic and blessing. Just what was it that had drawn people to Findhorn all those years before? Why does the very name "Findhorn" conjure up such warmth and hope for so many people, and how do those magical blessings live on in people's lives, even decades later?

Karin tells me about her first magic moment at Findhorn:

"I can remember it happened the day after I arrived in Findhorn. The shock of arriving there the day before had been horrible—this ugly, grey, dark caravan park. After living in the south of Spain for six years, Findhorn in December 1975 was an ugly place. We were given a small, cramped caravan to sleep in and I wanted to run away as fast as possible."

"And then it happened, a never to be forgotten moment! We joined an Experience Week and one afternoon we were shown an audio/visual called 'Love Is.' Out of nowhere, I suddenly knew what love was! It was the glue that shaped the universe, the energy that drew everything together, that created everything, from matter to emotions, to spirit. I knew that everything that exists is created by love, and therefore IS love. It seemed so simple, and yet at that moment it was the most incredible experience I had ever had. At that very moment I knew I had come home, that nothing else mattered, not the dark, grey winter nor the ugliness of the caravan park, I knew it was all love, and I was part of it. I was love, surrounded by love, created by love, limitless. It was probably the most exciting and intense moment of my life.

"That same love was not just a fleeting feeling, but through my years in the community, it proved true again and again. For instance, one day,

someone saying to me, 'I sense that you don't like me, is that true?' and I
having the courage to reply, 'Yes, it's true, I don't like you.' And both of us
looking into each others' eyes, knowing we did not like each other,
probably never will, and yet feeling incredible love. That was the moment
I understood that at the deepest level I do love everyone, even when I don't
particularly like them."

I sigh, understanding very well what she means. I have been very
lucky—perhaps truly blessed—to have many friends in my life, and I can't
even think of anyone I would call an enemy or an adversary. However, now
and again I run into someone I just don't like, and don't necessarily know
why. My own years at Findhorn taught me well how to work and be with
both those whom I adored and those I couldn't abide. Living "cheek by
jowl" in a community dedicated to personal and spiritual growth doesn't
necessarily mean that you get along with everyone, but it does mean that
you learn how to be true to yourself, clear and direct with others, and how
to sustain kindness. Learning and knowing deep down that every human
being is a child of God—despite their flaws—took daily practice in
acceptance, understanding and forgiveness—and most of all in learning
how to love myself.

Karin's voice at the end of the phone brings me back from my own
thoughts.

"I just want to tell you one more thing. Many, many magic moments
happened for me through music, mainly through singing. When I sing I feel
very close to spirit. One such moment happened one evening when I was
rehearsing with our madrigal group. We were singing "The Silver Swan," a
song that really moves me."

Karin's lilting voice fills the miles between us as she sings it for me.

> The Silver Swan, who living had no note
> When death approached unlocked her silent throat,
> Leaning her head against her weary breast,
> Thus sung her first and last
> And sang no more.

"At that very moment, someone came into the room, listened while we
finished our song, and then told us that Barbara D'Arcy Thompson had
died—drowned earlier that day at Randolph's Leap. There was a sense of
very deep peace in the room, and I felt that Barbara had been with us while
we sang. We sang it again, just for her."

Barbara had been a long-time, much-loved member of the community.

"Oh, Karin, there are so many memories, aren't there? We could spend all day and all night on the phone. I hope you're writing these things down?"

"You bet I am," she replies. "I really am seriously thinking about writing this book. How about helping me do it?"

"Well, it does seem as though we are on the same wavelength," I reply. "That you and I are on the same page, so to speak. Perhaps calling this Gathering will be the beginning of it."

∞∞∞

AMANDA'S RING OF GOLDEN LIGHT

Some weeks passed and the day of the Gathering arrived. After a blur of hugs and excited chatter about thirty women and men settled in to take their places in a circle to share their stories, how they came to Findhorn and how it had affected their lives. We began with an attunement—a practice initiated in Findhorn many years earlier—standing for a few minutes of silence, holding hands around the circle to connect with others in the room and with each person's own personal spiritual centre—to God within, to eternal Light and the beating heart of Love. There was no need for words, the silence and sense of unity were utterly tangible. Someone in the Circle squeezed their neighbour's hand, and in seconds the squeeze circled around, feet shuffled and everyone sat down, holding the silence in rapt awareness, many eyes glistening with the special kind of peace this Circle of friends evoked. Magic.

Gently I broke the silence, my voice choked with emotion, and suggested a simple round of names, "I'm Carly," I began, and looked at the person to my left. "I'm Doug, I'm Allison, I'm Amanda, Merv, Jack, Linda, Mary . . . ."

"Who would like to begin?" I asked, hoping I wouldn't have to speak much more right then, though adding, "Or perhaps the real question is, 'Where shall we begin?' I called this Gathering to delve a little deeper into what that Findhorn magic was—and is. To see how that magic has lived within us over the years, and perhaps to restore magic in our lives now. To remember the intent we set for ourselves on our spiritual journey and to check back in with our dreams and hopes. To consciously reignite our connection with The Angel of Findhorn. Perhaps the first question is, what drew each of us—perhaps called us—to the Community?"

Amanda was the first to jump in with her story.

"For me, Findhorn is a place in my spirit, something cherished by my soul, at times forgotten by my personality. It sounds a note that is dear, that can galvanise all of me. It is a pure note of selfless service with a planetary perspective.

"I had a "dark night of the soul" in my mid-twenties and had only heard the name 'Findhorn' once—from a woman who wrinkled her nose and said in a tone of ill-disguised disgust: 'Oh, it's a place where they practice some funny kind of Christianity.' I was not, however, perturbed. A few weeks later I heard some exceptionally endearing singalong music, and learnt that it had been recorded at Findhorn. I distinctly recall the time, the place, the sunny weather and my reaction—which was that I just had to check out a place that produced music like that.

"I visited Findhorn and immediately began to receive inner guidance in the form of visions and pictures, which gradually led me to becoming a member of the community. In an interview with the Personnel Department I was clearly enclosed in a ring of golden white light together with the Angel of Findhorn. I lived there for fourteen years."

Amanda settled back into her chair and waited quietly.

ELIZABETH AND THE BURNING SKIRT

"Hi, I'm Elizabeth," a blue-eyed, intense woman began. "I had been to Findhorn previously, but in September of 1989 I was living among the infamous Peace Convoy travellers. I was desperately unhappy, but I refused to see that it was my lifestyle and alcohol that were at the root of it. One afternoon, I decided to visit an old friend in an attempt to get some perspective on my life. I returned to the Travellers the following morning and, as I got within a mile of the site where we were staying, a magpie—a kind of omen, one of my 'special' birds—flew across the front of the car. Time slowed, and it looked straight into my eyes for what seemed an endless moment—and then was gone. I suddenly knew something disastrous was going to happen to a close friend or family member, but I couldn't work out whom. I also felt that something small but significant had snapped in me, but I didn't know what.

"I pulled into our makeshift campsite and went into my trailer to change my clothes, choosing an Indian print skirt that I liked. I felt distinctly prompted to wear it. It was my turn to help with the food, and I dragged a large pot over to the campfire where we cooked, raked the coals from the edge and placed the pot on top of coals. I was still deeply inside myself, acutely unhappy, and barely heard someone cry, 'Liz, your skirt's on fire.' I tried to get the skirt off, but couldn't, and started to beat at the flames with my hands but the skin on them burned straight away. I began to fall towards the ground and for the second time that day, time slowed. During the forever, a calm voice within me told me that my higher self had made a conscious decision for me to go through this experience to clean unhelpful patterns and karma. That it was a wonderful thing, but would be very painful. When I hit the ground, time reverted to normal and I immediately knew to roll around like crazy to put out the flames. For a brief instant I thought I was pain free, then the agony of deep and superficial burns hit me and I screamed—from the pain of the burns and the pain that I had built in my life but refused to feel.

"I recovered slowly in hospital, and convalesced with friends, knowing I was too raw and sensitive ever to return to the Travellers and my chaotic lifestyle. One day I remembered Findhorn. I thought of how the energy of Findhorn Bay, the beach, the meditations and sanctuaries, would help me heal. I had spent a few weeks there in 1987 and had taken the Experience Week. I had fallen in love with the intensely real and magical energy of the community lands and been intrigued by the possibility of living with people of conscious spiritual intent. The next morning an unexpected check from the social services department showed up and it was more than enough to pay for petrol and a week's visit. Within the week, I was recharged with a sense of my path and felt strongly that there was a place for me at Findhorn, even if I couldn't see clearly what that was. Almost as soon as I acknowledged that thought, I was offered a place to live in Forres among Community people and I accepted with joy."

LINDA'S ROMANCE

"I think it's my turn, now." A tall, elegant blond woman in her late-fifties began to speak. "We've heard from the former hippies!" Linda smiled a wonderful, honest smile that came from within. "However, unlike most of the people who visited Findhorn, I was a pure sceptic. I was not a spiritual seeker and hadn't read any of the books—except of course *The Magic of Findhorn*, which I didn't take seriously at all. I wondered how otherwise intelligent people could buy into such a line of, well, you know . . .

"I guess my journey into the other world began when I met Dr Elizabeth Kubler-Ross, who was the keynote speaker at a conference I was co-ordinating. I had never met anyone quite like her before. She was on her way to becoming one of the most famous people in the world and seemed to come from another dimension with some kind of deep sense of knowing. She was calm, open, totally in touch with the natural and spiritual world, very, very deep and wise, and with no ego.

"I, on the other hand, was all ego and persona, from my expensive manicure and false eyelashes to my serious business suit and briefcase—and to use a real cliché—was at the cross-roads in my life. As a county level executive director of a national health agency, the time had come for me to move onward and upward, and there was no job that attracted me in the slightest. I wanted to do something else, but what?

"The real saga began shortly afterwards at the Esalen Institute in Big Sur, California. It was Memorial Day weekend, May 1980, Mount St. Helens had just blown her top, and I decided that I was going to drop my straight, executive persona, and experience everything that went on at Esalen—from nude hot tubs to encounter groups. I bought some really great Moroccan clothing from 'Uriah Heaps'—this super little shop in Montecito—and signed up for a Gestalt Therapy workshop!

"There I met Hugh, the man who—for lack of a better description—was an ex-hippie from Rhodesia (now Zimbabwe), who had travelled the world and was living at a place called Findhorn in the coldest, most northerly area of Scotland. And I was boring and conventional—you get the picture—there were never two more unlikely-to-end-up-together people. But I had a very strong, almost immediate, sense that I had met the man with whom I was destined to spend my life. That weekend we talked for hours, walking the trails along the mighty Pacific Coast. He was on his way up to Oregon, I was on my way to train some new staff in San Francisco. I gave him a lift.

"I would never be the same again. I was on my quest to learn from spiritual people, and Findhorn was definitely on my list—I arrived on the windswept sand dunes six months later to participate in an Experience Week. I didn't even know if Hugh would be there—we had not stayed in touch—but, coming through the doors of the Cluny lounge—there he was!

"I loved my entire stay in the community. For me, it was all so totally freeing on all levels. Without a doubt, living at Findhorn were the three best years of my life. Part of this was because I had no expectations. I didn't believe any of the myths—still don't. I experienced a very special and irreplaceable group of people, each with his or her own beliefs, story and reasons for being there, and who could remain there just being themselves and not necessarily having to accept someone else's teachings.

"The magic of Findhorn was—and still is—partly in the location and setting, but mostly in the people. There is just something in the energy of that particular area of the planet that can be felt even by one such as myself.

"There is the sense of leaving one's persona behind and being open and honest and caring and making an effort to operate differently than the way the rest of the world does; but most of all it is in the people—all in one place—the most brilliant, talented, unique, spiritual, warm, open, friendly people in the world from all walks of life, with only one thing in common—they are seekers of something better and the creators of a whole new set of realities. This synthesis is, to me, the magic of Findhorn."

"And, I'm curious, what happened with you and Hugh?" I wondered.

"Oh! I didn't tell you! Hugh and I married in May of 1983. We left the community in November of that year to visit his family in Zimbabwe and South Africa and then settled in the United States."

MERV AND BELLA READ A BOOK

"Any more stories to tell?" I asked. "It seems we are gathering the magic—I wonder what's going to come of all this?"

"For me, it all began sometime in the Spring of 1978," Merv began. "My wife Bella and I were living in Greensboro', North Carolina. She managed a gourmet cheese shop and ran her own catering company, while I was engaged in leadership development work for a small consulting firm.

"One day, while browsing through a bookstore, Bella spotted a book entitled *The Findhorn Cookbook* which, after perusal, she concluded was all about how to prepare not very attractive but extremely healthy food for multitudes of people in a vegetarian commune—a book that she was not about to add to her already considerable collection of cookbooks. Upon returning this book to its place, however, another book accidentally fell off the shelf at her feet—a book entitled *The Magic of Findhorn*. Glancing at the blurb on the back cover, she concluded that this was a kind of Harlequin romance—a story about an English couple, Peter and Eileen, who found love and happiness in the north of Scotland. Now this was her kind of book—so she bought it.

"Bella is the speediest reader I have ever known. She devoured the book within an hour or two of our returning home—and then passed it to me, saying 'I think you'd better read this too.' 'Well, okay,' I thought, 'What the hell.' In fact, like Bella, I couldn't put it down. And that very evening, lying in bed together before turning out the light, we turned to each other and said, 'I think we've got to go to Findhorn and check this place out.'

"Which is exactly what we did. We had already decided to spend a couple of weeks that summer visiting Bella's family in Wales, and on arrival in Britain, we promptly set about making plans to motor to the north of Scotland with Bella's brother and his wife. Now, my brother-in-law was nothing short of allergic to anything that smelled of religion or spirituality, and was less than keen about visiting a hippie commune that must surely be lining the pockets of the ageing gurus (Peter and Eileen) who ran the place. However, he went along with our plans, and leaving Inverness, was heard muttering in his lilting Welsh accent, 'I'll tell you what. If the sun should happen to shine on our arrival at this magical community, then perhaps even I will become a believer in forty-two-pound cabbages and all this other spiritual mumbo-jumbo.' Which is precisely what happened: somewhere between Forres and the caravan park, the rain stopped, the sun broke through in all its radiance, and from the back seat I heard something about 'a bloody coincidence.'

"We arrived just in time to join the one-hour tour of the caravan park that was offered to casual visitors such as ourselves. While my brother-in-law proceeded to gather evidence to justify his cynicism, Bella and I were being blown away by all the evidence to the contrary. The members of the community seemed incredibly open and genuine. No one seemed intent on selling us a bill of goods. And folk seemed remarkably willing to live with a measure of trust or faith that I had not seen anywhere else. But what finally did it for me was sitting by myself in the community sanctuary. No sooner had I sat down than my entire body was literally humming with the energy of the place.

And when I emerged from the sanctuary just five or ten minutes later, there was no doubt in my mind. We simply had to come and spend some more time in this very magical place.

"On our return to North Carolina we determined that we would sign on for what Findhorn called an "experience week" and then stay on for an additional week to see if this community was in reality everything that our first impressions had suggested. But lest we be seduced by the now-legendary "magic" of the place, we decided to go in February, towards the end of what we presumed would be a most miserable season of the year in the north of Scotland. If ever this community suffered a time of depression and bitchiness, we reasoned, it would surely be in late winter—and, before we made any rash decision to terminate our comfortable careers in the "sun belt" of America to go in search of the holy grail, we wanted to experience Findhorn at its worst.

"As it turned out, we were right on at least one count. Findhorn was not a holiday destination of choice in mid-February. But despite the dark and cold of winter, nothing seemed capable of dimming the sunny spirits of those with whom we shared that time. They seemed every bit as genuine, the sanctuary was as palpably buzzy, and the spiritual intention of the community seemed just as pure as when we had visited so briefly eight months earlier.

"And so it was that those two weeks culminated in our shared decision to take the plunge. On the day before we were due to leave, we stood together in the snow-covered woods behind Cluny Hill and asked whatever gods may be whether indeed it was heaven's will that we should come to live at Findhorn.

Wanting to experiment with this business of "guidance" on which the community had been built, we stood in the silence, holding hands, awaiting whatever direction our inner voice might offer. I heard no voice. Bella heard no voice. Instead, a length of ticker-tape passed immediately before my mind's eye. And on it were the unmistakable words: 'That's settled! Get on with it!'

"And so we embarked upon a series of successive events and experiences that would change our lives forever."

CARLY'S 'AH HA' MOMENT

After this story, I called a break for tea and bikkies. Tea breaks were also the life and soul of Findhorn and, for me, conjured up memories of a specific corner of Cluny Kitchen. There, on a wooden counter top in an alcove over by the bean sprouts, lived a clutter of sticky jars of spreads— tahini, honey, raspberry jam, marmalade, peanut butter, and Marmite—the ubiquitous shiny, black yeast extract that tasted, well, like Marmite, and which American visitors naively thought was gooey chocolate spread! Loaves of whole-wheat bread, rye breads, Challah braids, Vadan's muffins or Sprague's peanut-butter cookies, all made their way directly from oven to snack corner and were consumed instantly by the hungry hordes of Experience Week guests on tea break. Over at The Park, the Blackpool Gardeners took their tea breaks year-round in the potting shed—sheltering from wind, rain and snow, with mugs of hot tea or instant coffee warming their hands and gladdening their spirits. If they were in favour with Mary Coulman (a senior member with pronounced opinions), flapjacks filled their bellies, and if not, a couple of packets of Chocolate 'Digestives' were opened and dipped in the hot brew.

Re-convening the Gathering, I decided to jump right in with my own story.

"I had one of those classic 'Ah ha's' the moment I heard the word 'Findhorn.' I had moved with my family to Blackpool in the north-west of England when I was a teenager and quickly became friends with a radical group of kids—most of them gardeners—and all of them musicians. This was the late sixties and I was in my element—we'd re-created our little corner of San Francisco's famed 'Haight Asbury' district, reading "The Tibetan Book of The Dead" and strumming away our summers, dreaming of going to India like The Beatles to sit at the feet of the Maharishi and learn how to meditate.

"One day, one of our group, Ian, took off to visit his grandparents in Scotland. He returned glowing—and not just from imbibing the local fare. He walked through the door radiant, and right away said he'd been staying at a place called 'Findhorn.' Just like Amanda said earlier this morning, I remember exactly where I was at the moment I heard the very word 'Findhorn.' I remember what I was wearing, where everyone was sitting in the room—the sounds of the street, the smells in the house! 'Findhorn.' Everything in me knew I was somehow connected to that place—even before Ian told his story. He described a retired air-force officer who ran a 'very clean commune' with his wife—who received guidance directly from God—along with a bunch of sweet old ladies and garden gnomes! We all fell about laughing—our friend Ian was hardly one to cavort with gnomes and elderly ladies—not to mention military types! However, later that day, Ian handed me a book he'd borrowed from the community library. It was stamped 'Findhorn Trust' inside the front cover. In that moment, I realised that Findhorn was the place I was looking for—a 'commune' based on clear, spiritual guidance—and organised enough to actually have a library complete with library cards on a Dewey Decimal system! A few weeks later—accompanied by Ian—I hitch-hiked up to Findhorn for the August Bank Holiday weekend—and stayed for eight years!

"The magic of Findhorn—from the moment I first heard the name—to this moment—has never left me. I worked hard there every day—but looking back over thirty years, those eight years were filled with a constant, incredible joy. I faced some difficult challenges then—and now—but my years at Findhorn, learning and living basic spiritual tenets about love and kindness, compassion, faith, and surrender, they keep me steady now. I am ever grateful. I can look back over thirty years and beyond and see the threads of my life interwoven with real magic—and the fabric is still being woven."

ShARI AND The LAWS OF MANIFESTATION

We all took a deep breath and looked around for the next person to tell their story.

"The magic started for me in 1974 when I was living in San Francisco. On Christmas Eve, a man nearly ran me down with his Porsche and ended up taking me out to dinner." Shari began her story dramatically—her blue eyes sparkling. "In making conversation, he mentioned Findhorn and that he had just read an article about it—in the San Francisco Chronicle, I think it was. I'd never heard of the place, but something deep inside resonated and I found myself saying, 'I don't know how I know this, but I will go to Findhorn before the end of next year.'

"I had no money to travel overseas and no idea how I would get there. But something inside me said to go ahead and act 'as if.' So I made travel reservations on a credit card and called the Findhorn Foundation to make a reservation for October. In September, I still had no money to go there. A few weeks later, I was at a party and was introduced to an Australian woman who had recently visited Findhorn. When she heard my story and my intent, she reached in her purse and wrote me a check for $500—no strings attached. I was on my way, having unknowingly followed the laws of manifestation—the law of abundance intrinsic to the running of the Findhorn Foundation itself.

"Of course, in my three weeks at the community I fell in love with the place and knew I wanted to live there. There was a deep knowing that my destiny was interwoven with this odd little community. I was staying in a small caravan in Pineridge and awoke one night to see lights at the foot of my bed. They were about four inches wide and moved in a dancing pattern around my feet. I looked to see if there was an external light source, but found none. When I put my hands into the midst of the lights, they gently scattered, and when I withdrew my hands, they returned to their pattern. I can't explain it, but it was most magical!

"During this initial visit, I was sitting in the library at the Park one night when a book literally fell off the shelf and landed at my feet. I picked it up to put back on the shelf and noticed it was an original manuscript of David Spangler's 'Laws of Manifestation.' It was clear that I had to read it!

"Back in San Francisco, I set about to incorporate the Laws of Manifestation into my life. I set a goal for the amount of money I wanted to raise—$10,000. That would allow me to pay off my debts and give me money to live at Findhorn for a few years. I was unemployed at the time, so I had my doubts. One day a friend asked me to help her distribute goodies which she baked and sold at a flea market in Sausalito. It was the inspiration I needed to start baking and selling things in the City, and I recognised it as one of the first Laws of Manifestation. The first day, I made a few loaves of banana bread and some chocolate chip cookies and walked around Ghirardelli Square and Fisherman's Wharf, selling goodies to the tourists and the vendors who lined the sidewalk.

"This continued for a few months, baking and selling about twenty dollars worth of goodies a day. It was fun and very low-key. Then Easter came. I baked my usual amount and sold out within half an hour. I realised I was limiting myself by the amount of baked goods I was taking out, went home, baked more, and sold out quickly. That night I baked more than I might have sold in an entire month before, and I sold every crumb the next day! It seemed that I could sell as much as I could bake—what an amazing concept—no limitations! Another fabulous 'rule' from the laws of manifestation! I was baking cranberry bread, banana bread, carrot bread, brownies and peanut butter balls, bringing home over a hundred dollars a day.

"In July, I reached my goal. I had made $10,000 in three months. I made my plans to leave. I was able to implement the Laws of Manifestation to reach my goal: to return to experience the Magic that is Findhorn."

ĐOUG'S SEARCH FOR THE NATURE SPIRITS

"Still to this day I don't fully understand how it is that the promises of Findhorn can become so very vivid and stick so hard for people," said a blond curly haired man called Doug.

"In 1979, the University of Wisconsin-Extension offered a course about nature spirits and the western mystery tradition—one look at the flyer and it was all over for me! The course was primarily for a university group planning to visit the community, but my wife-to-be and I knew immediately we would be going to Findhorn! It was one-way tickets on PanAm!

"In my imagination I expected everything at Findhorn to be slightly more roundish and cartoon-like. Maybe a bit elfin—with a few more muted pinks and greys setting the tone, and the air thick with whimsy.

"Was it sacred? You bet. There was not one aspect of Findhorn that did not seem to me radiant with beauty, simplicity, and meaningfulness. Every teapot, every tree-stump chair out back of the community centre, every errant twig, was permeated with purpose and life and joy. And every action taken in that realm—whether it was planting a seed, peeling a potato, waving hello, or taking a deep solitary breath—was a celebration, and a sense of connectedness, and a revelling in the very miracle of creation itself.

"And," Doug paused, "This experience was—in one form or another— shared by all the others there! It was alive in the smiles, the hugs, the driving of the bus and the vacuuming of the rug. Not only that, it was a very nice place, even in the non-sacred sense. The bungalows were clean, the meals were splendid, the grounds were pretty, and the scenery and views across the fields, the dunes and the Bay were enchanting. The landscape picked up full well on the aura of sacredness—it, too, was luminous by association with everything else miraculous. And the people at Findhorn were fascinating—the community attracted some very colourful people. There was also a library with the wisdom of the ages, which no-one made you read, and a sanctuary where no-one made you go, which contained no religious icons that anyone made you worship.

"During my two years there, the question always lingered for me: was the magic actually something externally manifest—a real objective phenomenon—obvious to everyone? Or had Findhorn actually been magical previously, but was now a shell of its former self, and I should have been there when it was really magical—when the carrots were eighteen inches long and the cabbages weighed forty pounds?!? Or did the magic not actually happen unless you personally had the tumblers fall and things click internally, and the veils get adjusted?"

We all sat quietly trying to digest Doug's stream of comments and queries.

RUE'S GREATEST TEACHERS

"When I got to Findhorn, there were a lot of surprises." Rue, who had been at Findhorn in the very early days, began speaking. "For one thing, the women's movement hadn't really reached there. Women were in traditional relationships in families, staying home to look after the children while the mates went off to work in the community. Mostly, the government of the place was run by the men. I was relieved to find two or three other women there who were interested in women's roles, and what it meant to be spiritual and a woman—we had no models except the traditional ones. We formed a women's group, which was seen as a pretty alarming move!

"I wasn't actively limited from doing non-traditional jobs, though. I ran the printing presses with two guys, and was the first woman to run the industrial strength dish-washing machine, which had always been run by one of the men on the kitchen clean-up rota. And as things changed, in due time I was invited to be part of the government of the community, and by then there was a good representation of women in the various groups. I never actually saw anyone prevented from doing anything at Findhorn based on their gender. And many men became involved in raising their children. Although, as in the larger society, more women stayed out of things to take care of babies than men did. Later—much to my surprise—I did too! Motherhood became my greatest teacher about love and the earth and intuition, and about what is important and what is divine about being human. I have been turned inside out by my children in a way nothing else could have done."

For the rest of the day we listened to the many amazing stories from people whose lives had been changed, often totally transformed, by going to Findhorn. Some lived there for many years, others for just a brief visit. But for all of them there was a moment when it seemed that they had come "home."

∞∞∞∞

WAKE-UP CALL

The following morning I was awakened by the insistent ringing of my telephone. It was still dark outside, and when I checked my watch I saw it was only 5 o'clock. Who on earth would call me at this time of the morning?

"Hello, Carly are you awake yet?" I heard as I lifted the receiver.

"I am now," I replied sleepily. "Is that you, Karin?"

"Yes, of course. Oh, dear, I've just remembered how early it must be over there. I just had to tell you, I've made up my mind, I'm going to Findhorn today to check it all out, to see if I can find the magic. How did the Gathering go? Did you get all the stories?" Karin's enthusiastic voice rang in my ear.

"Yes, I got all the stories and wrote them all down. It was absolutely….." I began.

"Great, wonderful. I'll hear all about it when I get back," Karin interrupted. " I'll call you when I get there. I have to hurry now to catch my flight. Wish me luck."

"Of course. Hope you find what you're looking for."

"So do I. 'Bye Carly, you can go back to sleep now," were Karin's parting words.

Knowing that would now be impossible, I got out of bed and put the kettle on for a cup of tea. "If anyone can find magic," I thought to myself "It's got to be Karin."

The Adventure Begins

There's Music in the Air

Yes, it had to be Karin. Me. I'm at the airport. On my way at last. I choose a seat by the window so I can watch my journey from the south of France to the north of Scotland unfold beneath me. I settle into my seat and put on earphones to listen to "Music from the Magic Garden" — wonderful music recorded at Findhorn in the seventies, which still moves my heart and soul. We soar into the clear sky above the snow-capped Pyrenees. The music enhances the mood for adventure.

> *"I dreamed a dream a long time ago*
> *About people who know how to live,*
> *Their words and their deeds are simple and pure*
> *And their love they most willingly give."*

The words sound so banal and Pollyanna in this cynical, fearful, post-September 11th world, but they had been true once. What if they still are? "And their love they most willingly give." I hum along, trying to ignore my fear that this may all be a waste of time. A month earlier, I had written to the management team of the Foundation, full of enthusiasm and excitement—letting them know I might be coming to Findhorn to write a new book about "the magic." The reply could not have been more discouraging, explaining that they were all very busy with serious finance meetings and the annual internal conference. The writer used words like "lukewarm" and "tepid." She wasn't sure the world needed a story about "the magic," as Findhorn was beginning to attract corporate clients who were more "grounded and useful."

I wonder if anyone will have time to speak to me.

I know I am going at a difficult time. The Findhorn Foundation is having big financial problems and difficulties balancing their budget, and some hard decisions will need to be made. I've heard rumours of selling some property, of people leaving, of cancelled projects. Nothing is new. I remember the last time this happened.

In the late seventies there was a huge and rapid growth in the community. Membership rose almost overnight to nearly three hundred and fifty, people had to share tiny caravans and sleep several to a room. At the same time we were also spending more money than was coming in, and trusted that "God would provide." After all, we thought, we were world servers, and surely the universe would send us all the funds we needed? Unfortunately, it seemed that we forgot to "tether our camels," and suddenly we had a huge debt and no foreseeable way to reduce it. Soon, many of the new members who had arrived with such enthusiasm and wonderful ideas left in droves, and by the early eighties we were reduced to around 120 members, a large debt and the same work and commitments as when there were over 300 of us!

I was running the kitchen at the Park at the time, and was asked to dramatically cut our budget. No more choice of two main courses, nor yummy desserts every evening. I had to learn to be creative with the humble potato and teary old onion. Things looked very bleak for a while as our accounts people struggled to pay the bills—though my culinary creativity improved amazingly.

The music continues to cover the drone of the jet engines. The mountains and sparkling snow have disappeared, and we are flying over the dark, winter grey English Channel. The New Troubadours are singing, "Change can come in the twinkling of an eye." Looking back at those difficult times, that's how quickly it all seemed to change—at least that's how it seems from a distance.

Those of us still left in the community in the early eighties refused to allow the fear of failure to rule us. I can't recall the details of how we did it, but I know we reconnected with our vision of being a centre of demonstration, of showing how we could live in harmony with nature, with ourselves and with spirit. We became once again that "One Incredible Family" that the Troubadours are singing in my headphones. And, once again, people were inspired and drawn to the community. This time we grew more slowly, organically, learning from our past mistakes.

Within a few years we were not only debt free, but had managed to buy the Caravan Park, the land that we had been renting for many years. Through the generosity of people around the world who were once again inspired by our work, we raised the funds and on our 21st birthday we bought our home.

∞∞∞∞

Emerging from my thoughts and memories, I peer out of the window to see the Scottish Highlands and Cairngorm mountains below me. Scotland is such a wild and beautiful country, where flora and fauna can still exist without too much interference by humans. I can see only craggy mountains and icy lochs—not a comfortable place for people to make their homes.

I am feeling a mixture of excitement and the anticipation of coming home: of meeting old friends and a fluttering nervousness in my belly. This is no ordinary visit for me, this is a quest, a journey of discovery. This time it will be different, and I have no idea what I will find. How will I be received? I have let many friends know why I was thinking of coming, that I will be asking questions and keeping my eyes open for signs, clues, hints and real evidence of "magic." Will people be cautious in speaking to me? Will I find resistance…or openness?

Time to buckle up our seat belts—no more time for wondering or supposing. As we descend into Inverness' tiny airport, the last track on the CD closes with a piece of music called "And There is More . . ."

"Yes," I think, "There probably will be."

cold arrival, warm welcome

Flying into Inverness in the north of Scotland in the middle of January can be either impressive and dramatic or dismal and cheerless. Today it seems more like the latter, both the sea and the sky are a slate grey, hard to see which is which. The mountains below are devoid of vegetation, resting during the dark winter months, nurturing the waiting seeds in the frozen earth and waiting for the light to return. The small lochs are all frozen, flat and grey.

But as always when the plane descends towards the lonely strip of concrete that is the runway of Inverness Airport, my heart starts beating faster as I identify the towns and villages we are flying over—Culloden, Dalcross, Nairn and Fort George.

"Welcome to Inverness," the stewardess tells us, "please stay seated until we come to a complete halt." It all looks so familiar; I have done this dozens of times—it only takes a couple more minutes before we are parked outside the new terminal, completed just the year before.

The stewardess opens the door and a blast of freezing air reminds me again that it is January in Scotland. The passengers wrap themselves in their coats and hats before rushing from the plane into the welcoming warmth of the terminal building. A few hurry to the smoking area, but most of us make our way to the baggage claim where the cases quickly appear—Inverness is a small airport.

Whenever I fly into Inverness, I inevitably find someone I know from the Findhorn community, and this time is no exception. There is Vita, an old friend who has been living here for many years. We hug each other, and can't believe that it is really so long since we last met. That's always a phenomenon among old friends in the community, the connection is always there, immediately picked up—even after many years.

However, it's not Vita who has come to collect me, it's my dear friend Judi. There she is in her little blue car; she has taken time off from her busy schedule to drive me to Findhorn. I wonder, silently, what she thinks about the purpose of my visit?

Judi has lived and worked for the Findhorn Foundation—the educational and spiritual centre of the community—for over twenty years. During those years she has been involved in many departments including the Kitchen, Education, and the Game of Transformation, as well as focalising two international conferences. Now, her major responsibility is in the department called Spiritual and Personal Development, affectionately known as S & PD, and a couple of years ago she began some very valuable spiritual mentoring by telephone and e-mail for people around the world who are not able to come to the community.

What I enjoy hearing about most is Judi's other job as a wedding celebrant. She says she is getting quite used to receiving phone calls from people asking, "Will you marry me?" She travels throughout Scotland helping couples create their own unique wedding ceremony—often in unusual and romantic locations such as castles, gardens, and even in a lighthouse.

So we have plenty to talk about in the hour it takes to drive to Findhorn from the airport. I ask dozens of questions about mutual friends and comings and goings. And all the while I see the familiar sights along the way, driving through the small towns with grey stone buildings so typical of Scotland, where the stores have names like MacGregor, MacDougal, Grant and MacKenzie. We drive across the small bridge over the River Findhorn where the brown, peaty water reminds me that we are in whisky country and through the small town of Forres which year after year wins a "Scotland in Bloom prize." No flowers now—the trees are bare and Grant Park is too cold today for even the children to play.

Suddenly, there it is, the small black and white signpost pointing to Findhorn—the same one I first saw twenty-seven years ago. My heart leaps with anticipation and excitement just as it did then. I can already see Findhorn Bay and the cluster of small cottages at the end of the peninsula that is Findhorn Village—a village that has been flooded and rebuilt several times over the past few centuries. The last mile takes us along the edge of the Bay, which—beyond the old Caravan Park—empties into the Moray Firth. On the right, we pass the Kinloss Airbase, an unlikely neighbour of the peace-loving Findhorn Community. One of the Nimrods is just taking off, blasting my ears with noise. I know this happens many times during the day, but no-one ever gets used to that sound.

I know that passing the Kinloss base is the last milestone before we arrive at my destination. And there it is, the first caravans at the lower end of the Findhorn Bay Caravan Park, an area that in the summer months is filled with holidaymakers from Glasgow, but is now deserted. Curtains are drawn, no tourists huddle in dripping tents on the watery lawns. Not until we turn into the entrance and drive towards the Phoenix store do we see people. I smile as I try to guess who will be the first person to recognise me, to ask the inevitable question, "What are you doing here?" But today I don't recognise anyone; perhaps it is the January darkness—already at 4 o'clock there is little daylight left. Perhaps everyone is busy working. I see very few people on the Runway—our main street—formerly part of the Kinloss airbase. I have mixed feelings: I'm sorry not to immediately see old friends running over to the car to greet me, but relieved that I don't have to explain myself quite yet, knowing I'm not here just on a friendly visit. I'm here to put their lives under a microscope, to understand what brought them here and what keeps them here.

When I arrived 27 years ago, after my initial horror at the ugliness of the grey and dismal Caravan Park, I fell in love with the people, the way of life, the spirit of joy and love I found here. What will I find now? It all looks so very different, how will it look and feel when I begin to explore both the outer and inner life?

We drive past rows of wooden buildings and caravans into the Field of

Dreams where I will be spending the next ten days in a bed and breakfast. Tonight I will allow myself the luxury of a calm, solitary evening, perhaps walk around on my own to visit some beloved old buildings and see what is new around the place.

"Now" is just for me, to let my body and soul make silent contact with this extraordinary place. I knock at the door of the B & B named "Sunflower" and am warmly welcomed by Susan. She shows me to my room and I let myself sink into the vivid feelings and thoughts that await me, looking out across the Field of Dreams. There are lights on in every house and I wonder what is going on behind those brightly-lit windows. I am not yet ready to go out and explore after all; tomorrow I will begin my quest, my search for the reality and perhaps the magic of what is here. Tonight is just for me.

THANKS FOR THE MEMORIES

I slept fitfully that first night and was visited in my dreams by the many dear, beloved ghostly spirits that were once part of this place and part of my life. People who have journeyed to other places, but whose imprint is still very much part of Findhorn's fabric today.

The first one to drift into my awareness was Jennie who lived in the corner bungalow by the entrance. By the time I got to know her she was already mainly confined to her bed, and no longer moved out of her house. Various people would visit her during the day bringing her food, which, except for a few oat cakes, she mainly ignored. Others came to wash her hair, which she resented, and still others to clean her house. I was working in our little Spar grocery store at the time, and once a week I would get a phone call from Jennie. In her very Scottish lilt—she was one of the very few real Scots in the community—she would ask, "Would you please bring me o'er a bottle o' whisky and some chocolate?"

I would fill a plastic bag with the goodies and walk the fifty yards to her house. She always wanted me to stay for a chat, and I was more than happy to listen to this fascinating woman who had so much wisdom and a hilarious sense of humour. I once asked her what she did with herself all day, worried that she might be lonely or bored. "Och, I'm always busy sleeping, and in my sleep I leave my body and let my spirit go where'er it is needed. I visit places where there is war or violence, and help the poor, shocked souls who have been killed to cross over." Though she could no longer use her physical body, Jennie was still hard at work on a different plane.

In a BBC documentary film made in the early days of the community, Jennie was interviewed in her living room, sitting with some other elderly folks. She was asked, "Do people die here often?" "Och, no," she replied with her impish grin, "Only once!" Eventually, when she felt her work on this planet was done, she, too, died—only once—and left me smiling with appreciation for this beautiful lady.

I slept for a while, and found myself again drifting into the past. I was standing on the runway outside Doris's bungalow. Doris was another of the older generation who had been living in the community long before I arrived. I remembered her as 'Doris in charge of the allowances'. Once a month on a Friday, we would all make our way to Doris's house to collect our monthly allowance. As staff members of the Findhorn Foundation, we would receive our housing, food and energy free, plus a small cash allowance which was supposed to cover our personal needs like toiletries, bus fares, and any clothes we had not been able to find in 'the boutique'— our free second-hand clothing 'store'. In reality, most of us spent our allowance on chocolate, beer, and the occasional movie. So it was always a happy crowd who met in Doris' living room at the end of the month. She would look sternly at the younger members, making sure they had wiped their shoes, muddy from working in the garden. Doris was the kind of woman who expected respect and good manners, and we respectfully signed her little list and left the house quietly before yelping with joy. It's extraordinary how very rich one could feel with £10 ($15) in one's pocket.

Doris died suddenly just a few years ago. We woke up one morning and she had gone. "How can collecting allowances ever be the same again?" I had wondered.

These days, the allowances are rather more than the £10 of those early happy days and are collected from the Accounts office, or even paid by direct debit into members' bank accounts. I suppose that is also magic of a kind, but how can it compare with Doris counting out the crisp bank notes and the friendly row of people queuing up patiently outside?

I woke up and padded down the corridor to the bathroom. The night was very black, the stars incredibly bright. There is no light pollution here, in this quiet field in the north of Scotland.

I slipped back under my warm bed clothes and allowed myself to drift into more wondrous dreams and memories. And of course, there she is— tall and slim, with a shy smile—Joanie. Joanie was another one of the amazing women who came to Findhorn in the very early days, to serve. I will always remember her as the 'linen lady', the guardian of the sheets and towels. The spare room and porch of her house were lined with shelves full of sheets, pillowcases, towels and blankets. In the early days, before we became responsible for our own laundry, we would go to Joanie on Saturday mornings with our dirty bed linens and exchange them for new, freshly laundered ones. She would humour those of us who requested matching blue sheets or white towels, but always insisted that the guests had the best and newest linen. She regularly drove into nearby Forres and went to one of the town's small shops to buy whatever replacement linen was needed. On these trips she would often take Eileen with her to visit the hairdresser.

Joanie's bungalow was directly across from the community kitchen, and my most vivid and wonderful memory of her recurred whenever I was cooking dinner. She would come over towards the end of the afternoon to exchange the kitchen towels and aprons, ask me what was for dinner, and then no matter what it was, she always thanked me for cooking. It was my job, it was my duty to cook for the community, and yet every time she came into the kitchen, she thanked me. I would be left glowing in her appreciation.

Joanie died some years ago when she was in her mid 80's, at home in her little bungalow, surrounded by people who loved her, most especially her best friend Eileen Caddy. I still remember Joanie every year on March 5th—her birthday—which is also my son Michael's birthday. Every year on their birthday she would give him some money, and every year he would give her a flower.

For the remainder of the night I greeted a procession of old friends who are no longer with us on the physical plane. Barbara D'Arcy Thompson, who threatened to give us our honey in brown paper bags if we did not return our glass jars! Barbara left us one cold winter's day when she was drowned in the dark rushing waters of the Findhorn River at Randolph's Leap. Evelyn, who was so determined to celebrate her 90th birthday that she did so a couple of years early, in case she died before she reached that milestone. She must have known something, because in reality she did not live to be 90. I'm so glad she had her day of glory—her special tea party in the Community Centre with all of us gathered around, holding her in our hearts.

There was also Elfreda, with whom I sang in the community choir for many years and who massaged my feet when I was sick; Inara, who spent the last years of her life in a nearby nursing home because she was too sick for us to care for her in the community; and Mary Coulman who disliked garlic and loved babies, and made pink sugar mice for the children at Christmas. So many special people who were so loved in this community.

The last person to visit me during that long and restless night was Elizabeth Grindley, my neighbour for many years. She suffered from a progressive disability and had never been able to walk unaided during the 27 years I knew her. Every day she drove a little three-wheeler car back and forth from her home to the Community Centre for lunch. Everyone who knew her remembered the pendulum she held over each food item on the buffet, sensing which foods would be good for her and which she should avoid. Elizabeth was a healer, always willing to help any of us. She died just a few weeks before I arrived here on my quest.

I lie awake, wondering why these women have visited me during the night, my first night at Findhorn. After all, I have come to find the magic of the place now, not as it was years ago. Perhaps, in order to find what is here now, I need to remember and learn from those who created and served this community from the very beginning. Many of these women came to Findhorn at a time in their lives when they could have begun to wind down, to relax into a comfortable retirement. Instead, they chose to come and build a community, a centre of spirit and love, a light centre of clarity and truth. They chose to change and grow and serve both spirit and humanity to the very end of their lives on earth. They gave of themselves completely, and passed on when their particular and unique work was done. I shall remember them as I begin my search today. I can almost hear them whispering, "Remember the past, but release all attachment to it. It was important at the time, we all had our roles to play, what amazing times we had, now move into the present and find the magic that awaits you."

It's still dark outside, but in my being I feel warmed and guided by the spirits of Findhorn past, encouraging me to open myself to the experiences ahead.

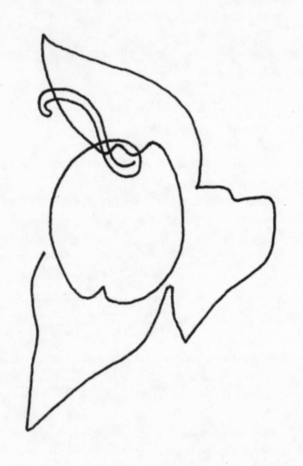

change can come

the field of dreams

It's 4:00 a.m. on a freezing cold January morning, but already a solitary light is shining from the small, yellow wooden house in the middle of the field—or rather, what was just a field a few years ago. Trevor the baker is awake and getting ready to walk the short, narrow path to his little bakery. He dresses quietly, so as not to waken his wife Birgitte and daughter Emma. Soon there will be the warm and delicious aroma of bread baking in his ovens, whole wheat loaves, rye bread, poppy seed rolls, all ready to deliver to the Phoenix shop and later to the Café where customers will come for lunch, eagerly devouring the crusty bread with their hot soup. Trevor slips his woolly hat over his ears, and, a lonely figure lit only by starlight, makes his way to work.

Twenty years ago this field on the edge of the Park would still have been covered with stubble from the barley that had ripened there during the previous summer. I lived in one of the old bungalows on the edge of the field and would often watch the luminous carmine pink and gold sunrises over the distant hills while drinking my early morning cup of tea. In the spring we could watch the tractors and ploughs digging up the soil. In fact, my young son's first word was "traktrak." Then came the planting of the grain, and just a few short weeks later tiny green shoots would cover this enormous field in a carpet of delicate green. By August, heavy golden grains waved in the summer breeze until the day arrived for the harvest; when huge yellow combine harvesters would travel up and down the field, followed by the shrieking gulls from Findhorn Bay. For the children, the best part of the year came after the harvest when they could run laughing and playing among the bales of straw, climbing to the top and daring each other to jump.

It is in this field that I wake up this morning, in a lovely wooden house called Sunflower, a house that was not even a dream twenty years ago, but is now home to Susan Gibson and her ten-year-old son Jonathan. The smell of fresh bread makes me realise that I am hungry and I make my way down to the cosy little dining room where Susan has prepared my breakfast. Sunflower is one of the new enterprises in the community—a Bed and Breakfast where people from all over the world can come to stay and experience the community for a few days or longer —whether or not they take part in a programme.

Susan is obviously going to look after me very well: my breakfast is a bowl of delicious fresh fruit salad and crusty, fresh bread rolls. I decide on real English tea instead of one of the large selection of herb teas.

As I sip my tea, Susan and I begin to get to know one other.

"How long have you been living here?" I ask.

"This house was finished nearly two years ago," Susan replies. "But I've been coming to visit the community with Jonathan since he was quite young. We participated in several Family Experience Weeks during the summers. Jonathan was born with a hole in his heart, and after heart surgery when he was five, I brought him here to recuperate and get well. I somehow felt drawn to bring him here."

"Where were you living at that time?" I asked.

"In Spain," she says. "I lived there for eighteen years, and before that in Tenerife in the Canary Islands. Jonathan was constantly telling everyone that when he grew up he wanted to come and live here, so one day I thought, 'Why not now, why should he have to wait until he is older?'"

"So it was Jonathan who brought you here?" I told Susan that I believed my unborn son, Michael, now twenty-six had brought me here for the first time many years before.

She nodded. "I cannot exactly pinpoint what made me come to live in Findhorn, except that I knew it was the place where I could bring up my son in a spiritual environment and try to live a simple and peaceful life, away from so much materialism and unnecessary conflict. From the moment I made the decision everything just unfolded easily, and here I am!"

"And are you happy to be living here now?" I wondered.

"Oh yes, I thoroughly enjoy being here, and while I am aware of the energy of this place, it's mainly the people I am living with that matter most. I can be myself—be totally accepted—and I can be me! The people are friendly and loving and the surroundings are beautiful. Yes, there are also challenges, as there are everywhere, but I feel it is the right place for me and have no longing to be anywhere else. Nor does Jonathan."

Chatting with Susan, I feel that my quest for magic here at Findhorn has begun without my having to step outside the front door. However, I am now ready to venture out into a surprisingly sunny day and see what it has in store for me.

Before I go anywhere else, though, I need to visit our Findhorn Press office and say hello to Carol. Carol is the manager of our office here. I have known her for over twenty years, and our children grew up here. Nowadays, one of our favourite things is showing each other photographs of our grandchildren. I don't know what we would do without Carol, she is so totally reliable and committed to Findhorn Press. It means Thierry and I can live and work anywhere, knowing that everything is taken care of here.

It's only a few steps for me to reach the top of the Runway and there is the Press Building. I always enjoy that first moment when I open the door of the office and am met by rows and rows of our books. Although it is still quite early, Carol is already at work.

"Hi, Carol, I've arrived," I call out, seeing her in the back office dealing with some orders. Next thing I know, I'm enveloped in a huge hug. Carol is quite a bit taller than me and she smiles down broadly.

"Karin! How are you doing? Did you have a good journey? When are you coming for dinner?" she asks, almost without a pause between questions. I wonder, which one to answer first? The dinner of course! Carol knows that I love her cooking—particularly the delicious organic veggies from her garden.

I make a little tour around the office. This doesn't take long, it's just two small rooms, with every available space filled with books and packaging material. From this small place our mail orders are dispatched all over the world.

I don't have much time to chat with Carol this morning, for my quest awaits me. But before I do anything else, I think I'm going to have a cup of tea in the Green Room Cafe.

The Cafe is a community meeting place. It is part of the Universal Hall, and serves not only tea and coffee, healthy organic snacks and lunches, but also scrumptious gooey French pastries. I can already guess who will be there so early in the morning—and there he is, sitting in his corner as usual—Ken. Ken is one of those people that no community can exist without, because he can fix anything. He has been my saviour on so many occasions, changing locks, repairing bicycles, putting up shelves, painting walls and fixing things nobody else could do. But his main job is to sit in the cafe drinking tea and smiling at everyone who arrives. Which is just what he is doing now. In a rapidly changing world, I'm so glad that there are still some things that I can rely on.

It's still too early for the morning crowd to be in the cafe, apart from Ken and Trevor the baker, who has just delivered a tray of hot bread. Now there is some magic—the smell of bread just out of the oven. I join him with my cup of tea and we catch up on community news before I leave to go on my walk around the Park. I'm interested to see what is new, and what is being built. There is also a very special friend I hope to visit in Pineridge.

PINERIDGE

Warmed by my hot tea, I start up the road to Pineridge. It is nearly ten o'clock and finally full winter daylight in this northerly latitude. In the morning light, I can see the whole Field of Dreams on my right, with all its new houses and others under construction. I notice one with a turf roof and I wonder who lives there. And there is the house that Mary Inglis recently built—looks like she is already living there.

Arriving in Pineridge, I see on my left an unusual, almost-finished house with what look like straw bales for walls—this must be the house that Karl and Deborah are building. I hope to talk to them while I am here.

A few yards further up the road is a small, lilac-coloured building with a huge ribbon painted around it. The boutique! That seems a rather grand name for this little place, but it is one of the most visited places around the community! The location of the Boutique has changed several times over the years since its humble beginnings in 1970 in a wardrobe in Mary Hilton's spare room, but for many years now it has been in this colourful concrete building. I step inside and recognise the familiar smell of ageing socks. This is the place where community members bring clothes and any useful items they no longer need, and where they can pick up anything that takes their fancy—for free. When my children were young, and we had very little money, it was invaluable to find 'new' clothes for them as they grew out of their old ones, and to bring back their used ones for someone else to have. Every now and again, I would have the luck to find something really good and new—usually something a guest had left behind. Some clothes could be followed around the community—I particularly remember a blue woollen dress of mine that I saw on several other women in later years. Not infrequently someone would come up to me squealing, "Ooh, that's my coat/jacket/skirt/scarf you are wearing." I half expected to see the blue woollen dress hanging on the rack!

I continue my walk around Pineridge; past the new greenhouse—though there's not much to see in there at this time of the year. On the corner is the maintenance building, and there are still a lot of the old caravans here, all of them familiar. Many of them were—and still are—the homes of some dear old friends. Here is the caravan where my friend Ann lived—she is now living in South Africa. There is Ludja's caravan—oh, I remember the fuss when she cut down some trees in her garden. This blue caravan was once Virginia's home—I bought her hair dryer from her when she moved to the USA. Here on the right is Maria's bungalow; she must have lived there for thirty years or more. And here is Anna's house. Anna became my friend right from the start, when I arrived here twenty-seven years ago. In this very small bungalow she brought up four children, all of them now scattered around the world.

At last, here is the old friend I am really looking for—my Christmas Tree. A quarter of a century ago I planted this tree. It had been decorated and displayed inside our caravan, and after Christmas, we planted it outside. And here it still is, now nearly thirty feet tall. Every time I come to the community, I visit my tree: we have a little chat, share how we're both doing and reminisce about happenings over the years. I like to think it will always be there, my piece of Findhorn that will survive me.

There in front of me now is Bag End where the first ecological houses were built. Real houses. Twenty years ago there were just caravans here. Tiny caravans like the one where Binka and Michael lived with their children, Elysia and Coren. And this is where Judi's caravan once stood. I stop for a moment, recalling a fun weekend together painting the inside walls bright blue. Now, in their place are large wooden houses, built close together for comfort. There is a central bicycle shed, and the gardens already look quite well established. They must have been there longer than I thought.

I round the corner and there are the Barrel Houses—five amazing buildings that are the mecca for every tourist arriving here. These houses, each uniquely different, were all built from old whisky barrels that one of the local distillers no longer needed. The first one arrived around fifteen years ago, and we all watched in amused astonishment as Roger built his Barrel Home—on a warm day you could still smell the aroma of whisky in the wood. Later Craig and May built another Barrel, which grew and grew as they added more rooms when their children arrived. Now there are five Barrel houses, including John's double Barrel!

Pineridge is a most surprising place, with something new and interesting around every curve and corner. Leaving the Barrel cluster, I now come to the studios. I glance into the weaving studio, which looks exactly as it did when I first arrived—even the same colours are on the oldest loom. I can't resist going in and having a closer look.

Inside, I find Kathryn at a spinning wheel. This is not an unusual sight, nor, as in some Scottish tourist attractions, is it a picturesque activity merely for the curiosity of visitors. Kathryn is just quietly sitting there on her own, spinning some yarn which she will later weave into fabric.

There are several old looms in the studio. On one is a small carpet, almost completed, and on the oldest and very large loom shine the distinctive colours and pattern of a Sunrise Panel. The original Sunrise Panel was a gift made to the community in 1967 by the Donavourd weavers, of Pitlochry in central Scotland, when the Main Sanctuary was first opened. The Panel consists of hundreds of brilliant colours radiating from an intense centre of sparkling, soft light. A few years later, the old loom, the unique pattern and the method of weaving the Panels, were passed on to the weavers in our community—and now—thirty years later—the method has been handed down and they are still being woven. Once more, I am amazed at how the delicate threads of colour are woven into a pattern that so magnificently replicates the beauty of a Scottish sunrise—like the one I witnessed a little earlier from the Field of Dreams.

Kathryn shows me around the studio, which seems not to have changed at all since I first visited it so many years before. I had lived in a bungalow opposite the weaving studio for a number of years and would sometimes be able to watch the weavers and spinners at work—often working outside on a warm summer day.

However, now it is mid-winter and I reluctantly leave the warm and tranquil atmosphere of the weaving studio. I notice how tall the trees have grown on the lawn opposite, and I walk past the Trees for Life building to my first appointment, the Pottery Studio.

THE MAGIC OF THE POTTER

I enter the pottery, and instead of the pungent smell of wet clay, I am met with the aroma of hot toast and jam. Brian is having his breakfast. There, sitting on one of the comfortable looking squashy armchairs, is the man I am looking for—toast in one hand and large mug of coffee in the other.

Hard to know how to describe Brian; perhaps I could try saying he looks like a rather large, roundish garden gnome, minus the pointed hat and boots! During my years of living in the community, I had often heard about a group of artists and craftsmen and women who had arrived in the early seventies to create the craft studios and bring the arts to Findhorn. One of these people was Brian Nobbs.

Brian is a quiet, jovial man, invariably cheerful and smiling, with a passion for good food and wine, which is something I share with him. He is also the community potter, and has run the pottery studio here in Pineridge for many years. Although he first came here in the very early days of the community—long before I arrived—he was away for a number of the years I spent as a member of the Foundation.

I would love to know more about Brian and hear the story of how he came to Findhorn, so I wait for him to finish his toast while I take a look at all the pots on the shelves—there are candle holders and jugs, mugs, plates, and vases, some ready to be sold, others waiting to be fired in the kiln. I touch some of them carefully; they are smooth and sensual with subtle colours.

I see that Brian has now eaten the last bite of his breakfast and looks ready to answer my questions.

"So, what do you want to know?" he asks, putting his dishes in the sink.

"I've heard that you have led a rich and fascinating life, Brian. I'd love to know how and why you came here to Findhorn in the first place."

"Well, it all came about as the result of a series of quasi-miraculous events. First, it was an experiment with a Ouija board with a group of friends that led to our having spiritual guidance to prepare to create an arts and crafts community in Scotland. That was in 1969. We were supposed to help 'prepare for the New Age.' You can imagine how strange that sounded to us!"

Even now, Brian still looks somewhat surprised. He rinses his cup and plate and puts them neatly on the draining board.

"Then, about a year later, we heard about this place called Findhorn and eventually decided to contact them. Imagine our surprise when they replied to us immediately, and told us that we were expected! Peter Caddy invited us to come to build and run the Studios. Eileen Caddy had received guidance that a group of artists would be coming and they had already been fund-raising for a year in readiness for their (our) arrival! They were convinced that we must be the expected group, and Peter told us to 'please hurry and come.'"

After living in the Findhorn Community for so many years, I am no longer surprised by this kind of story.

"What happened next, looks like you decided to come?" I ask him.

"Yes, I came up here to check it out, but I had great doubts about the whole thing. I had been a monk for some years, a Roman Catholic, and was not sure that this 'New Age' business was at all compatible with my spiritual path. In fact, I arrived here on a Sunday and the first thing I asked was where I could attend Mass."

"What did you do? Was there a Catholic Church in the area?"

"Well, a very odd thing happened—I didn't need to find a church. I found that Canon Andrew Glazewski, a man I greatly respected and admired but had not previously met, just happened to be here that day and was about to say his daily Mass right here in the Sanctuary."

Brian pauses for a moment, remembering that moment of surprise and delight. "After that I was pretty sure that I had been guided here, and decided to stay."

"What happened then Brian, did you find the magic?"

His face lights up when he recalls those early days. "We found it all right! I cannot remember any period in my life that had anything even resembling the intensity of wonder and discovery that those opening years of the seventies held for me and the others in the arts group."

I recall my own arrival and early experiences in the seventies, full of the newness of it all, the excitement, the wonder . . . we all felt like pioneers. Brian has more to say.

"Findhorn was an incredible awakening to just how beautiful it is to exist. For those first few years I could hardly believe the total renewal I felt within me. I commented to one member of the arts group that I felt like someone reborn. In some ways it even was a bit like the 'born again' experience among evangelical Christians."

"Is it still like that now? Do people coming here still have that experience?" I wonder.

Brian is thoughtful, trying to put words to his feeling.

"Today's experience for the newcomer is much more sober. 'Growing people' is clearly a much more serious endeavour than growing giant cabbages. A little of the old intoxication would actually be a fine thing, and sometimes the Experience Week groups are taken to that place for at least a peek, but, as many have said to me, the very things that had drawn their initial interest seem sometimes to be missing".

That sounds rather sad. I wonder what has happened. Has some of the magic slipped away? "What is it that is missing, is it something important or just the glamour of the early days?" I ask.

"In some ways we are well rid of the 'glamour' of those heady early times," Brian continues. "However, there really was a baby in the bath, and the danger is that it could be gone."

I am beginning to wonder if this may possibly be the case, and press him further. "Are there still people here who work consciously with nature spirits?" I ask.

"Oh, yes!" he replies instantly, much to my relief. "I think many still do, but it is often seen as purely a concern of the gardeners so that, for many people, nature spirits are set aside as not really relevant. Just yesterday, an Experience Week guest asked me why we developed these awarenesses if we didn't work in the gardens. I really wasn't sure how to answer her, though now that we are speaking of it again, I do have a clue."

I think about this for a while, remembering that when I lived in the community, I had always resisted any kind of gardening or outdoor work. I found the cold wind and rain a good reason for working in a warm kitchen!

"Do you think it would be of value for us all to work on our connection with nature—with the nature spirits?" I shiver at the thought of working in the gardens in the depth of winter.

It looks like I have now hit on Brian's favourite topic. "Yes, I think that would teach us all something. There is a universal value to this enlargement of consciousness. It really has very little to do with growing bigger and better cabbages. The true value rests in what it has done for my experience of reality, and the wonderful quality it has added to my whole life! I believe every person who becomes aware of the multitude of conscious life that surrounds them will experience an immensely increased joy and delight in being alive. One clear benefit of such consciousness is that we will see our place in the universe very differently."

Brian takes a deep breath and looks out of the window across to the Field of Dreams. "We could then interact with the world around us with total empathy and lose some of the cold, manipulative detachment that has allowed the exploitation of our beautiful planet. Ultimately this is the key to an ecological turn-around, because it also carries the truth that when we work together in co-operation with Nature, Nature itself will powerfully respond. Just imagine how much could be achieved when this happens!"

Both of us fall silent for a moment, letting the implications of his words sink in. The small pottery studio suddenly seems very peaceful—and very large—almost as if the ceiling has disappeared.

"What about you Brian," I ask quietly. "Do you still have this experience, do you connect with and 'see' nature spirits?"

"Yes, I still experience all this," Brian begins slowly, "but it is not usually so attached to traditional fairy-tale images like the experiences I had early on. My belief is that such powerful images from mythology are simply an expedient means to gain our attention, and of course they carry many layers of important symbolism."

I nod in agreement, and change the subject, aware that our time together is drawing to a close.

"There was a time when you left the community—for quite a long time, it seems. What led you to do that?"

Brian looks at the clock—I think he wants to get back to his pots soon. Then he answers me. "The reasons for my decision to return to a pretty rigid and fundamentalist Catholicism, and indeed to the Benedictines, are complex. It included a certain amount of fear, caused by my increasing level of penetration into other realms as my psychic awareness developed."

"I imagine there are shadow sides on the psychic levels?" I ask him.

"Yes, I wondered if I knew enough to avoid getting entangled in clever demonic snares. But the experiences also removed all doubt that spirit is real and that there are other habitations than the purely physical."

"What did you do then?"

"This led to several years of further experience within a Christian mystical ethos, which gave me greater confidence and was itself very enriching. In the end, the lack of a true vocation became clear to me, and it also became clear that I had every reason to trust in God's protection so long as my intentions were for goodness and truth. Within a few years of leaving the monastery I realised that it would be important to return to Findhorn. Many years earlier, ROC had told me that I was being prepared to fulfil a destiny similar to his and that I would be doing similar work at Findhorn after his death. At the time this had seemed unimaginable, but by 1992 Peter Caddy confirmed that a quite independent source had told him that this was so. Dorothy Maclean has also has said so publicly, and she invariably invites me into her workshops to talk to the group."

"So that's why you are still here, Brian?"

"Yes, that is why I am still around, talking to groups when invited, and generally keeping alight the flame that Dorothy and ROC lit and nourished."

We hug goodbye, and I leave Brian and his pots to continue on my way, wondering whom I will meet next on my adventure into the magic of Findhorn. As the cold wind greets me, I hope it will include a hot cup of tea. Checking my watch, I see that it is actually time for lunch and, wrapping my coat a little tighter around me, I walk hastily down from Pineridge to the Community Centre.

LUNCH WITH ROSIE

Still shivering, I arrive at the Community Centre. It's only a few minutes walk, but the wind is bitingly cruel and I'm glad to enter the cheerful warmth of the dining room. The kitchen staff are just putting out the dishes for lunch—two huge pots of soup, trays of hot vegetables, bowls of salads and fresh crusty bread. I've heard that, because of the current financial cutbacks, the food is not as good as it used to be. But then I notice that some of my favourites are still there, like roast parsnips, potatoes baked with rosemary, sliced beetroot—and a tray of tofu lasagne. What looks like a cream of tomato soup smells delicious, or perhaps I'll try the onion soup instead.

However, before we begin to eat, we take a few moments to attune together and bless the food. We create a circle around the tables and hold hands, while one of the kitchen staff says a blessing. Then I feel the well-remembered squeeze. When a blessing or attunement is over, the person leading it gently squeezes the hands on either side, and it is then passed on throughout the circle.

I pick up a plate, fill it with all my choices, butter a slice of brown, whole-wheat bread, and look around the dining room for someone I know.

The noise level is rising as more people enter the room. I see a group of hungry-looking guests who have been working in the garden—their cheeks ruddy, rubbing cold hands and obviously ready for a hot meal and some relaxation after a busy morning.

Then I notice my old friend Rosie and wave to her to come and join me for lunch.

"Hi, Karin, I'd heard you were here. Is it true you are planning to write a book about us?" she asks, sitting down on the bench next to me and looking at me somewhat quizzically.

"Yes," I smile. "It's true. Someone has to do it, why not me? I'm trying to discover if the magic still exists here. What do you think? Do you still work in Outreach?'"

"Yes, I still travel all over the world. In fact I'm off to Ireland in a few days time to give some talks and dance workshops. Mmmmm. . ." Rosie takes a few spoonfuls of her soup before she continues. "You know, Karin, Findhorn is still seen as a beacon of hope out there in the world. And there is enormous appreciation for Eileen and Dorothy, for their discipline and obedience to living a God-centred life. They are such an inspiration to others, and though they are now well into their eighties, they still continue to serve."

"Yes, I agree. I can certainly understand that. They have given their lives to listening to their inner guidance and following it without question. But what about the rest of the community, how is that seen from out there?" I ask.

Rosie continues. "Many people are awed by the fact that folks here have given up perceived 'normality', perceived 'security', to be part of this experiment—living and working together with others from different faiths, backgrounds, cultures, and age groups. Many people have all sorts of reasons for thinking they would love to live in community, yet they also realise the commitment, dedication, personal responsibility and learned skills that are needed . . . "

There is a happy interruption as a couple of people recognise me and come over to give me a welcoming hug.

"I'm really enjoying these baked parsnips, we can't get them in France, the potatoes are also rather nice . . . " I comment, turning to Rosie and switching on my tape recorder. We return to the purpose of our conversation, and I ply Rosie with more questions, hoping to reveal another strand of magic.

"You've been here for many years now. When did you first arrive?"

"Oh, it was the usual thing, we had read some books about Findhorn while we were homesteading in Canada, and became curious. We were bringing our children—all three of them under four—to meet their grandparents over here, and thought we'd come and visit."

I can still remember the first time I saw Rosie, with little Andrew in his pram and the two girls, Alexandra and Heather, hanging on tight to their mother's hands. What a courageous decision it must have been to move their young family here at that time.

"It was more Ian's idea than mine," Rosie explains, "I was too busy trying to cope with three little ones to make any decisions."

"And twenty years later you are still here, and the children are grown up. What's kept you here all these years?"

Rosie puts down her fork and thinks.

"I suppose we just kept getting more and more involved—when the children were little we were part of the group of parents who started up the Moray Steiner School. Later we got involved in running Family Weeks, where we welcome other families with children to come and participate in our lives and work. They were always very popular. As our own children grew up, they became involved in the Youth Project that our teenagers started. Later they also began running Youth Weeks for other young people."

My son Michael was also part of this group of teenagers who raised the money to build their own house where they could meet and have their parties, play loud music and talk all night, putting the world to rights.

"We certainly never came here with the intention of staying twenty years," Rosie continues. "We just were always busy doing things. Ian has worked in many areas—like on the Hall, and then he was inspired to build the Nature Sanctuary. My focus has been mainly in Education, Publications, and with Sacred Dance and the Iona group."

Rosie finishes the last parsnip and picks up her plate and soup bowl. She's off to one of her many activities.

"Karin, so great to see you—I'll catch you later . . . "

"But what about the children, did they benefit from living here?" Rosie is already half way out of the dining room, dropping off her dirty dishes in the washing up area.

"No more time now, ask them yourself," she calls back to me.

"But what about the . . . ?" I shout after her. But she's gone.

MEETING OF HEARTS AND MINDS

"Bus to Cluny!" Barnaby's head pops round the door, calling those of us waiting to catch the afternoon bus to Cluny Hill College. I pick up my things and make my way out onto the Runway where Herbie is waiting for us.

Herbie is a bus. As are Grace and Frances. Whenever a new vehicle is purchased for the community, it is given a name, usually by the transport department. I've never yet learned why these particular names were chosen, but it does make it easy when we can tell each other that "Herbie is doing the afternoon run" or that "Grace will be taking us to Erraid at the weekend." Because several miles separate the various locations of the community, these buses are invaluable, and generations of guests and members have been ferried from The Park to Cluny and back, from Cluny to Randolph's Leap, and from The Park to the west coast islands of Iona and Erraid. The buses also take the children to the Steiner school and pick up the new guests from the train station on Saturdays. There have been several generations of buses which have diligently driven back and forth—some like Jasmine, Daphne, Henry, and Woodstock have long since gone to that big bus stop in the sky—and before them there was Peter's faithful Morris Traveller, Sir Galahad!

In the past, the buses would also do a weekly run to the nearby town of Elgin where community members could go shopping or visit the dentist. At Christmas time there would always be several outings to Inverness or Aberdeen for the serious Christmas shoppers. In the summer, if the day was unexpectedly warm, it was not unusual for everyone to drop their work, quickly prepare a picnic and jump into the buses heading for the beaches at Rose Isle or Primrose Bay, or the magnificent rhododendron gardens at Black Hills. These buses hold some dear memories for me. Of course, it's different now. The buses are still here, but these days many community members own their own cars. Twenty years ago, I might have seen five or six cars parked on the Runway, but now it is often difficult to find a parking space. I suppose that is progress of a kind.

This afternoon, I am glad to be going on the bus. I see many old friends already in their seats, smiling at me from the windows. I spot India, Judy, Rosie (so that's where she was off to!), Mari and Dürten among them. And of course our driver, the smiling Barnaby. We are all going over to Cluny for the Internal Conference.

This conference has been happening each year ever since I can remember. It is a time when the Foundation takes a break from its guest programmes, reviews what has happened over the past year, evaluates how each work department is doing, deliberates on its annual budget, and makes plans for the future. Because there are no guests to care for, it is also a time when the members can relax and have fun together. There are special meals, evening sharings with particularly outrageous skits, and nature outings to local beauty spots. It is a time for the 'family' to get together and enjoy themselves.

This year it feels rather different. The conference is being held without the usual break from work. The guests are still here and the departments are functioning normally. I know there are big financial problems within the Foundation, and perhaps taking a week off is not appropriate or affordable. I have arrived on the third day of the conference, and this afternoon is the final session. The internal conference is only for the Foundation staff and members—not for the entire community—but, as a former, visiting member, I have been invited to attend as a silent observer. I am extremely interested in seeing how the Foundation is handling its financial challenges and what suggestions are going to be made to deal with them.

After a giggling, noisy five miles in Herbie, we arrive at Cluny, drive up the short drive and come to a stop right outside the front door. I haven't been to Cluny for a long time; it always seems to look bigger than I remember. Just inside is a reception area with notice boards covered with hundreds of little coloured sticky notes: nice to see that in these days of e-mail some people still prefer to write to each other.

I have half an hour before the conference begins so I take the opportunity to look around, have a cup of tea and see if I run into old friends. I walk into the lounge, filled with large comfortable armchairs and couches; there is a roaring fire in the fireplace and newspapers and books are scattered on the tables—seemingly exactly where they were the last time I was here! A few people are relaxing with their hot drinks, deep in conversation, others appear to be sleeping off a good lunch, but I don't see anyone I know. I walk through to the dining room, a very lovely, big room with many tables where members and guests sit and take their meals. At the south end of the room is an enormous picture window overlooking the town's golf course and the distant hills.

It all feels so familiar. I lived in the Community for twenty-five years, but I never lived at Cluny. However, I worked here occasionally and have participated in many workshops and numerous celebrations in this room. Through the swing door is the stillroom and kitchen. Some cheerful looking people are still washing up and filling the huge dishwashers with plates and cups from lunch. The kitchen already looks spotless and ready for the dinner crew to arrive and prepare the next meal. The smells of coffee brewing, fresh-cut vegetables and frying onions are all very familiar.

Everybody I know must already be in the Ballroom where the conference is being held this afternoon. I make my way down the long narrow corridor, going quickly past the Smoker's Lounge. That room is perhaps my least favourite place in Cluny—it is the only public room in the community where smoking is allowed. In the days of the Cluny Hill Hotel—and Peter and Eileen's first sojourn here—it was an elegant and popular cocktail bar, open to both hotel guests and local dignitaries. When the community took over this building in 1975, it became the "smoker's lounge." No magic in there for me—though I hear tell that for our first summer we kept the bar open to serve the coach parties that had been booked by the previous owners—with the indomitable Hugh Ferrar (yes, the same Hugh who later married the elegant Linda) as Head Barkeeper, polishing the brass fixtures till the wee hours of the morning.

The sound of many voices leads me to what was the largest ballroom in Forres when this building was a luxury hotel. Gentlemen in tuxedos and ladies in long, sequined evening dresses would dance to the music of a local orchestra. Nowadays, this room is mainly used for Sacred Dance sessions or Group Discovery games with the guests and, more occasionally, Scottish Country Dancing and celebrations.

However, today the ballroom is home to the last session of the Internal Conference, and the hundred or more chairs are all very nearly filled with people talking in small, animated groups or waiting quietly for the afternoon session to begin. I find a seat at the front of the room and look around to see who is here; I recognise many faces—several people wave to me across the room, obviously surprised to see me here. There are also many faces I don't know at all, people who have joined the Foundation over the past few years. But there are still enough familiar faces for me to feel at home in this gathering.

Sitting in the front row are the people who will be leading the session. I recognise Mari, who is the current Foundation focaliser and next to her is Geoffrey, the Finance Director whom I am looking forward to talking to later in the week. I have known Mari for twenty-five years—she is another person whose wedding cake I baked and iced when she married Loren on the island of Erraid. They have two grown-up children, Ona and Teva, and after many years spent teaching in the Steiner School, Mari is now head of the management team of the Foundation.

As I have mentioned, there is a time of silence and inner connection before all meetings and activities in the community, which allows us to release our day's busyness and bring our total attention to the present time and place. This attunement at the beginning of any activity is of prime importance; it now gives us a chance to open our hearts and minds to each other so we can accomplish the work of the afternoon as a cohesive group.

I have heard that earlier in the day a number of small groups brainstormed ideas to create a balanced budget for the coming year, to help reduce expenditure in all areas of the Foundation. The amount of money needed to fill the gap sounds impossibly large—I wonder what these suggestions are likely to be and how tough are the cuts needed to satisfy the bank manager.

One by one, the persons representing each group stand up to report on their discussions and recommendations. As a silent observer, I have plenty of time to watch and listen without having to worry about what I have to say. I see that many of the speakers are new faces and I also realise that some of them are saying things that I have heard many times in the past. But above all, what I notice is that everyone is listening with respect and attention. Nobody jumps up, saying, "But we've tried this before, we've heard this a dozen times!" Everything is heard, and each speaker is applauded and thanked for their input.

A lot of thought and courage has gone into some of the suggestions. Some speak of reducing allowances and holidays and working longer hours. Some speakers suggest consolidating departments in order to cut costs, others of selling property to raise money to reduce the debt. What amazes me is that every single person in the room seems to feel involved and responsible for what is happening. This is not just a problem for the management and financial team, it is a challenge for the whole workforce and the newest arrival is listened to with as much attention as the Finance Director.

This listening and respect gives each person the courage to speak out— even to recommend unpopular and difficult things, to take risks and move beyond their fear of being laughed at or not heard. Some people speak enthusiastically and with force, others speak softly, unused to public speaking and yet willing now to be seen and heard.

As always, there is a tea break, and we all make our way back to the kitchen where large pots of tea and coffee have been prepared. There is a lot of sharing and talking in small groups as everyone discusses the ideas put forward. I am very aware that this financial hurdle demands serious attention.

Then it's back to the Ballroom for the management team to make their suggestions. They, too, are listened to with understanding and support. These are the people who ultimately will need to make some possibly unpopular decisions. The Trustees have given them the task of balancing the budget and reducing the debt—not easy at this time: Guest numbers have fallen after the September 11th attacks in the United States, and they were also affected earlier the same year by the foot and mouth epidemic in the United Kingdom. Findhorn is not impervious to outside influences.

The afternoon's discussions seem to be coming to an end. There is obviously still much to do and much to say, but for today what could be said and done is over. We finish in a very typical Findhorn ritual: the holding of hands, closing our eyes and singing together.

"All is well, this I know,
It is always safe for me to change and grow."

As we sing the words over and over again, I am deeply moved at being once more part of this amazing group of people, connected in love and spirit. There seems no doubt in everybody's mind that this present obstacle will be overcome, that they are willing to do what it takes to make sure this place will continue to inspire future generations of spiritual seekers. I may not be living and working here now, but I know that this is my family and I hold them in my heart and lend them my support in overcoming their present challenges.

DAY'S END

Herbie and Barnaby drive us back to The Park. I'm beginning to feel somewhat overwhelmed by all my experiences today. This is what I have come here for, this is what I have invoked, but the mixture of meeting so many old friends, the intensity of the energy here and the need for some quiet time on my own tell me I should withdraw to my warm little room in Sunflower. I want to stay in my room tonight and let the experiences of the day sink into my mind, make some notes and begin to find the first clues on my quest.

Just two more things to do today. It is already dark when we arrive at The Park, so I leave the bus and walk down to the Phoenix—our community store. The Phoenix sells everything from organic foods and wines to clothes, crafts, cards, books and music. It always amazes me how much can be put into such a small space. Now walking into the store, I am once more confronted by what looks like an Aladdin's cave, full of colours and smells and sounds. Around every corner there is something new to find. I've decided to buy a few food items for bed-time nibbling.

Walking through the narrow maze-like passages, I eventually find the cheese counter where a wonderful array of cheeses is displayed. No difficulty in finding something I will enjoy here! Beside the cheeses are shelves with a large selection of organic fruits and vegetables, and I also find some tubs of yoghurt in the fridge. Kneeling on the floor in front of me is David, the manager of the shop, filling some shelves while he talks to Harry, the manager of the Holiday Caravan Park. I say, "Hello," and then make my way to the cash desk where Jan is on the till. Nice to see all the old faces here. Jan points to some rather delicious looking muffins on the counter, and I decide to give in to the temptation and include one in my purchases.

Just one more person to speak with before I let myself collapse into bed. I want to call my friend Carly in New Mexico. Carly is going to help me write my book—I'm the one who is having all the adventures here, and she will be helping me put it all together. I check the time, remembering that it's seven hours earlier where she lives—I don't want to wake her up again in the middle of her night.

I can hear the phone ringing, so very far away on another continent. Then a soft voice answers, "Hello. This is Carly."

"Hi, Carly, it's Karin. I've just come to the end of my first day at Findhorn."

"Karin, yeah, I've been thinking of you all morning! I'm so glad you've called me, how's it all going? Have you found any magic yet?" Her voice is full of enthusiasm.

"It's been such a busy day. I've already done so much, talked to so many people. I'm finding magic oozing out of everywhere. But, *the* magic, I don't know yet, I think I still have a long way to go. But the clues are there, I think."

"Are you going to tell me what they are?" she asks hopefully.

"Not yet, I need to do a lot more detective work over the next few days. But now I need to relax and let it all sink in," I tell her. "I'm beginning to feel very tired."

"Keep in touch, let me know what's happening," she asks.

"Oh, I will," I assure her.

"I'm sending you lots of good energy, Karin! Wish I was there, too!" she adds.

"Goodnight, Carly. Oh no, it's not night for you yet. Have a nice day!"

"I will. Thank you. Goodnight, Karin, sweet Findhorn dreams!"

Wearily, but full of inner excitement and expectancy for what will happen over the next few days, I make my way to my room. I lie down, relax, switch my mind off and drift into a deep sleep. Now that feels like magic.

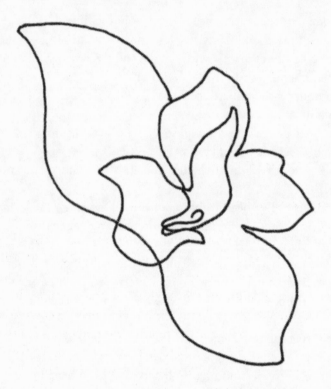

SUNRISE, SUNSET

JULIA IN PARADISE

For those first few moments after awakening I'm not quite sure where I am. I must have slept very deeply because the last thing I remember is sliding gratefully into bed last night. It's still very dark outside, but when I check the time I find it's already 8 a.m. Just time to have a shower and breakfast before my first appointment today.

When I arrived here, several people advised me that I really must speak to Julia. She is not someone I know at all, although I seem to recall seeing her around the place over the years. Of course, as often happens here, I bumped into her on my first day and asked if she would be willing to talk to me. She seems to be one of those people who say "Yes!" right away, so here I am, watching another amazing Findhorn sunrise and waiting for Julia to arrive. Better put the kettle on for another cup of tea.

A few minutes later, a laughing, dark-haired, energetic, vigorous looking woman bursts into the room and greets me with a warm hug. Julia and I curl up in front of the open fire, make ourselves cosy and sip our tea. In the comfortable way of people who don't need all the polite preliminaries, who don't need to explain who they are, we immediately feel like old friends. Of course, I want to know what brought her here in the first place, why she is at Findhorn.

"It's the way we live together, it's knowing that we are all on the same kind of track," she answers, without me really needing to ask the question. Although she is Argentinean, she speaks perfect English, albeit with a delightful accent. She has a deep, throaty voice. "I have lived with other groups, was very politically engaged, been part of women's movements, worked with refugees and immigrants, it was my passion. But there was a piece missing, the piece about self-realisation, the piece about my connection with God that never existed in all that. And here I can have everything." She speaks with great energy.

To me that sounds pretty amazing. Then she remembers something else. "Except maybe the political things, those are not so present here, but perhaps I can be the one who can bring them in."

Yes, I think to myself, I'm sure she will!

"Does it matter?" I ask, "the lack of the political thing?"

"No, perhaps not, because it is superseded by the work we do, by what happens to people when they come here."

"So what does happen to people here, what do we do to transform them?"

"Bah, I don't think we transform anybody!" she explodes.

I'm already laughing, I find Julia refreshingly different and irreverent.

"I think people are transformed by the energy and the atmosphere of this place," she continues. "Something happens to them when they come here. It's part of the willingness that people themselves bring, wanting something to happen, and here the terrain is propitious, so then it happens."

"What happens, and how?" I really want to know.

"I don't know what it is. If I knew, we could bottle it and make a packet!" She laughed heartily, her dark eyes glistening. "Sometimes I wonder about it. When the community is going through difficult times and things are tough, like they have been recently, and I talk to the guests who have been here during that time, I'm always surprised. While we have all been struggling and agonizing, they all seem to have had this fabulous experience of feeling love, open-heartedness, something of that magic. And then I realise that it definitely doesn't have anything to do with us!"

She chuckles gleefully, and I'm delighted and amazed at how willing she is to share her perceptions of how it is here with such humour and delight and openness.

"We may all be fully engaged in the budget, which is not a particularly uplifting topic, and yet people are still having that experience. So it must be something above and beyond what we do or say, or how the energy of the community is at any particular moment." She is suddenly quiet, thinking deeply. Then she continues, "It is grace that comes. I think it is because of the expectation that people bring or the desire, which then gets met with grace—and it happens."

I notice that the sun has now risen fully above the horizon, or at least as high as it ever gets in the north of Scotland in mid-winter—it looks like it will be a sunny day. But Julia continues speaking, full of excitement. "And it happens forever. Once it has happened, the person cannot go back to being a fully closed person, and not remembering. That's what I like most. When I talk to people who have been here a long time ago, even for just one week thirty years ago, it is still there, whatever it was. It has nothing to do with any individual person here, it has to do with something that is collectively held here. I don't know why it happens here, or if it happens anywhere else, but it certainly happens here."

Julia pauses again, and I'm wondering if I will now hear what is the "it" that happens. I break the easy silence with another question.

"Is it love, is it the way you treat each other with such respect and caring, is it the way you listen to one another?"

"Yes." Julia is becoming animated and lively again. "This listening thing is something we do all the time. Every day, in every department, everyone has a chance to share how they are and what is going on for them, so that this can be heard and held. We also have a weekly attunement in every department, which allows us to go deeper."

I remember those weekly attunements, when everyone who works together in a department—the kitchen, the garden, maintenance, the accounts department, or wherever—all take one afternoon off from their working week to talk, to share, to discuss business. But more than anything, to make time to create a loving circle of support, where everyone is held and everyone is listened to. This time is just as important, perhaps more so, than the time spent cooking the meals or weeding the garden. This is a time to create a group out of a number of individuals, to meditate together, to share fun and laughter, to touch the spirit that is here and to ground it in our work and lives.

I come back from my memories and to Julia. She is talking. "It took me a long time to realise the benefit of articulating how I was feeling at the time, because it did not seem to me that this could make any difference; maybe because I have always been pretty self-contained and not relied too much on other people for support. So what, I thought—if I said I was feeling rotten, who cared? How could that change anything? But then I realised that it did change how I felt about that feeling, person or situation. Suddenly, if I just speak about it, it is no longer only my problem, it is with someone else also, and that helps. It is held by the group. And people will remember, and will come back at a later time and check with me to see how I am doing.

"More than anything, the bonds that we create together come by working together—I know that I can absolutely trust those people, that they care for me, I care for them. What I felt when I first came here was the feeling that I was accepted just as I am—that's totally delicious. That has allowed me enough self-esteem, so that I can move and change and explore how it would be if I stopped behaving in a particular way, or stopped doing something. I feel nobody is judging me. It's fine for me to be the way I am, and it's also fine to change. This touches my soul, this acceptance. It's pretty unique, the willingness to be accepting of each other, the whole group, the whole community."

I'm beginning to feel out of breath, trying to keep up with Julia's enthusiasm. She has an enormous heart beating in that ample chest. I also know and resonate with what she is talking about. "Yes, Julia, I know. I have not found this anywhere else. Not even close. Lots of great people everywhere, but not how it is happening here. Then I come back here, and 'whoops,' there it is again, waiting for me."

I'm starting to feel that we are getting a bit too sentimental, too much into how wonderful it all is. There must be another side to this. "Julia, is this all for real, or is some it is just glamour, illusion? The 'glamour of Findhorn', does it still exist?"

Julia is thoughtful, trying to find an answer that is real for her.

"I'm not really sure if it exists, this glamour. Perhaps, yes, occasionally, when we go over the top trying to say how wonderful it is to live here. The other part that I personally find very difficult is when I feel that we live and function here without any reference to the outside world: in other words, that it all begins and ends here, and we make comparisons only with ourselves and don't position ourselves with everything else that is happening around us. I find that tough.

"We sometimes get a bit self-congratulatory. I get very nervous when we say we are doing all this world work. I think there are many people doing world work in different ways, maybe even better than we. From the practical point of view, in the physical world, many do it better than we. On the spiritual level, I think we are doing very well, but even with that, others are doing it just as well. But in our understanding of the material world, I don't think we are as excellent. I would like for us to move further there. I think we are reaching a level of maturity where we really can bring matter into spirit and vice versa, and that, I think, is the missing link."

I am finding it so very refreshing to listen to someone who loves this place with all her heart, and at the same time can realistically see where there is still a lot of work to be done.

"After six years you are still here, Julia. Why is that? "

Her answer is simple. "Where else could I live with people who all—in one way or another—bring more consciousness and awareness into our lives? That's what we are doing here. Working with the principle of respect for each other, to remind ourselves that we are permanently in touch with spirit and we can draw from that connection. We can also hold a space for other people to come and tap into that, which is such a gift."

Julia gets ready to leave and puts on her shoes and coat. She looks back at me with a broad grin.

"When things are tough, I always need to remind myself that here I get to live in Paradise, with all the difficulties of Paradise, but nevertheless, Paradise."

That seems like a good way to say goodbye.

I put the cups away, and check my schedule. I've really had to organise myself while I am here, to make sure I get to speak to as many people as possible. I have also scheduled in 'serendipity' time—time to just hang out, wander around, let whatever happen that wants to happen. However, my next appointment looks as though it will be interesting. Time to get ready and make my way out into the cold, bright morning.

EXPLORING THE SACRED

Right in the centre of 'downtown' Findhorn, at the Park, there stands a smallish, dark green caravan. What is often called 'downtown' is actually a collection of buildings—the Community Centre, the food sheds, the General Office and Reception, the Main Sanctuary and a few other small wooden buildings that seem to change their use every time I visit. All these buildings are set right next to the original gardens, where all the famous giant vegetables were grown, and right next to what had been the legendary rubbish dump where it all began. And there is that smallish, dark green caravan—the one that Peter brought here forty years ago, where the family lived "cheek-by-jowl" during those first years—Peter and Eileen and their three young sons, Christopher, Jonathan, and David. Attached to it is the small annex where Dorothy Maclean once lived. This humble caravan was the small and very lively heart of what was to become the Findhorn Community.

A few years ago, the old caravan began to look somewhat the worse for wear. Since the Caddys had moved on to bigger quarters over thirty years before, various other community members had lived there and they too had come and gone, and in later years it became an office space. Even I worked there in the eighties when it was the personnel office. So when the floor was collapsing and it looked as if it were about to fall apart, a decision had to be made about its future. Should it be towed away to make room for something new? Or should it be left as it was, a shrine to our founders and to our history? In the end, the decision was made to renovate it—a long and lovingly executed task—and now it is once more an office space. Today I am going to join a meeting of the Spiritual and Personal Development group, who are currently using it for their interviews and administrative work.

I pop my head round the door, and see four people squeezed into the larger of the two rooms. I remember that this room was originally the living room when the Caddy family lived here—as well as the dining room, and at night the master bedroom! With some difficulty the four make room for me—no problem about getting close here. How on earth did the Caddy family manage to fit into this small space for so long?

There is no need for introductions. I know these people well, and they know why I am here. However, it does feel strange to be sitting here with them, asking searching questions.

"Hi folks," I begin cheerfully. "Thanks for seeing me."

Nobody speaks immediately. I think they are waiting for me to ask the questions.

"Perhaps you could tell me how you all came here, what drew you to this place, how long you have lived here?" I suggest.

Margo is the first to answer me. She is a Dutch woman, with a soft, gentle voice. "I've lived here ten years now," she tells me.

Hard to believe it is so long, I think. It seems like only yesterday that she moved into my old caravan in Pineridge, just as I was moving somewhere else with Thierry.

"How did you come here, Margo, what is your story?"

"A friend of mine had been here, and when she told me about it, I just knew I had to come and visit. So, like everyone else, I came for an

Experience Week, and during our tour around the Park, while we were in the Nature Sanctuary actually, 'something' told me, "You are going to live here." When I returned home, I kept the memory of that voice, but I am a cautious, even suspicious, sort of person, so I came back to visit a couple of times to check it out. But finally I realised that I was ready to come and live here, to share in the life here."

"What was that realisation? What made you decide that it was right for you?

In her quiet, sincere and deeply thoughtful way, Margo answers, "More than anything, I loved the spiritual values and spiritual practice and how it is brought into our daily life and work. And the interaction with people, how we deal with daily challenges and work through them on the highest possible level."

Suddenly, a very loud noise interrupts our sharing. One of the Nimrods from the Kinloss Airbase is just taking off. We smile—we are all used to this happening several times a day, and we just stop talking for a minute while the noise abates. Then Margo continues, "I have been involved with Buddhism for a long time. I love the spiritual life, but also love the normal daily human life. I often go to Buddhist centres to recharge, but always come back here to live and work."

I ask her what her work involves as part of the Spiritual and Personal Development Group.

"We support the staff and students who live here, we create training programmes and supervision. Another thing we do is to hold self-evaluation interviews with our people, as well as life coaching, and of course spiritual mentoring."

"How did you decide to do this particular work?" I ask her.

"Oh, I saw the job advertised in the Rainbow Bridge and it sort of jumped out at me. I just had an inner knowing that it was right for me".

"There is a lot of that around here," I comment. I thank Margo with a warm smile, and turn my attention to Judy, sitting next to her.

I'm wondering what Judy *has* not been involved in during her long career in the community! She is outstanding as a Game of Transformation Guide of enormous experience; we worked together in Personnel; she has focalised the community for several years, has been a Trustee, and has brought up two children. She is also a terrific cook. I 'borrowed' my favourite recipe from her—Spaghetti with Gorgonzola sauce—and she also bakes wonderful cakes. Years ago, on one unforgettable occasion when our friends Pauline and Alex were married, we created a very beautiful and elegant wedding cake together, iced in white and turquoise.

I would also describe Judy as a very private person who has worked hard to overcome her innate shyness in order to use her skills in service to the community and the planet. We smile at each other, the interviewer and the interviewee.

"Why are you still here, Judy? It's been a long time." I'm asking this question a lot, hoping to find answers that will help my quest.

Judy thinks for a moment and then replies, "Because some part of me still hears that this is where I'm supposed to be. I originally came out of curiosity, and stayed because I just knew that this is where I belonged. It was the last thing I would have expected. I have tried to leave a couple of times, and invariably what happened was so dramatic that this was not supported inside me, in the greater sense. I would not say it is a sense of magic, or a sense of awe. What keeps me here . . ."

Judy pauses and smiles as she realises the truth of her own words. "What keeps me here is God. I sometimes argue against it, I rail against it even. I sometimes think it is the ultimate joke that God could play on me, to keep someone like me, who is not particularly social or gregarious, in a community!"

Judy laughs at the joke God has played on her. "I'd be much better off as a hermit," she continues, "That's the irony, that I'm still here."

"You came here when you were very young. How has it changed you?"

"Well, I've spent my entire adult life here—twenty-five years now. A lot of who I am, how I think and how I look at the world and interact with people and the skills that I have acquired, they have all happened here. I can't imagine having been anywhere else, and what that would look like. I feel very much like part of the place."

I seem to have heard that before somewhere.

"Do you like that? Do you like what has happened to you here?" I press her.

Judy looks out of the window, at the branches bending in the strong wind outside. "Most of the time. I like what has happened to me as a person, I like who I am. I like the way that I look at the world. I think that I have been shaped by this place, polished and at times disturbed, battered and bruised by this place. It's not all sweetness and light being here."

After twenty-seven years, I also know that to be true. "Judy," I say, "what do you mean by 'this place', what does that mean to you?" I know I will be asking other people to really define what 'this place' means for them.

"The land, the people," she replies. "The processes that go on between people, the evolution of structures. It's a bit like watching a child as she grows up. Seeing all the cycles that she goes through, and then seeing how a whole group of people also go through those cycles. I can live here as an individual, as part of a department or the community, and I can watch this amazing story unfold in front of me, an infinitely complex story. It's almost like watching a play."

Yes, a play, a movie, a continuing drama. (With a secret little inner smile I wonder if it isn't also sometimes like a soap opera!)

"The story has a sort of repetitiveness to it, but the leading men and women are constantly changing. Everything is the same and everything is changing—both are true. The process of living inside that, sometimes being a leading lady, sometimes with just a walk-on part with no lines—I've stopped trying to explain what it is. Anything that I can say is completely inadequate."

I think she is actually doing very well—and she has more to say.

"Then there is the whole inner world. The exploration of what or who is God." Judy now starts asking the questions. "And what is the Network of Light, what is the Landscape Angel? What is the Angel of Findhorn? How are they all different? Will I ever see a Deva? I feel them, but will I ever see them? The sum total of all these things, and much, much more, that's what this place is."

But what are the answers?

"They defy description," are Judy's final words to me.

I shake my head in puzzlement. "I think that people had it easy when they tried to write a book about this place twenty-five years ago," I say. "With the complexity now, it's impossible. I can't do it. All I can do is watch and listen, and the more I watch and listen, the more I realise I don't know anything."

The dark-haired young man opposite me is laughing. Perhaps he has some answers for me. Perhaps he knows something. Javier is Spanish, has been here a number of years and now has two young children.

"Well, Javier," I begin, "What do you think is special here? Why are you still here?"

"What brought me in the beginning was the sheer beauty of the place. The beauty I found expressed through nature, through the people, everything around us here."

I look around this tiny caravan, and while it is a place with an interesting history, I can't quite see the beauty of it now, but I do know what he means. He is talking about an inner beauty, that you can only see when you are in touch with that part in yourself that is beautiful.

"Now, it is working with guests and new members that keeps me here. I find the magic of Findhorn seems to be strongest at the beginning, when people first come here. After a couple of years we seem to get used to it."

"That seems a pity," I reply. "But that doesn't mean it's not here any more. If it's here for the guests and new members, then it is here. It must have something to do with what you expect to find. That sounds sad to me, though—getting used to magic."

Javier continues to tell me his story. "I was taken very much by surprise by what happened to me when I first arrived here. I was very closed down and suddenly, out of nowhere, I began to connect with joy. It was very beautiful. The culture here provides a lot of conditions that allow people to bring forth elements of who they really are and share that with others. It's a combination of awareness, of sensitivity, the caring that is here, and just ordinary community life."

I'm beginning to feel that Javier does still sense the magic.

"People seem to find more of a sense of self here, and feel more empowered. Some people, when they first come here, they tell me that they want to be closer to God. Some want to learn how to connect with their intuition, or receive guidance. Others feel that they have just come home. People who get the most out of being here are those who keep their priorities very clear, remembering what they came here for. Then, when they leave, they go back to their lives with a greater sense of purpose, knowing who they are and what they really want out of life."

Javier seems to know quite a lot about the magic here, perhaps he is not quite so used to it after all, as he concludes with great enthusiasm.

"I'm very passionate about my work here. This is a sacred place."

I look at the woman sitting next to him, my dear old friend Judi, and ask her, "What do you think Judi, is this a sacred place?"

Judi is not to be drawn to answer that one easily. "I'd first need a definition of sacred," she replies.

"Is this place special? Is this a place of God? Is this a place of spirit?" I am hoping that this is what she wants to hear. Now she seems willing to answer me.

"If I were to take all of these words, I would say, 'Yes.' But it is not the only place that is sacred. For me every place is a place of God, special in some way. What is true for me in this particular place is that there are a lot of people here who put their attention on their connection with God. And because there are so many people doing that, it becomes in some way more tangible on the form level. It's not underground, not something seldom spoken about—it is spoken about as part of everyday life. As it says in the Bible, 'In the beginning was The Word,' and if you want to bring something into form, you need to speak about it—first it is an idea, and then it becomes a word. There are a lot of words around here to help make spirit tangible. So, yes, it is more tangible to access, easier—especially for people who don't normally do that, like our visitors and guests. It's a very special spiritual place, it's in the atmosphere and it is talked about."

"So, if every place is sacred in some way, why and how are people drawn here in particular?" I ask.

"A group I was in recently was asked why they were here," Margo responds. "There were so many different answers, each person had a different reason for being here. They also defined living in community in many different ways. Some people just like coming here to hang out in the café for a few hours, others have lived here for twenty years and are a hundred percent involved. This community is so many things to so many people. And we are all continually creating this community, all in our different ways."

"Thank you Margo, I know what you mean," I reply. "Tell me, if the Foundation no longer existed, would the community still be here? How important is the Foundation to what is happening here now? I see you, the Findhorn Foundation, taking steps to transform yourselves. Does the Foundation need to continue existing as it is?"

This question has been with me for some time. Now that the community is getting bigger and stronger in itself, does the Foundation still need to be holding the energy, as it has done for the past forty years? Judi seems to have some answers for me.

"I first want to answer the previous question, why people are drawn here—and get into quantum physics!"

Uh, oh, I think. Quantum physics? I haven't even read *The Dancing Wu Li Masters* yet!

"I think we are actually a living example of what Transcendental Meditation master Maharishi Mahesh Yogi talks about," continues Judi. "He has always said that if one per cent of the population meditates, it will affect the whole area. That was proved when it happened in New York and the crime rate dropped. That's what happens on a vibratory level to an area around places where minds are attuned to a certain way of thinking. Here, while we still have our distress and fear or whatever problems we have—at some point we always go back to spirit. Each day we connect with spirit. That actually affects the vibratory level of this part of the world. Since it then vibrates at a certain level, people are attracted to that, because their own vibratory level is at a certain rate and this is what they are looking for. They harmonise with it."

"But what about . . ." I begin, but Judi is in full flow and continues to speak.

"Then they think up a lot of good reasons why they are drawn here, but the reason they are here, why they fit in, is because their vibrations harmonise with it. We still continue to do that, it is around us and ever present. Now, if the Foundation were not here, and the community around here consciously continued to maintain the vibratory level, then the energy would stay. If they continued to meditate and keep their connection with Spirit, and continued with their spiritual practice like Taize singing and all the other ways that people here connect with spirit, then it would stay. If they didn't, because they forgot, then it would not stay, because the vibratory level would actually change; the meditators would be gone. So the  answer is, yes, the Foundation is important as a constant reminder of the central core that keeps this vibratory level going, and no, it's not important provided that everyone else would pick it up and do it."

"So there need to be guardians of the centre, whose work is to keep the vibrations on a high enough level?" I comment.

I am thinking about all the committed people who spend long hours meditating in the Sanctuary, holding the energy that is created here. I particularly remember Eileen and her willingness to continue this work.

"Yes, and if indeed they forgot it and the vibratory level wasn't here, the people who came, who built houses here because of it, would feel very uncomfortable and would eventually want to leave".

I wonder if all the new people building their houses on the Field of Dreams are aware of the debt they owe to the generations of deeply committed people who have created and cared for the vibrations of this centre over the past forty years—and who still continue to do so.

For now, my time with this group is over. I squeeze my way out of the caravan, wondering again at how the founders of this community lived in this tiny space for seven years. It was those three people, Eileen, Peter and Dorothy, who dared to start this adventure into spirit, and it is people like Margo, Javier, Judi and Judy who continue the work today.

IF HE BUILDS IT, THEY WILL COME

The four members of the Spiritual and Personal Development Department squeeze their way past each other and follow me out of the room. I can understand why they usually call themselves just S & PD; it's a bit of a tongue twister of a name. Looking at the time, I realise I have missed both the noon Sanctuary meditation and lunch in the Community Centre. It looks like I'll have to go up to the Green Room Café and see what they have to offer today.

Luckily, everything is close by, here at The Park. So just a few steps through the central gardens, past the Press Building, and I arrive at the Café. In the summer this would be filled with hungry people, sitting both inside and outside on the terrace where a dozen tables would be set out in the hope of some warm, sunny weather. Today there are just a few people in the Café eating lunch. In one corner, reading the newspaper and eating a sandwich, is the familiar bearded figure of David from the Phoenix. On another table I see Alex quietly eating his bowl of soup and some bread. This is something I know I can rely on, seeing the regulars in the Café for their meals and coffee.

Walking into the Café just behind me is my old friend John.

"Hi, John," I greet him. "Shall we have lunch together. I'd love to chat with you."

"Oh, yes," he replies. "You're writing a book. Hello, fellow author." Some years ago, John penned *Simply Build Green*, a book about the ecological buildings here in the community.

"Not yet I'm not, just an aspiring author. Perhaps you can help me," I say hopefully.

"Sure, let's pick up something to eat and sit in the corner over there."

I check the menu. I know that everything served here is probably locally grown and organic. I order a baked potato with cheese and a side salad. John chooses a slice of quiche and orders a cappuccino. We make our way to a table in a quiet corner and wait for our food to be prepared.

John is an American. It's hard to guess his age; he has a handsome, boyish face, dark curly hair and a cheery smile. I know he has lived in the community since around 1980, so he can't possibly be as young as he looks!

"OK John," I begin, "down to business. Let's talk before our lunch arrives. What brought you here to Findhorn in the first place?" I ask the familiar question.

"I came originally mainly because I felt called," he replies. "It felt right, as if on purpose. I was meditating in my little home sanctuary in Portland, Oregon, and asking where I should go as part of my spiritual path. I got the sense that I should call the British Consulate and find out about visas for Americans in Britain, as that would be a sign whether Findhorn would be the 'right' place. I had previously visited twice as a guest, in '78 and '79. Well, to my complete surprise I discovered that I was actually considered a British citizen, having been born in England, even though my parents were Americans. My father was stationed in Britain with my mother for a couple of years in the early '50's. This seemed a pretty clear 'sign' that I should go to Findhorn."

My mind is trying to work out how old that would make John now, if he had been born in the early '50's. With a shock I realise that must make him nearly 50 years old! I look at him a little more closely to see if I can find any wrinkles. John is still talking.

"I was working as an engineer for a large multi-national company, but I realised early on that this wasn't my career path. I needed something more fulfilling, that had a sense of meaning and purpose. When I visited Findhorn, I found that sense, though in my first visits here I wasn't sure if I would ever live here. And when I eventually did come, I thought it was going to be for just a year or two."

"How did you get involved with the ecovillage?" I ask him.

Our lunch arrives, brought over to us by a young blond girl wearing a nose ring. It seems that our youngsters here have the same strange habits as their local friends. Our food looks very fresh and delicious, and I begin eating my baked potato while John continues to speak.

"A few months after I moved to the community there was some talk about turning the Caravan Park into a demonstration of co-operation with Nature on all levels—not just the gardens, but to create an ecovillage. We began to talk about replacing all the caravans and having clean energy and ecological houses. I remember thinking, 'Uh oh, this is the reason I came here,' knowing that this was going to be a long-term project, not just one for a year or two. I certainly couldn't have predicted that it would last the 22 years that I've currently been here."

John sips his cappuccino as I remember something.

"Wasn't there a conference about all that in the early '80's?"

"Yes, that's right, my first official involvement with the ecovillage was as part of the group that was organising the 'Building a Planetary Village' conference in the autumn of 1982. We worked on it for about a year, and there was a lot of activity building up to the actual event of planning and dreaming what an ecovillage would actually look like."

I only have to look around me to see what John's dreams have created.

"You have to remember also that the community was in the worst crisis of its life, with a huge overdraft and debts, and no foreseeable way of paying them off. Over half of the 320 people who had been living in the community in 1979 had left by 1981, and there was a real crisis of mission and purpose. It really looked black for a while."

I remember it well, we even wondered if we could survive as a community at all. But throughout our darkest moments, there were people like John who continued to dream and hold the vision for the future. John takes a bite of his quiche and brushes aside a lock of hair.

"Then the vision of the ecovillage came along. It actually first came from David Spangler, through a transmission from the being he calls 'John,' who spoke about the need for Centres of Demonstration where the principles of living in harmony with nature, ourselves and spirit could be worked with. When the idea took root in the community, it gave us all a new sense of hope and vision. Immediately after the conference we began the fundraising appeal that raised the money to buy the Caravan Park."

I remember that at that time we were still renting the land from Captain Gibson who owned the Caravan Park, and we were unable to put up any permanent buildings.

"Two years later," John said enthusiastically, "we had done it and actually had completely turned around our finances."

I remember that time so well. The whole community was involved in the fundraising; we all brought our ideas and energy to the project. Eileen had personally signed 10,000 letters that went out to friends and supporters everywhere. By November 1983 we had very nearly raised the £300,000 needed to buy the caravan park and we hoped to do so by our 21st birthday—it seemed a symbolic act of faith to own our home by that time. People from all around the world sent contributions small and large, and all felt part of this inspiring project.

The day of our twenty-first birthday arrived, November 17th, 1983. There were many celebrations and parties happening, and at one point the whole community gathered in the Universal Hall to meditate together. It was at this moment that someone—I don't remember who—got up and told us that we had very nearly made it, we just needed a small amount of money to reach our goal. We all got up and put whatever money we had into a bowl. We had achieved what seemed impossible.

Later that day, at the 11th hour, we signed the Deed that would allow us to own our land, to be custodians of this small piece of the Earth.

My recollections give John time to finish his lunch.

"Of course, it took a long time before we were ready to build," he begins again. "It really was not until 1990 that we started Bag End. But it was valuable dreamtime, researching and learning about what building an ecovillage was all about. And it gave us time to come up with our basic philosophy and understanding of the concept."

John looks at me intently. "You really should read all the papers about this, it's important stuff you know."

"I know, I know," I reply, "But I don't have the time right now. I need to rely on you to tell me all about it."

John laughs and I continue my questions. "When did you first dream that the field would be filled with ecological houses?"

"When we were putting up the windmill in 1989, the Bichan family, who owned the farm next to us, decided they wanted to apply for planning consent to build a few houses on six acres of their field. Initially we didn't like the idea, but they had just allowed us to put up the windmill on their land and run the cable across the field, so we didn't object and they did receive planning permission. This meant, however, that the field would never again be used as farmland. Eventually, after about five years of somewhat tense relations as we nervously watched various developers weigh up the potential, we were able to agree a price and buy the field ourselves. This was in 1995. I think it was about 1993 when I personally saw how it made sense for us to develop the site, and it felt like it was part of the plan. That was the year Patrick Nash and I set up Eco-Village Ltd to carry out the development."

I remember that at one time Thierry and I had considered building our Findhorn Press offices and a house on the Field of Dreams. At the time, it all felt as if it were taking too long, but looking at what has been done since, it all seems to have happened in the twinkling of an eye.

"How many houses are there on the Field now and how many more are planned?" I ask him. I know I could go out and count them, but it's very cold outside and I expect John knows all the information by heart.

"There are now 11 houses completed, two under construction and another 31 to start building. In all, there will be 44 dwellings—and 14 of them will be one and two bedroom terraced flats, not detached houses," John tells me. Glad I don't have to leave the cosy Café and do all the counting myself.

John himself lives in a Barrel House at the end of Pineridge. It is the biggest of the five Barrel Houses—tall enough to have a second story, and John has his living room upstairs with a magnificent view across the Field and Findhorn Bay.

"I started my Barrel in July 1993 and moved in a year later. We got the barrels from the nearby Craigelliche cooperage where they were being stored. Originally they came from a distillery in Dundee that had closed. They were 'spirit receivers', where the whisky was blended, not the fermentation vats which are quite smelly and foul. These have an amazing aroma and were in service for about 60 years. The wood comes from the Northwest of America and is Douglas Fir, or as it is sometimes known in Europe, Oregon Pine. Exactly the place I grew up in."

"John, I know another of your personal successes has been to build our first wind generator, named 'Moya.' And I've also heard a rumour that you are planning to build another one. Is that true?" I ask him.

"We bought Moya in 1988 before we had even got planning permission, and she was erected and commissioned in October 1989—Friday the 13th to be exact. Would you like the basic 'specs.' for your book, Karin?"

I was relieved he was about to offer the information, as I really didn't want to wade through all the technical data.

"Moya is 32.5 metres (107') tall, and rated at 75 kW capacity. She has now faithfully supplied us with about twenty percent of our electricity, generated 1.5M units of electricity, and saved some 2000 tons of CO_2 emissions."

I know that John, more than anyone else in the community, has held the vision and done much of the hard work to create the reality of an ecological village. I listen, filled with admiration, as he continues.

"This year we are hoping to erect a much larger machine, in the order of 850 kW, that will fulfil all our electricity needs and more. And yes, I was the main man for the project. I had a vision in 1985, and championed it. I can't say it was 'my' idea, only that the idea came to me. I think it happened because it was part of the larger plan for Findhorn. Our job—my job—is to tune into what that plan is and bring it into form. That's what it means to work in co-operation with spirit and nature. But we're not doing this alone."

This somehow reminds me of what Brian was telling me yesterday. Both John and Brian know that they need to work with the unseen realms of nature and spirit, both doing very different work and yet with the same commitment to service and spirit.

"And you are still here after 20 years, John, why is that?" I ask him finally.

The girl with the nose ring has cleared away our plates and the Cafe is having its early afternoon quiet time between lunch and tea. Perhaps it's time to leave soon.

"I'm still here because I'm still inspired and feel called to be here," John tells me. "The vision of carrying on the experiment of co-operation between the three kingdoms—human, devic and elemental—and of aspiring to create a model of true sustainability for the 21st century, is a compelling one. Findhorn, as a relatively mature intentional community, is still a leading light in this exciting field. Humanity badly needs positive examples of what we can do, and I think we are breaking some new ground."

I don't know what we could add to that. John leaves to return to his work. I think I'll just go and wander over to the Field myself to count the houses.

ROGER'S BARREL

I walk back towards the Field and my cosy room in Sunflower B & B—counting the houses as I walk. Yes, John was right, there are 11 of them. I'm trying to imagine what it will look like when there are 44 homes here, when the trees have matured and each home is surrounded by flowerbeds and little vegetable plots. We will hardly be able to remember when it was a field of golden barley.

I rest on my bed for half an hour, absorbing all the new information and sorting my notes from the morning. Then, my energy renewed, I make my way to my next appointment—at the other end of Pineridge again, where another 'pioneer' lives inside something very different. On my way I pass some of the 'mobile' homes that have never moved anywhere and are still in place after more than 30 years. Then I arrive at the Barrel House cluster. John's house is on my left, and in front of me is the very first one to be built—Roger's.

I seem to have known Roger forever, and yet always feel as if I don't really know him at all. We have both been part of the community for over 27 years, but our paths have rarely crossed; we've never worked together in the same department or even socialised within the same group of friends. To me, Roger has always been the intellectual guy with a deeply furrowed brow, who talked very fast and at great length in community meetings. A philosopher type with very strong opinions—often at odds with everyone else's point of view. The man who many years ago built himself an elegant home out of a giant whisky barrel—an exploit so unusual that even the respected Observer newspaper came to photograph it, and Roger, for a Sunday colour supplement. I realise that Roger probably has no idea about the two occasions when he had a genuine impact on my life.

The first time was in my very early days in the community. Roger was then the focaliser of the Education Branch, which seemed to me a very important position. I worked in the kitchen, preparing meals for the whole community and was walking home after a long and tiring shift when I met Roger on the road to Pineridge. Quite out of nowhere he gave me a hug and thanked me profusely for cooking such delicious food. He was not to know how low and discouraged, tired and depressed, I was feeling at that particular moment. I have remembered his few words of gratitude for 25 years.

Many years later I was working in the Public Relations department, and one of my tasks was to show journalists around the community and introduce them to interesting and articulate members. Of course, journalists always wanted to visit the Barrel House, which in those days still smelled of whisky, especially on a hot day. I would try not to disturb Roger unnecessarily, for I imagined he must get rather tired of having people peer into his home. But that day Roger saw us and invited us in, made a big pot of tea, and was willing and very happy to talk to the journalist. And talk he did. He told us so many stories I had never heard before, and held our attention rapt for a long, long time. The journalist was most impressed. So was I.

Today I am well prepared to interview Roger. I have already marked both sides of a blank cassette tape, "Roger," knowing he'll probably chat for quite a while! I arrive at his Whisky Barrel House, now surrounded by four other Barrel Houses—each uniquely designed—knock lightly on the door, and am met by a beaming, six foot tall American. He invites me in and puts on the kettle.

Let me describe my surroundings. I can't imagine that many people have actually seen the inside of a house made from a whisky barrel. A very large barrel of course, where huge amounts of whisky were once blended. When it was no longer used for that purpose it was dismantled, brought over to Findhorn and then re-assembled at this far end of Pineridge, with a large picture window on one side and a handsome copper roof above. Of course, everything inside is curved. The living room takes up most of the space, and built around the curve is a small kitchen. The only part of the house that is at all straight is a wall which divides the living area from the bathroom. Behind the couch is a ladder which leads up to Roger's bed in a loft about three metres above us.

"What on earth do you do when you need to go to the loo in the middle of the night?" I can't resist asking, apologising for being so personal and inquisitive. "Isn't it dangerous in the pitch dark?"

"I'm used it," Roger laughs, and invites me to make myself comfortable on the couch.

The tea is ready, and Roger informs me that we really don't have very long—there's a good football match on TV soon. I remember that in the mid-seventies Roger was one of the very few people in the community who actually owned a television. When very

important things were happening in the world—such as the Watergate scandal and the final episode of MASH—Roger's TV became an essential community item.

Knowing our time will be short, I get right down to business, speaking a little faster than usual to keep up with Roger's pace.

"Why are you still here after all these years?" I ask right away.

"I've been here for 27 years, and this is my 15th year in the Barrel. I don't know why I'm still here, wish I did, then I could gush and enthuse with the best of them. But to be candid, I think it is because I have invested so much of myself in Findhorn—27 years is a big investment. Particularly building my own home here. That's an act of putting down roots."

He picks up his mug of tea, still talking at great speed. "The truth is, I have not found any place that's any better. And I've looked extensively, on several continents. Every place has its own distinctive quality, but Findhorn's distinctive quality is a vibrant sense of the collective, which still abides. You can partake of it to the degree you wish, but that sense of the collective is still pervasive. Which means being part of a bunch of people who are substantially like-minded even if oftentimes bull-headed, territorial and difficult as ever. But the basic aspiration and commitment abides, to provide a human, ecologically sensitive, spiritually aware, personal growth-oriented town that is able to pay its own bills. At the moment, the part about paying its own bills is a challenge. So, we are having to recut our coat to fit our cloth. The miracle is that we, the community, are still here after 40 years."

It takes speed and a lot of mental agility to say all that in 30 seconds! I'm glad I am recording this instead of trying to take notes.

"Why am I still here?" Roger repeats my question. "I am obsessed. My attention is fixated mainly on the collective, much less on the personal. This is simply where my attention always returns. I feel married somehow to Findhorn. I also have the luxury of reviewing that marriage every year, to renew or change the conditions of contract. I also constantly seem to get involved in new projects, which keep me fresh."

"OK, Roger, now I know why you are still here, but what do you think brings new people and guests here?"

"There is a certain mythical resonance here that engages people, attracts them to come here. It usually happens at a point of transition, a point of opening in their lives. And the original myth is still intact, this brings people here. And then there's the endurance factor, that we're still here after 40 years."

"Yes, that's pretty special, so many other places have fallen by the wayside. Is there really something unique here?" I look around this rather strange and certainly different house. This is pretty unique. Roger has more to say.

"It's the atmosphere around here. Findhorn's distinction is the ambience in which any programme is held, it's the atmosphere here."

"Yes, all right, but what is this atmosphere?" I want to know,

"It's the whole approach to life here, where the spiritual dimension is not only spoken about but is an integral part of life and offers a significantly greater quality of life and connection between people."

It's tough trying to pin Roger down to give a complete answer to my questions. I glance out of the window and notice that it's getting darker, nearly time for his football match. "So people come more for the atmosphere than for the workshops?" I ask.

"Absolutely, it almost doesn't matter what the workshop is, it's the total experience here that matters."

"So, what *is* this place Roger, what do you think we are?"

"We've never been able to agree about what it is. It's not a church, not a monastery, not an eco-village—at least not yet—nor is it a business organisation. We are all of the above and none of the above. That's the nature of the place. A mystery school perhaps, it's even a mystery to us! We just don't know how to describe ourselves: we are holistic, synergistic, collective, communal, spiritual, getting more businesslike, educational in a distinctive way, not conventional, and unique. We are a centre of sorts, nice word, centre, that seems to fit, a centre that lives by its values."

"What are these values?" I press him further.

Roger arches his eyebrows, rubs his nose and has a quick sip of tea before launching into his answer. "Of course this is my version only. There have been many attempts to answer this question and they tend to be the most controversial discussions we have, even though we all know what we are talking about and we all agree. But basically it's to create a centre that is primarily focused around universal spiritual values, values that seem to inform all the world's religions or spiritual paths, or are common to all those paths. Like honouring self, others, nature and God. To live life as we all know it can be, in a common yoke, to create as heavenly a place as we can, that's how I would describe it. To take that experience of connection and peace and unity that we have in Sanctuary, in meditation, and bring it into our working life, our social life, educational life. Practising the presence of God, that's how I would name it. Which is not unique to the New Age, it's the classical spiritual aspiration, it's what every organisation that is dedicated to a sense of spirit attempts to fully realise. We are a community which endeavours to cultivate a sense of connection and wholeness."

Roger glances at a clock on the wall, picks up the remote control clicker from the coffee table and turns on the TV, muting the volume.

"Roger, I know you're about to watch the football match, but do you have a few final words for me?"

He grins and quotes a famous line by Christopher Fry: "'Affairs are now soul size, an exploration into God.' That's the name of the game."

Roger hugs me warmly, towering at least a foot above me, and as I leave the Barrel House I hear the sounds of cheering football crowds and the voice of a commentator speaking even faster than Roger himself.

SENTINEL BY THE SEA

As I leave Roger's Barrel I'm aware that there's only about another hour of daylight left in this Scottish winter afternoon. However, I feel the need for some quiet reflection and fresh air after the intensity of today's conversations. I decide to walk to the sand dunes and the long, sandy beach that skirts the Moray Firth. Findhorn is on a peninsula, with Findhorn Bay on one side and the much larger Moray Firth on the other. We are lucky here that it takes only a few minutes to walk to the beach on either side. The old fishing village of Findhorn sits at the very tip of the peninsula, with the Bay providing a safe harbour for the many sailboats and skiffs.

This afternoon, I choose to walk the 'back way' to the beach, past the Barrel where May and Craig and their children live, then across the fence and down a short path through the woods. On my right Moya the windmill is doing what she is supposed to do, going round and round in the wind, of which there is plenty, and producing the electricity that will keep us warm. Then I turn left and make my way towards the sand dunes.

There is a well-trodden path here that will take me down to the beach. This is a favourite walk for community members and guests who need some space and quiet time. It is not unusual to find 'cairns', little mounds of stones or patterns of shells and pebbles, which some contemplative walker has left by the side of the path. The dunes are covered in heather and gorse which in the spring and summer create a beautiful carpet, first golden yellow and later purple. But now, in the January twilight, I see nothing but straggly bushes and bare roots.

I continue walking along the sandy path until I come to the place I have been looking for. In front of me is a very large sand dune, much taller than any of the others, like a sentinel waiting for the explorer. I have been here so many times in the past. In the winter, when we had snow, I would bring the children here with their toboggans which we would drag up to the top of the dune, and then, shrieking loudly with excitement, we would slide down the steep side. Over and over again, full of energy, they would continue to run up and slide down again.

In summer this was a perfect place for sunbathing, with its golden sands high above the beach and the amazing view of the Moray Firth and the mountains beyond. Today, there is neither snow nor warmth, but as I reach the top of the dune I catch my breath in wonder. Before me is the most beautiful sunset—carmine red, soft purple and coral pink with the glowing red globe of the sun sinking into the distant mountains. I sit in the sand on the highest point of the dune and allow the beauty and serenity of this moment to wash over me and through me.

As often in the past, a moment like this is similar to the deepest meditation I might experience in the Sanctuary. Both have an exquisite beauty, when I can touch the most inner and precious part of myself. Alone here on this dune, I am at one with the universe, I can sense the infinity of time and space. I am connected to all that is.

Then I remember that I have come here to think, to contemplate what it is that I am doing here, and how I am going about my quest. I have begun to ask questions and listen. Yes, I need to listen and listen. I am visiting as many people and areas of the community as time allows, and letting past memories and present experiences speak to me. Is there something else I should be doing, I wonder.

The sun has almost completely disappeared, and across the Moray Firth I can begin to see the lights coming on in the houses, perhaps 20 miles away. I shiver and realise that I am starting to feel very cold up here on this exposed dune, with the wind blowing even through my thick coat. I stumble down the sandy slopes until I find the path again and slowly make my way back, walking carefully in the gathering dark. By the time I reach Pineridge it is almost completely black, not even the moon is out, just the first stars lighting my way back home.

Home? Is that what this place is—home? It certainly felt like that for many years. It is also a word I have heard a lot over the past few days. Many people here speak of this feeling of 'coming home'. The realisation dawns on me that I am no longer the same person who left France. Findhorn has been changing me even in the short time that I have been here. I can no longer pretend to be the objective reporter searching for "magic." The magic is part of me. Henceforth I can only report what I feel and what other people tell me, and not try to stand outside the process. In a way that's reassuring. In one of the Alice Bailey books, DK says that "theology is a vice of the academic mind," meaning that one cannot understand the divine by observing it from the outside. If I am inside the process, it follows that my reporting will be more truthful.

I can now see the lights of the houses on the Field and make my way to Sunflower. What a lovely name for a house, particularly in the darkness of winter. I enter into the welcoming warmth and remember that tonight I'm having dinner with Carol and David who live in a small village some miles away. I anticipate a delicious meal, some good wine and a relaxing evening with close friends. I think that tonight I will put aside my task and just enjoy the company and the food. Tomorrow the quest will continue.

OLÒ FRIENÒS, NEW FRIENÒS

GAPS ANÒ SURPRISES

Susan is beginning to know my morning habits now, she knows the tea I like and she toasts my bread to perfection. The marmalade is on the table and every morning I find a different bowl of fresh fruit waiting for me. Today there is Kiwi Fruit and Banana. While I am having my breakfast I hear her urging her son to get ready for school. I too need to get ready for my first interview this morning.

Geoffrey has recently been appointed Finance Director of the Foundation, which must be the most challenging job at this difficult time. There is an enormous debt, which the bank would like reduced, and the Trustees want to see a balanced budget. At the internal conference I saw that the whole workforce felt involved and responsible, yet in the end it will be Geoffrey and the rest of the management team who'll need to make the decisions that will turn the situation around.

Yet, here is Geoffrey this morning, willing to spend some time to help me with my project. In fact, he even offered to come to the B & B for our interview. I open the front door and invite him to take off his shoes, though I regret that I can't offer him a pair of slippers. The house is warm and perhaps he won't need them.

"Hello, Geoffrey, nice to have an English person to talk to at last," I begin.

"I'm not English," he replies. "I'm Cornish."

"That's English," I insist.

"Not, it's Cornish. In Cornwall we consider ourselves Cornish."

For the non-British reader, I need to explain that Cornwall is the region on the extreme south-west tip of Great Britain. All I know about Cornwall is that it produces a delicious, thick clotted cream, was once famous for its pirate caves where they stored brandy smuggled over from France, and that its tip at Land's End is the southernmost part of Britain. I decide not to argue further with Geoffrey, and so Cornish he will be.

"But actually I feel more Australian than anything else. I lived there for 18 years and am working hard to keep my Australian accent," Geoffrey tells me.

He still sounds very English to me, but I'm quite happy to let him be a Cornish Australian!

"It's the pioneering spirit of Australia that's more to my liking than the establishment of the UK."

"What did you do in Australia?" I ask him, intrigued.

"I worked in real estate for a while. I also trained volunteers to help people with AIDS. And I worked for some cancer charities."

"So what brought you here then?" was my next question.

"The charity I was working for was downsizing, and I knew I would be made redundant soon. So I began to wonder, where will life be taking me next? I have always been drawn to community living, so I spent a few months around spiritual communities in various parts of the world."

"Was Findhorn one of them?"

"Yes, I liked the diversity here, and that it encompassed all belief systems. In other communities, I felt that I had to adhere to a particular belief system, which was not the case here. It soon became clear that I should move here, and I eventually arrived in 1998."

Geoffrey looks across the Field at the newly-built houses. "My entrance into the Foundation was pretty uneventful at first, just the normal way people arrive here. But as soon as they found out I had a financial background, I was asked to help with the budget."

"So that's what you've been doing ever since?" I ask.

"No, in fact I had a very hard time living here and eventually returned to Australia. Then I came back for a visit and realised once more that this is where I had to be."

"Oh, arrival number two. How was it different this time?"

Geoffrey's voice suddenly changes; it becomes soft and vulnerable as he continues. "When I came back this time, I felt so loved and appreciated, just so very loved. And suddenly I realised that I didn't want to be anywhere else. The people I had got to know in the nine months when I was here before were so genuinely pleased to see me that this time I knew for sure that Findhorn was where I needed to be."

"So, now that you are here, right in the thick of it all, how do you see what is happening in the Foundation, in the community?"

"In my experience there is an organisational life cycle as well as a personal life cycle. It's a parabolic curve. Every organisation goes through it. From what I can see we seem to be near the end of the downward slope, just heading towards the end. Now we have a choice."

I am aware of how differently Geoffrey is describing his perceptions and experiences than some of the other people I have spoken to.

"If we can redefine ourselves in the world, integrating spirituality and business, and then actually grounding the different aspects of our being, then we have a relevance. When we talk about love in action, yet have guests going into our work departments where we do only token things, it does not relate to their work back home in the office."

I suppose he is right. Certainly the working habits here are rather different to the 'outside' world. I am surprised and fascinated at what I am hearing and ask him to continue.

"Unless there is some intensity about the work experience, then there is no real grounding of our motto that "work is love in action." Their work experiences here are so different from their normal life. Do we continue to have tea breaks and long sharings during the work day, or do we modify that? Life is much more pressured out there now than it was 20 or 30 years ago. We need to give people real skills to take home to help them cope with the reality of their everyday lives and work."

I find myself struggling to say something that is on my mind.

"I have found such a mixture of people here, most of them are very committed and hard working, but there are also a few, well, flaky ones."

I'm hoping that I have not offended anyone.

"Yes," replies Geoffrey. "We are very good at the compassionate holding, but we don't really seem to deal with some of the harder issues. We talk about them and then they drift away."

I'm aware that I may be 'drifting away' from one of the harder issues, but I'm not sure I want to go any further with this train of thought—at least not for right now. I make a note about tackling it later. So, I come back to my particular interest and purpose.

"Geoffrey, despite all its problems and challenges, I know you will agree that there is still something unique and wonderful here. What do you think is the magic?"

When Geoffrey smiles, his face totally belies the 50 years I know he has lived. "For me, it's made up in lots of magic moments. Singing is my way of connecting with spirit, so leading the Taizé celebration is a magic time for me. I frequently have tears running down my cheek, I feel so blessed and beautiful."

I am planning to join the Taizé singing tomorrow morning and look forward to seeing another side of Geoffrey. However, he has more to say. "For me, the essence of community is established in the Community Centre, and in eating together. It started for me in Cluny dining room where I had a sense of it being the temple where we come to commune with God through each other. I actually get annoyed sometimes with people who come with their dishes and pick up food to take to their rooms. I want to say, 'If that's how you feel, why are you still here? If you can't take the intensity any more, if you need to put up these walls around you, why are you here?'"

While I understand what he is saying, I also know that at times most people here feel the need to withdraw from the intense energy and the constant stream of people. Living in a community can be a lot of fun, but sometimes I know I need some quiet time alone. Geoffrey seems to be a person with enormous amounts of energy, who is constantly willing to give of himself.

"And joy," he continues. "I tend to be more with people who are new here, because that's often where the joy is. Some of the people who have been here a long time seem miserable. Surely they then need to make some changes in their lives. I particularly enjoy Nitzan, he's a young, inspiring, vivacious, enlivening and joyful soul. He has been working in the Hall and organising evening sharings. He is just delightful. I hope you will get to talk to him."

I hope so too. I must find out where he lives.

"Do you know," says Geoffrey, "there are some people here who say they don't want to get close to new people because they will leave, and then they'll be sad. That's foolish. We need to appreciate this gift. I am sad that Nitzan is leaving, but I celebrate that he has been here. What an extrovert personality! I want more of that alive energy. I am inspired by the people who come through here."

Geoffrey knows of still more magic that he wants to tell me about. "I also get a very clear knowing about my next steps here. That's part of the magic. And it's a place of like-minded people, a distillation of people I can have fascinating conversations with. The magic is also in all these traditions we have here that allow us to connect with spirit. Like attuning before a meeting. It sometimes feels like a habit, but I'm really glad we do it. And sharing briefly, so we connect. When we do this we create a chalice for our meetings."

"Looks like the world is full of magic for you here, Geoffrey." I think I must be right because he is still finding more.

"Then there is KP on Thursdays."

Now this I really want to know—the magic in washing dishes—especially those enormous pots and pans with cheese sauce or bits of scalloped potato stuck to the bottom.

"I have been doing the washing up in communities around the world, so when we get a little blah about another plate to wash, I begin to whistle a little tune. That helps me find the joy in washing up—even in the pot sink. The guests always love it and join me, but the staff sometimes feel embarrassed about it. But for me, it's magical."

Geoffrey's face lights up even when he is talking about KP. "You know the thing about looking for magic," he tells me, "it really happens when you are not looking for it. It's in the gaps, the surprises."

"You're probably right," I say. "But I feel I need to look for it, so I can put it into words."

"That's going to be a challenge for you." Geoffrey smiles, then makes one more attempt to give me what I need. "The magic of Findhorn is that we have an opportunity to help demonstrate and experiment with integrating spirit and humanity. It's no longer about the monastic, separate, hippie commune, it's about how can we can work with mainstream business, mainstream people. How can we help connect hearts? How can we make a positive difference in the real world?"

There seems to be a lot of magic in Geoffrey's life and I'm glad that he has managed to put it into words for me.

Though I'm still wondering how to tell him that 'monastic' has never been a word that could describe this community.

ALAN'S HAPPY BUTTON

Saturday morning at The Park is a very busy time. It is the day that the weekly programmes start and finish, and participants of the previous week's workshops are getting ready to leave while new guests are arriving. The members of the Foundation are all out in full force for the Saturday clean up. Groups of people move into the bungalows and caravans with mops and buckets, vacuum cleaners and dusters. Others are carrying trays of freshly baked bread, marmalade, cereals and tea to replenish the stores of breakfast essentials in the guest accommodation.

The Community Centre is also a hive of activity. Lunch is being prepared in the kitchen, the dining room is being given a thorough clean and polish, and guests are arriving to sign up for their Experience Week or workshop. Everywhere, there are groups of people hugging each other and saying goodbye after a week of getting to know and love each other.

I see Geoffrey on a cleaning crew (KP). One of the unique traditions here at Findhorn is that everyone, no matter what their primary job or title—from Finance Director and Foundation Focaliser to the newest member working in the gardens—is expected to be part of the Saturday guest accommodation clean-up crew. Each person also takes a turn one day a week washing the dishes in the CC or Cluny Kitchen. There are some people like Geoffrey who love this community service, but it is not everybody's favourite part of community life. I well remember how I sometimes struggled to get up early on a Saturday morning to clean the guest accommodation. Yet somehow, after the initial resistance, it always turned out to be fun when we all got together and put our hearts into the job.

Geoffrey spots me from a distance and notices that I'm empty handed. "Karin," he calls, grinning, "Put down your tape recorder and give me a hand in Evelyn's Bungalow."

All the bungalows now used for guest accommodation are named after the person who originally lived in them; in this case it was Evelyn.

"Geoffrey, I'm on my way to see Alan J. in half an hour," I plead, feeling a bit of the old inertia.

"C'mon Karin, that's a whole half hour away, don't you remember how much fun this is?"

"OK, Geoffrey, of course I will, I forgot," I say, genuinely perking up on hearing the enthusiasm in his voice.

Geoffrey hands me a mop and we make our way over to the bungalow. Another person—a guest staying on for a second week—is already busy making the beds. Geoffrey begins sweeping the kitchen floor and I turn on the vacuum cleaner in the living room. In no time at all the little bungalow—one of the original cedarwood bungalows in Eileen's vision—is spick and span and ready for new arrivals.

Soon I am making my way to Pineridge, to one of the small bungalows there. I am looking for an old friend who is no longer able to participate in the physical work of the community. The house where my dear friend Elizabeth Grindley lived for so many years is now Alan's home. I have known Alan since the very first day he arrived here.

One of my most vivid memories of him is the way he celebrated his 60th birthday. Unbelievable that it was 20 years ago. On his birthday he decided that he would run in the 100 metres sprint at the upcoming Highland Games in nearby Forres. It was difficult to imagine Alan doing that. He was a short, stocky man, perhaps a little overweight and definitely not the sporty type. But he seemed determined to do it, to prove to himself that he could. He is that kind of a man—when he makes up his mind about something, he does whatever it takes to achieve his goal. Not long before, after having been a very heavy smoker for years, he had decided to quit smoking. Not another cigarette passed his lips from that day onwards. It was tough going at times, but his determination carried him through.

Over the next few months he was often to be seen training for the race around the community or on one of the local beaches. While I supported and encouraged him, I was secretly worried that he might hurt himself. The day of the race arrived, and my little son Michael and I accompanied Alan to Grant Park where the Highland Games were being held. It was a sunny, warm afternoon, unusual for Scotland where occasions like this are all too often accompanied by rain and cold winds. Eventually they announced the big event of the afternoon —the 100 metres. Alan lined up with the other runners. I remember noticing that most of them seemed to be under 25, and all looked very fit. I knew Alan must be nervous, but his face reflected total confidence. He grinned at us broadly, his 'devil's eyebrows' raised in salute.

Then they were off, and in just a few seconds it was all over. Alan had come in last, but I could tell by the look on his face that, for himself, he had won. He had done what he set out to do for himself. I still have a photograph, taken just after the race, of Alan looking radiant and filled with joy.

Over the next ten years Alan continued to live and grow with his inner courage and determination. As a member of the Foundation he worked in the kitchen, ran the long-term guest programme, became General Secretary, was in charge of Public Relations and later also chaired the Management group.

Some 12 years later, then aged 72, in the early stages of Parkinson's disease and losing his sight, Alan went to Nepal. He had served with Nepalese Ghurkas during the Second World War, and was now drawn there too by a growing interest in Buddhism. Little did he realise how this trip would change his life once more. He was so appalled at the lack of any kind of health facilities there that, when he returned to Findhorn, he used the inheritance his mother had left him to set up the Nepal Trust, which began building health posts in some very remote villages. In his mid 70's he had once more found important work that he could be involved in.

Alan now lives on his own in this small bungalow in Pineridge, and he has invited me to drop in for a cup of tea. (Perhaps I should say something here about all these cups of tea I am drinking everywhere. For a start, I love tea, all kinds of tea from green to herbal to black. It also helps to warm me up, here in the bitter cold weather of Scotland in winter. And finally, it's part of the culture here. It's what people invite you into their homes to share, not coffee, not wine or fruit juices, but a "nice cup of tea.")

Alan is waiting for me and has already put the kettle on. We make our tea in his little kitchen and then move to the living room. Alan is now nearly 80. He can see very little these days, plus he has to cope with his Parkinson's disease. Yet here he is, still living alone, and his house looks immaculately clean and well cared for.

"How are you doing?" I ask.

"Not so bad. I can't see much any more, but I somehow keep going. And there's always something new to do."

"What is it that you are doing these days, Alan? Do you get out a lot?"

"Well, I'm an elder in the community now. I find it difficult, not having a proper job any more, but I am still involved as much as I can be. When I become aware of things that I don't like, I still make sure my voice is heard."

"Are you still running the Nepal Trust?" I ask him.

"No, I've left that to others now, but of course I am still involved in it and will continue to be so, as long as I can." He picks up his cup and sips his tea before continuing. "I seem to spend a lot of time just sitting here, in a constant state of reflection. Now that I can't work in the physical realms any more, I can do a lot of inner work. One thing I have found is that I can now totally indulge myself in the spiritual dimensions. I now have all the time I need to explore my inner world. That's very exciting."

"Do you hear much about what's going on in the community?" I wonder.

"Of course," he replies. "I have a lot of visitors, people bringing me food, or just dropping by for a chat. I like to keep in touch with everything that's going on."

"So what do you think of it all now? Have things changed?"

"Of course things have changed, some for the better, others for the worse. I remember years ago we all trusted one another much more, just got on with our jobs and did things together. Nowadays, they have contracts of employment and managers. I always thought we were trying something different here, a new way of living, but now we are becoming much more like just any other business." Alan looks somewhat sad as he is telling me all this.

"But you're still here, Alan. What has kept you here all this time?"

"Well, the love and inspiration that brought me here initially is also still here. We may be struggling on some levels, dealing with many challenges, but there is still a lot that is very special here," he replies, looking a lot happier. He pauses for another drink of tea and continues, "I don't know anywhere else where there are so many special and wonderful people, and so much love. I feel I am living in a kind of brotherhood and sisterhood with all these like-minded souls. And of course the spiritual dimension here is very important to me. I'm just very happy to be here. Let me tell you a story which will show you how happy I am."

I can feel his joy, and am looking forward to hearing this story.

Alan's smile broadens as he begins to speak. "Look, can you see this button I am wearing, it's a panic button. If I am in any kind of trouble, I just have to press it and someone from the community will immediately call me or come to see me to make sure I am all right. The other day I suddenly got a phone call from someone asking if I was all right, telling me that the panic button had been pressed. I certainly had not done so, but then I remembered that a friend had been to see me and when she left, she had given me a huge hug, and that must have pressed my panic button. So now I call it my 'happy hugging' button." He laughs as he points to his button. "So you can see how happy I am here. I have wonderful friends who care about me, and give me big hugs. What more do I need?"

I think he has a point there.

"I suppose that means we are going to see you around here for a long time yet?"

"Yes," he nods, still smiling. "I'll be here—just another old codger. But the evolution of the community will to a large extent depend on the younger people. We mustn't dwell on the past too much. They have to get on and continue building the new."

I think he may be right, but I am glad that we still have our older, wiser people to hold this place on the inner. People who know the stories from the past, who have helped create this very special place, and who are willing to contribute whatever they can in spite of old age and failing health. There is great magic in that.

∞∞∞∞

[A few weeks later, when I was back in France writing this book, I heard from my friend Judi that Alan had just celebrated his 80th birthday in great style. He had asked for a 'fun evening' in the Universal Hall, and all his friends performed songs, skits and dances to a packed audience throughout the evening. Judi herself sang a song from the musical Pippin, "Time to Start Living," which sounds like a great song to sing to an 80 year old, particularly this one! A group of men came out in tutus and performed a dance from Swan Lake, and the teenagers, not to be outdone, danced a number from Saturday Night Fever.

In the interval, it took several people to blow out the 80 candles on Alan's birthday cake and there was an enormous line waiting to wish him, "Happy Birthday." Later, when the performances were over, the audience was invited to appreciate Alan and, one after another, people told stories and thanked him for his gifts to the community.

It had taken dozens of people to organise this event: the performers, the bakers and coffee makers, and of course those who cleaned up everything afterwards. This is one of the things the community does so well—the celebration of its heroes and heroines, the ordinary members of the community who over the years have given of themselves. It is at times like this that the love and appreciation we feel for each other is most tangible.

I'm sorry I missed Alan's party. Maybe I'll be there for his 90th.]

NETWORK OF LIGHT

I check my watch and see I have just enough time to get down to the Main Sanctuary for the noon meditation. I give Alan a hug, making sure I don't press his 'Happy Hugging' button, and quickly walk back towards the central area of The Park where the Sanctuary is. It is normally very quiet around the Sanctuary, for everyone knows that there are likely to be people meditating there at any hour of the day or night. Work departments, groups of all kinds as well as individuals, will come to this place for some quiet moments of spiritual inspiration, some inner reflection, some inner listening. Three times a day, in the early morning, at noon and early evening, there are community meditations, often with a special focus.

This was the first Sanctuary to be built—in 1968—and it was the place where Eileen shared the daily guidance she had received earlier in the day. The guidance was often very specific; telling the early community members exactly what work was to be done that day. Peter always made sure that this was done exactly the way the guidance had advised. One day, Eileen's guidance said that the community should build a kitchen and dining room for 200 people, which was rather amazing as the community at that time only had ten members! Peter immediately set in motion the designing and building of what was to become the Community Centre, and soon the timber-framed building was erected. Within a year it was already too small for the rapidly growing community and since then it has been extended several times.

Then came the day when Eileen's inner voice told her that she should no longer share her guidance with the community, and instead people should learn to listen to their own inner voice. Eileen still maintains that this inner listening is one of the highest ways in which we can serve the planet, and of course she herself continues to meditate daily and receive her guidance.

I enter the anteroom of the Sanctuary and remove my shoes, placing them on the shelves below the benches. I notice that there are already several other pairs of shoes there, as well as coats and scarves on the hooks above.

On the door that leads into the Sanctuary itself is a notice which reads.

Peace
Be unto all who enter this my
Sanctuary
May My Peace descend on you,
May My Love infil you,
May My Light guide your every step.
Cast all the old aside and become new in My Spirit.

I open the door and see two ranks of golden velvet covered chairs and some cushions set in a circle around a burning candle in the centre of the room. A light is shining on the Sunrise Panel opposite me and fresh flowers are in the corner. There are already a number of people sitting around the room, their eyes closed in silent meditation. I find a seat and make myself comfortable, take one more glance around me and close my eyes. I am aware of more people entering the room. The atmosphere is unutterably peaceful. Generation upon generation of community members have sat in these seats in stillness and listened to their inner guidance, prayed, sent healing energy into the world, focused peace on areas of war and sometimes just sat quietly, waiting to connect with higher beings.

Today, at 12.15 p.m., like every day for the past few months, there is a Network of Light Meditation for Peace. As I allow my attention to move inward I hear Carol's soft voice speaking.

"Welcome to our daily Network of Light Meditation. This meditation began as a spiritual response to the terrorist attacks in the United States in September and is now ongoing as an act of service to the planet.

"Let us each come into our heart centre, that place of deep inner peace in the centre of our being, setting aside all that has occurred during the day, in order to be here and be fully present in this Sanctuary.

"Let us connect with everyone else in the Sanctuary at that heart level.

"And with everyone else in our community.

"And raising our awareness to just above the crown of our heads, let us connect with our soul, seeing it in its beauty and truth and knowing we are all part of the one great soul.

"And from that soul level we align ourselves to the network of light, to all those groups and individuals meditating in service to this planet. We see the network of light as a glowing web surrounding and protecting our planet with light.

"We align ourselves with the angelic realms and we welcome the presence of Michael and Raphael, those two great angelic beings who guard and ward humanity.

"And we align ourselves to Shambala—the centre where the will of God is known.

"And having created a group vessel to receive the divine qualities of love, light and power, we open ourselves to act as channels to receive these energies and to ground and anchor them in the Sanctuary."

For the next 20 minutes or so I allow myself to go deeply into the silence, to take these words with me and let them become one with me. For a while, I am still aware of my breathing, of the sound of the wind outside, of my body on the seat. I try consciously to release all sound and sensation, but as always, the more I try the more difficult it becomes. It is only when I release all striving and let myself just be that I can touch that silent centre, the inner stillness where, for a few blissful moments, there is nothing but peace.

Later, after these timeless moments, I once more become aware that Carol is speaking.

"Now is the time for us to radiate out to the planet the divine qualities of love, light and power which we have anchored in this sanctuary. We will do this by reciting The Great Invocation with intent and purpose, followed by sounding OM three times."

Together we recite The Great Invocation, a prayer given to humanity in 1945 and now recited around the world in nearly seventy languages.

> *From the Point of Light within the Mind of God*
> *Let Light stream forth into the minds of men.*
> *Let Light descend on Earth.*
>
> *From the Point of Love within the Heart of God*
> *Let love stream forth into the hearts of men.*
> *May Christ return to Earth.*
>
> *From the Centre where the Will of God is known*
> *Let purpose guide the little wills of men—*
> *The purpose which the Masters know and serve.*
>
> *From the centre which we call the race of men*
> *Let the Plan of Love and Light work out*
> *And may it seal the door where evil dwells.*
>
> *Let Light and Love and Power restore the Plan on Earth.*

As we complete the last stanza, Carol quietly continues,

"As we sound the first OM let us visualise the quality of love radiating out from this sanctuary to touch the hearts of every human being, and especially those who are suffering and oppressed—no matter what race, colour or creed. Let us also see love transmuting the thought-forms of fear, hatred and violence."

Together, everyone in the Sanctuary sounds that first OM.

"As we sound the second OM, let us see the quality of Light flowing out from this Sanctuary to the whole planet and especially to the military, political and spiritual leaders, so that enlightened decisions may be made."

Sounding this OM, I try to visualise some of the world leaders who are currently making decisions that will affect the lives of millions of people.

"Finally, as we sound the third OM, let us visualise the power radiating out from this Sanctuary, so that the Divine Plan for the earth unfolds for the highest."

We continue to sit quietly for a few minutes, and then, one by one, each person gets up to leave the Sanctuary. Outside in the anteroom, still in silence, we find our shoes and coats and make our way back into the busyness of our day, all of us richer for the experience we have just shared with each other and the planet.

THE QUEST

Still filled with the peace of the Sanctuary, I walk quietly down to the Community Centre for lunch. I'm quite hungry after my busy but lovely morning and am very pleased to see that my favourite roast parsnips and potatoes are on the menu again. I appreciate the fact that most of the vegetables are grown locally and organically, and that the bread is baked right here by Trevor and his colleagues in the Bakery.

I choose a table next to someone I don't know. We greet each other and he introduces himself as John. Not the John who lives in the double Barrel house, but the John who lives in the turf-roofed house on the Field of Dreams. Seems as if the Johns here like to build unusual houses! I have noticed the turf roof, which happens to be right opposite the house I am staying in, so it is interesting to meet my neighbour. I learn that John had originally lived here in the very early days of the community and had already left before I arrived in 1975. Now he has returned to live here again and has built a house with grass on top. Eileen calls people like John her 'homing pigeons'—former members who are deciding to return and live here for a second time around.

John tells me a lot about the very early days of the community. He used to tutor the Caddy boys after school, and was an avid outdoorsman, taking community members on hikes and climbing expeditions. After our lunch, I return to Sunflower to find that Susan has already lit the fire, so it's very cosy and warm for my next visitor.

Over the last few days, I've been hearing about a new project called The Quest, and now someone from this group is coming over to talk to me about it.

There's a knock on the door, and a very English-looking woman introduces herself as Joycelin. I offer her a cup of tea (of course), and we make ourselves comfortable by the fire.

"What is the Quest?" I ask her right away, knowing nothing about it.

"It's a home-based programme for exploring your spiritual and personal development. The written, self-study materials can be used alone, with a partner, a community group or even through Internet-based discussion." Joycelin has a very clear English accent, which stands out at Findhorn amidst the German, American, New Zealand, Scots and many other inflections.

"So everyone does it at the same time?" I ask.

"Oh, no," replies Joycelin, "Everyone can do it at their own pace—over six months to a year—and continue for a lifetime! The Quest doesn't tell you what to think or believe, but interweaves questions and activities that focus on what matters to you."

"Tell me more." I ask intrigued.

"There are six sections to guide the person through the course. One of the first things you do is explore yourself and your own life story, all the things that have happened to you, the good and the bad, and how your values and spiritual experiences have evolved. Later you learn ways to make positive changes and how to live your daily life as a spiritual experience."

"In a way that sounds like life here in the community," I say to Joycelin.

"Yes and no. We are not just trying to capture the essence of Findhorn, but the essence of contemporary spirituality in a very non-dogmatic way. Which of course is what Findhorn is also about."

I get up and put another log on the fire. There is something so soothing, calming and comforting in watching an open fire.

"The problem was to capture and express all this through the written word in a way that people can easily relate to. It was difficult to put on paper something that's almost impossible to describe."

"I do understand. That's just the challenge I am having at the moment, trying to describe the magic of this place." Perhaps if The Quest has managed it, so will I.

"One of our biggest challenges was having to do all the research and writing and testing of the material so quickly. In the end we realised why it had to be done like that. We had no time to start thinking and agonising, we just had to find a different way of working, and do everything intuitively."

That sounds very much like the way I am searching for my answers—using my intuition, and hopefully having the help of the Angels.

"Why was The Quest researched and written here at Findhorn?" I wonder.

"Because Findhorn is a place where you can actually talk about things that matter—like inner listening and spiritual experience. In most other places you have to be careful before you talk about God. Here it is part of daily life."

"Is that why you have chosen to live here?" I ask her.

Joycelin looks out of the window across the Field. "Yes, it's partly that," she replies. "And it's also the beauty of this place, the wildness. And feeling held and supported by the community. There is a very special sense of acceptance here. There is an unseen but tangible web that is around everything, it's here for everyone, but people experience it in different ways."

"Tell me more about this web you are talking about."

Joycelin takes a moment to reflect and then answers. "I think in terms of pictures and colours," she begins. "I experience a fine web that is made of tiny little particles of a multicoloured rainbow, creating a web of white light. Here you can somehow feel closer to it. The veils are thinner here."

In the fire I can also see sparks of many colours, which sometimes blend into a flash of white flame.

"I am a Quaker you know," Joycelin continues. "I know what it is like to make a commitment to sit in silence. Being in the silence gives each one of us the freedom to search for and find our own inner truth. And of course it is of great importance to take your truth and then put it into your daily life

"You are a Quaker, and I know many people here have different beliefs. What do you feel we all have in common?"

"Yes, people from all backgrounds and religions come here, and everything is accepted. Our belief system is that we can all work together. There is a profound respect for each one, and acknowledgement and acceptance of our differences. We listen deeply to each other."

That's just how I would have put it, I think to myself.

"What would you say is the magic here, Joycelin?"

"Ah, you mean the 'something else factor'," she replies, smiling softly. "Yes, there is something here, there is more than will ever be apparent."

"But somehow I have to put it into words, to tell people out there what it is," I say.

Joycelin thinks for a moment, and I know she's trying to help me. "If you can centre yourself in silence, you can sometimes contact that 'something else'. The really important thing is that when you discover what it is, that you learn what to do with it," she advises, looking directly at me.

As Joycelin gets ready to leave, I realise I had better think about that. What do I do with the knowledge, if and when I find it?

The Littlest Magician

I've been invited out for dinner again this evening; tonight it is with the Featherstone family—Cornelia, Alan and their six-year-old son Kevin.

I've known both Alan and Cornelia for a long time. Alan arrived in Findhorn in 1978 and has always been one of my heroes, although it is unlikely that he knows that! Alan is one of those people who has an enormous vision, whose work is planetary while at the same time he can act locally. In the 80's, during the conference "One Earth: A Call to Action," Alan stood up in the Universal Hall and made a commitment to launch a project to help restore the Caledonian Forest in the Highlands of Scotland. This led to the founding of the "Trees for Life" project, originally as part of the Findhorn Foundation, and later as a separate charity based in the wider Findhorn community. For many years Alan has been taking groups of volunteers to plant native trees in Glen Affric, and to date they have planted close to 500,000 new trees.

This, to me, is often the way that magic works. Alan's commitment to his work seems to bear out what the philosopher Goethe said so eloquently, "Whatever you can do, or dream you can do, begin it! Boldness has genius, power and magic to it." Alan's boldness and commitment is making a huge, positive difference not only in the Highlands of Scotland, but in many other places around the world. Alan and "Trees for Life" have justifiably received many awards for their work, including the Schumacher Award of 2002.

Another of Alan's projects is the "Trees for Life" calendars and diaries, which he began in the 1980's. Alan has travelled throughout the world photographing endangered tree species, and offers them to us in the form of exquisitely beautiful photographs on calendars and engagement diaries. At the time I visited he was also busy with preparations for the conference "Restore the Earth" where he, and many others also passionately concerned about healing the Earth, intend to declare the 21st century as the "Century of Restoring the Earth." Knowing Alan, I am sure that he will commit himself as much to this project as he does to "Trees for Life," and will inspire future generations to continue, and hopefully complete, this work.

Cornelia, a medical doctor, came to Findhorn from Germany in 1987. Like most new members, she worked and learned new skills in community departments—in the kitchen, the gardens and in the accommodations office, taking bookings from new guests, as well as driving the community buses. However, it was not long before she was also looking after the health and well being of her new 'family', and she soon became the focaliser of the Holistic Health Department. Cornelia's commitment and passion lie in healing the whole person, and in using her skills and compassion on every level. I well remember Cornelia giving me an amazing massage in the Bodhi room at Cluny Hill, and the many times over the years that I have sought her advice.

One of her heroic projects was to put together, in 1997, a very valuable book called *Medical Marriage*, which brings together the wisdom of both complementary and orthodox medicine and has been an invaluable resource for doctors and nurses as well as holistic health practitioners. Cornelia is now working as a general practitioner in the nearby town of Lossiemouth, bringing all her skills to serve the local area.

The Featherstone house is right at the top of the Runway, next to the Universal Hall. As I enter the porch, I can already see the signs that a child lives in this house—a bicycle, toys, small shoes and coats. I hear the excited squeals of a couple of young boys playing. Kevin and his best friend Clancy are on the floor doing something very interesting with some little wheels. I join them on the floor for a while, until delicious smells from the kitchen tempt me to visit Alan who is cooking our dinner. I know Alan eats vegan food, so I am particularly interested to see what is cooking tonight. It certainly smells good.

Kevin's little friend has now gone home, and Kevin is helping Cornelia lay the table, trying hard to remember which piece of cutlery goes where. He decides it does not matter too much anyway, and places the knives and forks in his own unique way. Dinner is now ready and I get to taste all the interesting dishes coming out of the kitchen. Potatoes with a sauce that tastes like blue cheese, but I know it can't be dairy as it's vegan. There is also curry soup with poppadums, and a platter heaped with a variety of fresh veggies.

Throughout dinner we talk about happenings in the community, new projects in Alan's and Cornelia's lives, and of course the book I am writing. From time to time, between mouthfuls of his food, Kevin joins in the conversation. I am particularly interested in getting to know Kevin; I have been away from the community for most of his young life and only know him as one of the small, lively children running around. We seem to be looking at each other with a certain amount of interest. My own children grew up in the community and now, as adults, are making their own lives in the world, as are all their friends who also lived here. I wonder how a young child today copes with community life in the 21st century.

Cornelia tells me that, although Kevin began his schooling in the community's own Steiner school, it did not suit him and he is now going to one of the local State run schools. This is also what happened with my son Michael. Now, Kevin can't wait to go to school, and is doing very well. It shows me again that each child has a unique need and if we listen to them we can assist them in their particular evolution—and they, in turn, will assist us.

Towards the end of dinner I ask Kevin if he has learned to read yet. He smiles indulgently at me and runs to his room to find one of the lovely Roald Dahl books. With no hesitation at all he begins reading it to me, fluently, and with a lot of expression. He understands what he is reading and is enjoying it enormously. I'm sure he also enjoys the fact that I am sitting there with my mouth open, astounded and very, very impressed at his expertise.

When we can persuade him to stop reading (not an easy task), I begin to talk to him in German. Cornelia is German and I know she frequently speaks to him in her native tongue. Again with no hesitation, he chats to me just as happily in German as in English. Whatever he happens to be doing, whether it is reading or talking in various languages, he does it all with an impish grin. He knows I am impressed, and is quite happy to humour me some more.

Eventually it is time for Kevin to go to bed, and I have been given the task of taking him up the ladder to his loft bed, and this time to read to him. He has chosen a book of German bedtime prayers. As I begin reading the one he has chosen, he quietly reads it with me—he can read in German as well as English. Another delighted grin tells me he is enjoying this as much as I am. "OK, Kevin, I am impressed," I say, and gently tuck his duvet closer around him as his eyes begin to glaze over. Carefully, I make my way down the ladder and return to the conversation with Alan and Cornelia, still hearing an occasional sleepy comment coming out of Kevin's room.

I'm beginning to feel sleepy myself, it's been another long and busy day. I thank my hosts for a delicious dinner and a fascinating evening, and walk the short way to my own bed. The sky is clear and the stars are twinkling at me very much like little Kevin's eyes. I smile to myself—I now have three heroes in the Featherstone family—Alan, Cornelia and Kevin, the little magician.

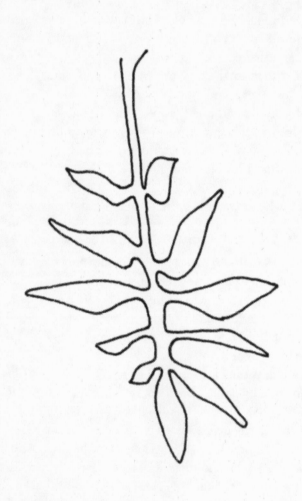

SUNDAY SWEET SUNDAY

THE HALL

How can I describe my experience in the Universal Hall this morning? Was it magic, or was it just emotional? Was the experience real in the here and now, or just some memories from the past?

After a leisurely Sunday morning breakfast I had walked over to the Universal Hall to participate in a ritual that I had somehow always missed in the past. However, today, in the interest of experiencing everything—or as much as I possibly can in the time—I decided to give it a try.

Walking into the Hall, particularly after I have not been there for a while, is always a deeply moving experience for me. I have been part of so many important, creative, fun and inspiring events in this building.

So many memories, so much joy and creativity, so much fun, laughter, tears, weddings, farewells—all such an important part of my community life. And the interminable meetings when we would share, and disagree (yes, we did disagree!) and talk and talk, until it seemed impossible to make any decision at all. Then we would remember what help there is in silence, and we would close our eyes and let our inner knowing guide us. Strange how easy it was then to make decisions with our hearts, as well as with our minds.

When I first arrived in 1975, the Hall was still a shell, with a concrete floor, a roof and walls. For the children, this was a magnificent place to race around on roller skates, until the day came when the permanent floor was laid and skating came to an end.

I was not here when the construction of the Hall began, but I do know somebody who was. Lyle has been a friend for 27 years. He arrived in the community some years before I did, and I remember him as always being involved in building and construction. Eventually he created a business manufacturing solar panels, which today is run as a private business by another community member. I felt that Lyle could tell me about those early days in the Hall and I wrote to him asking him how it happened, how it all began. How was this magnificent building first created? Now, standing here at the main door, seeing the stained glass and crystal wall of colour and light, I remember what he wrote. I will set it down here just as he wrote it:

> Dear Karin,
>
> You asked about the Hall. Construction was started in July 1974. I am quite certain that it was July 1st. Peter wrote me in February that year, asking if I wanted to come back and help build this simple all-purpose hall that was to be finished in 3 to 6 months.

I remember reading that line and chuckling: the Hall eventually took more than 10 years to complete and it is definitely not a simple building! To continue with Lyle's letter:

> When my wife Elizabeth and I had left after a short stay in Feb. '71, we planned to return, and this seemed to be a signal that it was time. Elizabeth, Sara (then 1 3/4 years old) and I arrived in May, but the construction was delayed because there was a shortage of cement for making concrete.
>
> Angus was busy running maintenance and Richard and some of the others who became part of the Hall crew were just finishing off the publications (Pubs) building. I was building the new food storage shed that finally ended up opposite Reception.
>
> The land that the Hall and Pubs were built on were traded with Mr. Wilke for some land behind The Park that was part of the original sale, which I think happened in the spring or summer before my first arrival in Nov. 1971. The construction group were part of maintenance, with Angus as overall focaliser. But it soon became clear that new construction was a different energy, and the Hall became it's own department with Richard V. as focaliser. I must acknowledge Angus for staying with maintenance and providing the

focus for that in the community, when his heart was clearly with the Hall.

Anyway, back to the cement strike. Cement is the grey powder that is mixed with sand, gravel and water to make concrete. Usually concrete arrives in big mixers and is poured into trenches for the foundations of buildings, without hardly being touched by human hands. To get around the shortage we bought something like 25 tons of cement which was then stored in Pubs. By the time we started pouring the foundations the cement shortage was over, but we had to use up all the stored cement. The big concrete mixers arrived with sand, gravel and water, and we added the cement by hand at Findhorn, which was a lot of extra work. This concrete was then poured for the foundations of the Hall.

At our attunements we wondered why circumstances seemed to dictate that we had to do all this extra work of putting in the cement by hand. We realised and agreed that it was important that more love be put into the foundations through our handling of the cement, both into storage in Pubs and into the cement mixers. This was important especially for the foundations, but was also the beginning of a process of blessing and loving all the materials that went into building the Hall.

As I look back, I see that almost all the materials were handled or touched by as many people as possible. Whenever loads of concrete blocks arrived, we would have a community block-stacking event with most of the members passing the blocks in human chains around the building. Every square inch of the beams in the roof was burned and then carefully brushed to bring out the natural beauty of these magnificent Douglas Fir trees.

There were countless days, weeks and years that went into lovingly and perfectly shaping the sandstone walls of the many sides of the Hall. All the trim wood around the windows and doors, and the fronts of the seating platforms, were first sanded with a machine belt sander, and then finished off with hours of loving hand sanding by members and especially guests. Even the plywood on top of the roof was brushed to bring out the texture and radiance of the material. One of the most fundamental lessons we learned on the Hall is that the energy you put into creating a vessel or a space or a 'temple' is reflected back every time you go into that space. If that energy is love, respect and attunement to the Beloved and each other, then that is what is returned.

In the Hall we had a clear sense of this and made it a priority as we worked together to keep our relationships with each other and God conscious, clear and harmonious. And if it didn't happen in the moment, we made time at the end of the week to sort it out.

One story that I remember clearly: we were waiting to get started building. Peter had just returned from his first trip to the USA and was followed a few days later by Wayne and Bella, two sensitives he had linked up with in California. Peter told Angus and me to set out stakes to accurately mark the corners of the Hall. Bella, who was sensitive to these things, would check them to be sure that we had the building in the right place and properly orientated on the energy lines there. Angus nodded knowingly, and I just did as I was told—not having any understanding of, or sensitivity to, 'energy lines' and power points.

The Hall is a five-sided building and only just barely fits on the site with all the appropriate setbacks required by the local planning office. We were given the criteria that the centre line of the building was to line up with the power point on Cluny Hill five miles away in Forres. Neither of these were visible from the hollow in the sand dunes where the Hall was to be built. Angus got up on the very top of a 6 ft step ladder perched on top of the highest mound of sand behind the site. I pulled a long white tape measure from the centre corner at the back of the building along the ground away from Angus towards Cluny Hill. I moved it from side-to-side until Angus confirmed that it was in alignment with the power point, which was a bit to the left of Nelson's Tower on Cluny Hill and which he could just see through the trees from his vantage point on tip-toes at the top of the step ladder. With the centre line of the building 'skilfully' established, we then proceeded to measure and very accurately mark out (to within 1 to 2 millimetres) each of the corners of the building, using nails in the tops of stakes hammered into the ground.

When we finished, we reported back to Peter and the Core Group. Peter and Bella came down to check that the building was in the right alignment. Bella first walked to the area of the building that is now the auditorium. She stood on a spot about ten feet away from the centre of the auditorium, toward the back of the Hall, and announced that this was the *Power Point.* She said all the energy in that area flowed toward that point. *Angus* and *Peter* tried it and nodded knowingly, agreeing with her. *I* stood on the spot and turned 360°, didn't feel any energy, but thought "well maybe." *I* asked why it was not dead centre in the middle of the auditorium. *She* said that if the power point was right in the middle of the building, the energy would blow the building apart. *It* is interesting to note that now speakers and performers naturally seem to stand near "*Bella's power point.*" *Some* singers say—and this is my experience too—that they have a sense of being able to project out to and fill the whole room from that spot.

But that is not the end of the story. *Bella* checked all the other corners by standing beside them and tuning in to them, and then confirming that they were 'spot on'. *She* came to the last corner, the one beside the chimney and nearest the *Publications* building. *This* stake was on top of a tall mound of sand, about 10 ft higher than all the other stakes which were down in the hollow. *After* she attuned, she said that when we actually built the building, this corner would go out a bit further, closer to *Publications*. *I* was taken aback and my mind immediately jumped in, arguing, "*No I* am sure it's right. *We* double-checked all the dimensions. *Besides* the excavators are arriving this afternoon, and we are going to break ground tomorrow. *We* can't change the plans now, too much red tape at this stage and no time."

And then *I* realised that we had measured uphill from the reference stake, and if you dug the mound away and lowered the tape down to the level of the other stakes, that same dimension would in fact be closer to *Publications*, in the same way that the hypotenuse of a triangle is longer than the longest of the other two sides. *And* with this realisation there came for me an inner acceptance of another reality. *If* an elderly, grandmotherly lady could intuitively perceive the error in our measurement (without a tape measure), then, for me, there certainly also had to be something to her perception about the power point and the energy lines in the *Hall. And* most importantly for me, this experience was the beginning of opening door upon door to new understandings of myself and *God*, while working with many brothers and sisters in joy, love and grace, discovering who we really can be.

With love, *Lyle*

I open the doors that look like two multicoloured Angel wings, and then walk up the curved, wooden staircase. At the top I look back at the stained glass wall. With the light behind it, it is a blaze of colour. The American artist James Hubble, assisted by the local artist Janet Banks as well as many other volunteers from the community, combined to create this amazing and glorious piece of art in glass.

JUBILATE DEO

I am now joined by other people entering the Hall and we make our way into the main auditorium. As always, I catch my breath as I walk into this space. I know how much love and care went into the building of it, how many hundreds of people shared their skills with tenderness and generosity for its completion. I can sense how this love is part of the walls and beams and the very seats I am about to sit on. There is a feeling of sacredness in this place, to which people like Lyle and Richard and Dieter and Ian and so many others have contributed.

While most of the seats are covered in purple, there are also some larger, very comfortable chairs covered in golden velvet. I remember when all the upholstery was made and fitted over 25 years ago by my friend Elfreda. She would be glad to know that it still looks as good as new. These chairs have been put out in readiness for us, some with yellow booklets on them. I also take a quick glance up at the ring beam that goes around the top of the Hall, making sure that the colour is still the basic stone that it has been for many years. A long time ago some well-meaning member had covered the ring beam in a very lurid pink material because he felt it represented the colour of unconditional love. There was a huge outcry from the rest of the membership and eventually the pink was removed and replaced by the more sober stone colour.

There are already about a dozen people here. I sit down and open the booklet to see the words and music of the Taizé chants. These chants originally came from the Taizé ecumenical international community in France, where hundreds of thousands of people from around the world visit every year to sing and pray together. This is especially true in the summer when many groups of young people are welcomed there. Listening to and singing these inspiring chants can be a deep spiritual experience.

I look around to see who is leading this morning's celebration and am not surprised to see that it is Geoffrey—one of the Finance Directors of the

Foundation, bungalow cleaner and dishwasher extraordinaire, who also leads young people in sailing courses in his 'spare time'. It is now Geoffrey who leads the Taizé chanting and dancing, and I am struck that it is often the busiest people who have the most time to serve and give of their skills to others. Geoffrey seems to be one of these special people.

More and more people arrive until all the golden seats are taken and people move further up onto the purple benches. I am surprised to see that there are at least 60 or 70 people here.

Geoffrey asks us to stand up and create a circle, by now a very large circle, and we all hold hands. There are a few moments of silence as we all sink into this experience, letting ourselves enter totally into the present moment, and then one voice begins to sing. First one, then another, then more and more voices join in the song. I recognise the melody and also join in the singing. As we sing, Geoffrey leads us in a spiral dance that allows us to make eye contact with each member of our group.

"*Jubilate Deo, Jubilate Deo.*"

I look into the eyes of the person in front of me.

"*Jubilate Deo, Jubilate Deo.*"

I feel my heart opening, I allow the being before me to know me.

"*Alleluia.*"

After only a few minutes, I already feel profoundly connected to this group of people. We are all here to share our love, to see God in each one of us. This is what I miss in my daily life, this is what I find again here today. Through the music, in this special place, surrounded by like-minded souls, I feel so at home here. I can see from the shining, open faces passing in front of me that this is how they feel too. It is a moment of deep connection each with the other, with the spirit inside each of us. Through our hands and our eyes we recognise that we are one in spirit.

The dance is over, we release our hands and return to our seats. And with our hearts opened, we move into more silence. Some people pray, some meditate, and some are inspired to speak the words they feel move them.

We sing again, we sing in harmony, we sing until our hearts and voices are one. The joy and peace and beauty are utterly tangible, right there in our midst. Spirit is here with us—and we send this energy of love and healing out into the world.

"*Gloria in excelsis Deo.*"

An hour later, I leave the Hall feeling immensely happy, joyful and at peace. I have touched my soul, I have opened my heart, and I feel soft and tender.

Walking through the gardens towards the Community Centre I also begin to feel something else. Pangs of hunger. Time for brunch. I have fed my soul, time now to feed my body.

hAppy FAMILIES

Sunday brunch in the Community Centre is a popular time for the whole community to get together. It's more relaxing than meals during the week, and the cooking crew usually make something special. People like to hang around drinking coffee and talking to friends. So it's no surprise to me that there is already a large crowd milling around when I arrive with the others from the Taizé celebration.

Some of the food is already out—tasty cereals, a selection of dried fruits, a big batch of mouth-watering cheese scones and baskets of freshly baked bread, but we are still waiting for the kitchen to open the shutters to serve the surprise hot dish.

More people arrive, and we begin to line up at the counter in the hope of collecting our food. The door to the kitchen opens and one of the cooks puts his head around the corner.

"Sorry folks," he tells us, "it's going to be a bit late today, the eggs are not cooked yet."

There's a good-natured groan, and people make their way to the coffee urns or pour themselves one of the many herbal teas. The children run outside and play, laughing and shouting as they are released from the restraining hands of adults.

I'm hungry, so I butter one of the cheese scones and seat myself at one of the tables where two old friends, Trevor and Stephen, are chatting. It seems a good opportunity to join them, see how they are doing and meet their children. I often find it hard to know which children and parents belong together, as all the children are comfortable relating to any of the adults. Often children from several families will sit together for meals.

Half an hour later we are still chatting and waiting for hot brunch to appear. The cereals and fruit are vanishing into hungry bellies, and the scones have completely disappeared.

At last the kitchen shutters open. We all stand up and try to create a circle where we can hold hands for the blessing. There is a moment of silent grace—as there is before every meal—and one of the cooks says a blessing. Then, a rush of people pick up their plates of scrambled eggs and what looks like some sort of vegetable—perhaps carrots and courgettes? Hard to tell. Amidst the crowd I spot the people I have arranged to meet and we all make our way into the dining room, hoping to find an empty table— somewhere quiet. We eventually give up on the quiet, but find a table to ourselves next to a noisy but cheerful group of guests.

With me are Karl and Deborah and their two children, nine-year-old Jake and four-year-old Kezia. We make sure the children are eating, then settle down to talk. I first remember meeting Deborah about fifteen years ago, when she was twenty. We participated in a workshop called "The Mastery" together. This was some years before she met Karl, and she was a very attractive young woman just starting out in life. She does not seem to have changed at all, and is just as lively and energetic. Hard to believe she's in her mid thirties now.

I met Karl when I was working in Personnel, and he, wishing to join the community, came to me for an interview. We had a very hard time of it. In those days—fourteen years ago—I believed that in order to join the community one had to do so in a particular way, follow a certain path. He wanted to do things his way, and the two of us clashed. He was a strong minded and independent young man, and I was a more conservative, older woman who expected him to follow the rules

"How long have you all been here?" I begin.

Deborah turns to Karl who's hungrily tucking into his scrambled eggs. "Shall I talk while you're eating?" she suggests. He seems happy with that arrangement.

"Well, we came back here to visit about three years ago, just for a couple of months. We had been living in London for seven years and had bought a house there. We knew we wanted to live in a community and work with dance, but absolutely did not think it would be here. We didn't even want it to be here. In fact Karl was quite adamant that it was not going to be at Findhorn."

We all smile, knowing full well what can happen when we are adamant about something we don't want to do.

Jake, bored by our conversation, decides to take his plate of food and go and eat elsewhere.

"If you felt so strongly, why did you come back then?" I ask.

Karl has finished his eggs, and takes over the conversation to let Deborah begin eating. "We took a year to travel around and decide where we wanted to live. We knew we wanted a community-based lifestyle, incorporating some of the things we had learned here, but we didn't want it to be here! Our work includes a lot of travelling and we felt Findhorn was too isolated and too far away from London."

Kezia now needs some attention and Karl checks to make sure she has everything she needs before continuing. "Then we came back here for a visit and I found myself beginning to lighten up, to be happier than I had been for the last few years in London. We found Findhorn just reeled us back in, and I recognised the changes only after they had happened. Bit by bit, it became harder to separate the dream of living 'somewhere' in a community, doing everything we wanted, and actually doing it here. It just began to make sense to stay here. When I eventually gave up my resistance, I found that so many of the elements I was looking for were actually here, but I had not been able to see them."

"What were you looking for, Karl?" I ask, aware that it's quite difficult to keep our conversation focussed with all the noise around us. People are calling across the room to each other—and all the friendly, cheerful goings-on of a community meal. However, Karl bravely tries to answer me.

"Having a life which included the arts and dance—to be able to bring people up here to do that. And to live in a community that was not isolated."

"And is that what you have found?"

"Yes, definitely. Over the seven years we were away, the community here had changed and things had shifted from being just the Foundation to becoming a broader community with many groups and businesses. The population is more diverse, and there are lots of people I can relate to on an artistic level. And everything here is centred on core spiritual values. I need to be constantly reminded of God, of spirit, of working on myself. I need to be challenged, that's one of the things I like about being here, people are constantly challenging me, demanding more of me. In London, my spiritual life had become hidden and private and complacent—I could not share it with anyone else. Here it is not only accepted but encouraged. For the first time in my life, at age 39, I am getting a sense of integration. I can bring together my family, my dance work and my social life, all around a spiritually-centred life. Before I came here my life was very fragmented, and now I have a chance to bring it all together."

Right in front of me, he is bringing some of it together. Looking after his children, answering a colleague's questions about his work, smiling at his beautiful wife, and doing his best to help me find some answers to my questions.

He begins again, "The thing about Findhorn and knowing that you need to come here—that it's right for you—it's not always comfortable when it happens. It might be accompanied by total panic, emotional fear and breakdown, or it might bring huge relief and joy to know that it's right."

That's something I remember myself, and have heard from so many others.

"It is also knowing how much I can contribute, not only what I am given to do. I just love being here—for me it's just the way I want to live."

Kezia runs off to play with some friends and Deborah picks up the story.

"It's always been home for me here, ever since the first day I arrived. The reason we left was because Karl needed to finish his training. So I was very happy when we decided to come back."

"What do you find so special here?"

"I love this most fantastic mix of people whom I can engage with so fully, intellectually, spiritually, and emotionally and with all my heart—and all in the most beautiful landscape. That's one of the things that is so special, that there are great people and we have clean air and glorious surroundings. I need all of that."

She looks across the dining room where her son is running around with a group of other children.

"I see Jake when he is down at the Bay, and he has the vastness of the water and the mountains. And the sky—he needs to be held by it, it's bigger than he is. He can expand into who he really is, which is a child with an enormous amount of energy. The freedom he has here works for him. In London we always had to rein him in, and while we still have to do this up to a point, he has a lot of freedom to express himself fully."

"Does he go to the Steiner school?" I ask her.

"Yes, he is in class 3, and Kezia goes to the Kindergarten. Jake also went to a Steiner school in London, which was great for me too, as it was the one place where I felt at home."

Karl comes back into the conversation. "Here the parents at the Steiner school are more strong willed, stronger minded, more skilled at communicating, so at school meetings the level of experience in communicating and getting things done is much greater than it was in London."

"And I also like the fact that I am living in an experiment—that is what this is all about," Deborah adds. She goes on, "It's neither right nor wrong, we are all doing our best. We make mistakes along the way, but we take responsibility for making things better. What we do makes a difference. It's exciting. Who knows what the bigger picture will be or how it will all turn out?"

I ask Deborah where she works.

"I teach dance here, and sometimes I also work away from home, so I love coming back here. I need to get away, I couldn't be here all the time, I need to travel. But what a fantastic place to come back to!"

"Yes," I agree with her, "I always feel like that, too."

"One of the things that I really want in my life, what I have dreamed about, is to be able to see the stars at night and still be within cycling distance of a hot chocolate; those are two of my prime criteria for a good life, and that's possible here. I can cycle to work, then go to the hot tub and see the stars; it has everything that I want. I also need to get into nature often, that's where I get my strength."

I love listening to Deborah's enthusiasm and joy of life, and seeing the way her face lights up when she talks about her dreams—dreams she has made real for herself. I suddenly remember one of the most important things I've been wanting to ask them.

"Your house—the straw-bale house—I've been to see it being built in Pineridge. How did that all happen?" I ask them

Enthusiastically, Karl tells me the story of the Solus House.

"The history of the house is actually longer than our history with Findhorn. It was originally designed for the Foundation, to create accommodation for single members of the community. Each bedroom was going to be very big and would have a loft bed. It had gone through all the necessary stages, planning permission, drawings, building warrant—and then it stopped. There was not enough money to build it, so the whole project lay dormant for a while."

"Is that when you took it over?" I ask.

"No, not immediately. When we returned, we wanted to explore a co-housing development, and had a group of others to do it with. However, for many reasons, it just didn't work out. So we had to ask ourselves where we should live. And then it came to us, why not the Solus House? Everything then moved ahead at a rapid pace. We took on the whole project. It's not our ideal dream home, but it provides us with somewhere to live for the next few years until the co-housing development happens. It also gets a house built that deserves to be built, so while we are building our own home we are also serving the community by supporting this particular project."

"So you can serve yourself and the community at the same time," I said.

"Yes, it does feel like that. The money came to us through a miracle, and now we can bring together our money and enthusiasm and desire to move quickly and get this particular house built. So whatever we do in the future, we feel we will leave something behind, a beautiful, simple way to contribute to what is happening here. We will leave something concrete behind—except that it's not concrete, it's straw!"

We all laugh.

"It's also shown me how we can make a difference," Karl continues. "Just choose something, and do it. It's actually very easy to make a difference in the world in many ways. And it's a gorgeous house. And we also have the opportunity to release our attachment to the way we wanted our home to be. We always come back to the fact that it's all about service, not just about providing our dream home."

"Yes," I comment, "I have heard so much about this house, there is a lot of excitement and inspiration and life around it."

Deborah agrees. "It's such an incredible experience to be building something that so many people are excited about. We have had people telling us they are looking forward to spending time in our home. We'll probably never be alone in there! I was looking forward to a little bit of privacy, it doesn't look like it's going to happen."

"It's all been such a wonderful experience," Karl adds. "I had all these ideas about my life, what was best for me, or best for my family. The kind of house I wanted, and where it would be, and that it was not going to be at Findhorn! I have had to surrender all of that, and do what Eileen patiently and timelessly tells us—to turn within. I need to take all my ideas, let everything go, sink down inside myself and be quiet, receptive, and listen. And then trust what comes, whether it's words of guidance, whether it's inspiration, an impulse, whether it's a door that suddenly opens. So often for me, it's completely different than anything I ever imagined. But the result and benefit is always amazing and rewarding. Building the Solus house, working in the Universal Hall, living where we are now, having children."

There is a crash of crockery from the washing-up area, it sounds like brunch is nearly over and the dishwashing crew is at work. A small baby is crawling towards the noise and an older child picks her up and turns her around to crawl in a safer direction.

"So, all is very, very well?" I ask, and smile at my use of this very 'Findhorn' phrase.

"I do sometimes panic," says Deborah, "I definitely panic. Karl gets overwhelmed and I panic! There have been times when we've put a lot of energy into a project, like the co-housing project, and it doesn't happen. I had my panic then, I needed a home. I had let my house in London go, I had wanted adventure, but then, suddenly, I needed a home. It's all taken much longer than I thought and, with two children, that's difficult."

It's interesting to hear that not everything here is sweetness and light.

"But I have always been taken care of," Deborah continues. "I have to remember that. That's the reality. My panic is not the reality, just an emotional response I have when difficult things are happening".

Kezia has returned to her parents and is crying loudly. She climbs onto Deborah's knee, still sobbing, not yet ready to be consoled.

Karl turns to talk to a friend, and Deborah's attention is now all with her daughter. I whisper a quiet, "Thank you all," to this extraordinary little family. They smile back, and I know that the time they have given me is precious. I also know that they are willing to serve in any way they can. They know and accept that they live in a centre of demonstration and are willing to open their lives not only to me, but also to anyone who wants to share in what is happening here.

We seem to be the last people still eating and the washing-up crew want our dishes. I also realise I am late for my next appointment down at the Living Machine, so I say a quick farewell to Deborah and Karl and quickly make my way down the Runway, past all the empty holiday caravans and there, right at the end of the street, is the place I am looking for.

THE LIVING MACHINE

Puffing from having run all the way, I arrive in front of what looks like a very large greenhouse. However, I already know that this is something very different—this is a sewage plant. But not the usual, common or garden type of sewage plant—it is an ecological sewage treatment system. I will not even attempt to describe what that is, for although I do know what sewage is, the rest is a complete mystery to me. Nor can I imagine how I might find the magic of Findhorn down here, but I feel I must try everything! If anyone can help me find the magic in the Findhorn sewage, it's my friend Pauline.

And there she is, waiting for me. Pauline has been part of the community for much longer than even I can remember. She came to live here with her parents when she was a teenager, is now married to Alex, and has two sons, Barney age 22 and Craig who is 11. I have worked with Pauline on the One Earth magazine and baked and iced her wedding cake when she married Alex, but it is mainly through singing together that Pauline and I have shared many, many happy hours. We have both been part of a number of choirs here in the past, and for many years we also belonged to a Women's Barbershop group. I still find myself beginning, "He was a famous trumpet man from out Chicago way," as soon as I see her.

Over the years, Pauline has contributed a huge amount to the life of the community, from cooking meals for hundreds in the community kitchens to focalising the Park campus, and of course through her singing, which is how I will always remember her. She is a very popular and well-loved woman. She even focalised the brunch for my wedding reception when Thierry and I were married in 1992.

I am delighted to see her, and we promise to have a cup of tea together later. But for now a group of men and women have just arrived for the 'tour', and I will join them to learn something about the Living Machine. This group of people are from the Social Venture Network; they are visiting for the weekend to learn what happens up here, and to have a "Findhorn experience."

"Welcome to one of the most attractive sewage works in Europe," Pauline begins. "Here at the Park the waste water is treated in this greenhouse, here in these tanks in front of you. In the summer you would see an enormous abundance of plant life and flowers growing in these tanks."

We look around and find that even in midwinter there are many plants growing.

"Many diverse communities of bacteria, algae, micro-organisms, numerous species of plants and trees, snails, fish and other living creatures interact in these tanks to create an attractive environment and cleanse the water," Pauline's clear, soft and very English voice informs us.

The warmth in the greenhouse, even now in winter, is making me somewhat sleepy and my mind wanders as we walk through the building, until suddenly I hear Pauline say, "And here, at the end of the series of tanks, the resulting water is pure enough to discharge directly into the sea."

"So it's not pure enough to drink?" asks one of the group.

"Living Machines can clean the water to drinking water standards. We don't, because in this area we would be obliged to add chlorine before we were able to re-use it. We are currently working on a recycling use for the water—probably a tree nursery."

"Are there other Living Machines like this anywhere else?" someone asks.

"Yes," replies Pauline, "there are now more than 20 operational Living Machines in the world. Depending on the climate, Living Machines can be located outdoors, in protective greenhouses like this one, or under light shelter. Some of these machines produce water for washing or irrigation, and most also produce useful by-products like fish and plants."

Pauline smiles when she now tells us, "When you flush the toilets here, you feed the fish and snails and other creatures, as well as the plants of course."

My thoughts are wandering again, and I wonder if those people who began the educational programmes here many years ago would have imagined that Findhorn could one day be a centre of demonstration for sewage!

At the farther end of the greenhouse there is a small waterfall of what looks like crystal clear water. I also realise that there are absolutely no unpleasant smells in here.

Our tour is coming to an end, and the Social Venture group are off to their next experience. Pauline and I make our way back to my B&B for a cup of tea and a long chat. As I fill the kettle I look questioningly over at Pauline.

"It's all right," she laughs, picking up my thought. "That's not the water from the Living Machine. However, next time you flush the toilet you'll know exactly where it's all going."

FROM PARIS WITH LOVE

My very full appointment book tells me that my next stop is Cluny Hill College where I will be spending the rest of the day, though getting over there could be a problem. During the week there are regular community buses that carry people back and forth, but today is Sunday and there does not seem to be one I could use. And because it is Sunday, there aren't any of the local buses which run from Findhorn Village into Forres. My other choices are to walk the 5 or 6 miles to Forres and then another mile up to Cluny Hill, or to hitch a ride, or to call a taxi. I decide that the easiest and most convenient choice is the taxi.

Then I realise I have another choice. I have seen numerous announcements on the community notice boards offering rides in private cars. Should I follow up that option or call one of the local taxi firms in Findhorn Village or Forres? Decisions, decisions! In the end, I decide that the easiest and quickest way is likely to be the local taxi firm in Findhorn Village. I know the taxi drivers there are very friendly and helpful.

Five minutes later the taxi arrives and another ten minutes later drops me outside the main doors of Cluny Hill College. I am just in time for my next meeting—Viviane is already waiting for me by the reception desk.

I first met Viviane more than 10 years ago when my husband Thierry and I were visiting Paris. I remember her small apartment full of enormous plants and how, when we stepped outside, we could see the Eiffel tower right in front of us. What I remember most was Viviane's warm and gracious welcome, and that she gave up her living room for a week to give us somewhere to sleep.

Over the years, I have seen her at various times, and was once able to welcome her into our home at Findhorn. Last year we had a delicious dinner in her Paris apartment, and as always, enjoyed her hospitality and warmth.

I am delighted that she happens to be here at Findhorn during my stay, and that I can perhaps get another perspective on life here. As an occasional visitor, Viviane will probably notice the changes more than do the residents—either for better or worse.

She is staying at Cluny Hill College, participating in a workshop there. I have been trying to catch her between sessions, knowing how busy they keep workshop participants.

We greet each other in the typical French way, kissing each cheek at least twice. Now that I live in France, I've had to get used to all this kissing. Conversing for the first few minutes in French, we make our way into the lounge and find a comfortable couch in front of the roaring, open fire.

I turn on my tape recorder and switch to speaking in English.

"Thank you for taking some time from your busy schedule, Viviane. I'm so glad you are here, and I can get your thoughts and feelings about what is so special and magical here. Tell me about the first time you visited Findhorn."

"That was in 1985, I seem to remember, and it happened in a very roundabout and miraculous way. I had read the book *The Faces of Findhorn* and had also taken a workshop at Eourres—a Findhorn-inspired centre in the French Alps. I felt it was the right time to go and see the real thing."

"What did you expect to find here?" I ask her.

Viviane smiled at my question. She is a very beautiful woman and does not look anywhere near 78 years old, which I know she is. I can't believe that the 'inner Viviane' will ever be older than a very curious and childlike 21!

"I was looking for something—God, I suppose, or a reason to live. So I registered for Experience Week and as soon as I got to Cluny, I suddenly felt—like hundreds before and since—that I had come home."

She is right, I have heard this many times.

"And I have been coming back on and off ever since. I love the place. I need to know it is there. Sometimes, when I have been back in the 'real world' for few months, I stop believing it really exists. Then a letter with the postmark 'Expect A Miracle' arrives, and I decide to come back for a few weeks."

"Has Findhorn changed since you first came here?" I ask.

"Yes, it has changed, it keeps changing, but then so do I. Some changes I don't like: the Cluny gardens are nowhere near what they used to be—and still are in the countless pictures I took during the first years. Many people I knew have left, but there are new ones. It is neither better nor worse; it is in a state of ongoing evolution. I come back because I love the place and always hope it is going to heal and nurture me—and it always does."

I am so pleased to hear this. Viviane deserves to be nurtured and cared for. She is such an extremely loving and giving woman. I know that still, several times a week, she leaves her apartment late in the evening to spend the night as a Samaritan, one who listens on the telephone to people who are in distress and often desperate, having nobody else to turn to for help. I still laugh when I recall the story she told me about her neighbours, who see her leave late at night and return the following morning. They have grave suspicions about what Viviane gets up to during the night time! If it were true, this might make her the oldest lady of easy virtue in Paris!

I'm still smiling at the thought and put another question. "You work with the Samaritans, you practice Yoga, you raise amazingly beautiful plants, and you translate books from English into French. You also have a lot of friends, you travel whenever you can, and you love to come to Findhorn. What else is important in your life?"

"What else is important in my life?" Viviane thinks for a moment and then continues, "Even though I lead a reasonably active life for a woman my age and have many friends and interests, I feel the need for a different dimension of some kind. You might call it spirituality. It may be that I want to have another go at unconditional love!"

I suppose "having a go at unconditional love" is not a bad ambition, at any age.

Viviane looks out of the window, across the golf course and to the mountains in the distance.

"There are also more mundane considerations," she continues. "I have always lived in a city, but I yearn for a place where nature is respected, where beauty has been nurtured for years, where I can look out at the sea and dig around in the soil of the Cullerne gardens. Moreover, I am fairly sociable and curious about human nature. Findhorn is a place where I meet a wide assortment of fabulous people from all over the world and all walks of life. Some of them have become good friends. However different we may be in life 'outside', we have Findhorn's spirit and magic in common."

"Can you help me define what that magic is, Viviane, what is unique here?" I ask her.

"Of course, there is something unique in Findhorn, but how to define it? First of all, it is so obviously a power point and a point of light. That is built in. It may have been that long before man appeared on earth. I am not very sensitive to mysterious vibrations and never see—much to my regret— elementals hiding in the trees, but I can feel that there is something here."

I am like Viviane, I have never yet seen a nature spirit or elemental being. And I, too, know that there is something here. And somehow, very soon, I need to find out exactly what this something is—and be able to put it into words. I'll think about this some more later, but for now I'd like to hear more from Viviane.

"What about challenges, have you come across any here?"

"Challenges? Well, sometimes, but not often. I do not particularly enjoy the close proximity of shared accommodations, but lately, due to my old age, I have been granted the privilege of sleeping in solitary splendour. At other times, and this is not as contrary as it seems, I have felt lonely in Findhorn. Everyone is so busy, busy, busy, and I miss the chance for long, meandering conversations."

That is certainly something I can relate to. With so many people around, all of them busy and involved, it can sometimes feel quite lonely.

"You're participating in a workshop this week. How is that working out for you, and do you see Findhorn as just another workshop centre?"

Viviane looks appalled that I could even suggest that.

"Findhorn is certainly not an ordinary workshop centre, whatever that is," she replies. "However, over the years it has perfected a truly impressive way of organising workshops and dealing with groups. It works every time. I am thrown in with a bunch of total strangers, all of them usually far younger than I am and with whom I seem to have nothing in common, and by the end of the week we have become closer than close friends. To use a French culinary metaphor, "*la mayonnaise a pris* (the mayonnaise has set)."

Ah, yes, I remember I am speaking to a very good French cook here. Alas, she needs to leave me and return to her workshop group.

"Just one last question, Viviane, and then I'll let you go. How has coming to Findhorn affected your life?" I ask.

Her eyes are shining as she answers me. "Very simply, Findhorn has changed my life. Once, at a time of great pain, I thought I would like to leave my life behind me and come to live in Findhorn. I went to see Carol Riddell, a member here at that time and a very wise being, who said to me, "You are not meant to live in Findhorn, but why don't you take Findhorn home with you?"

"Is that what you did?"

"Yes, that is what I did and what I continue to do, bring something of the spirit of Findhorn—the love, warmth, understanding, peace, and healing—to my ordinary world, and do you know something?"

She got up from her chair, kissed me on both cheeks again, and then said, "It works!"

ANJA AND THE EXPERIENCE WEEK

I have some time to spare before dinner, so I decide to walk up to the power point, which is on a mound behind Cluny Hill College. I leave the building through the back door, and in the gathering dusk I find the entrance to the spiral path that leads to the top of the mound. I have heard a lot of stories about this power point—the strange experiences people have had here. Some mention communications with space brothers, others talk of seeing an intense light up here. It is many years since my last walk up here, but, as I make my way up the winding path, it still seems very familiar.

I reach the high point and find myself surrounded by bushes and trees. I look around nervously, but find nothing strange or unusual here. Perhaps I am not sensitive to the energies here. But the silence is welcome, a moment in nature to be savoured before I return to the bustling energy of the building below me.

Slowly, I make my way back down the path, and after dinner I am back in the welcoming warmth of the comfortable lounge. In just a short while I'll join the "Experience Week" guests in the room just above me.

The Experience Week is the "welcoming programme" for all first-time guests who find their way to the community. I have been told that if I am to find "the magic" anywhere, this is where I will surely do so. For around thirty years this seven-day programme has been virtually unchanged, and thousands upon thousands of newcomers have enjoyed (or sometimes not!) their first taste of living and working in a spiritual community. The programme has several elements, all of which make up a rich and profound experience.

One of these elements is the synthesis of all the different personalities of the participants; people of all ages, backgrounds and cultures come from every corner of the world. Everyone comes to Findhorn for their own special reason, and of course everyone has their own expectations. Each group is unique and is always woven together by "the magic," the "Factor X," which is what I am here to pinpoint. Each Experience Week group has two focalisers who facilitate and encourage everyone to share about their lives, their dreams, their hopes and fears, their challenges and successes. Every week emotional and spiritual breakthroughs occur, and a huge amount of trust, support and love grows between group members.

Part of this 'group coming together' is brought about by fun, laughter and dancing. Early in their Experience, there will be Group Discovery games that help break down barriers and allow people to re-discover and enjoy their inner child. Sacred Dance is another opportunity, with circle dances and beautiful music that join the group together without words or thoughts.

Another important experience for the first-time guest—as with all guests who come to Findhorn—is the work experience. Everybody works for half a day throughout the week. Each person is asked to go within to discover which department or work area they are drawn to. When led through attunement, it is usually surprisingly easy to choose the right place. Often, people who normally hate housework will find themselves strangely but irresistibly drawn to joining the home care department, and will find themselves cleaning toilets with great joy! The office worker may find himself pulling weeds in the gardens, and the teacher may join the builders and start laying bricks!

The third element in the Experience Week is education, providing opportunities to hear talks by community members who have special skills. During the week, the group may learn about eco-building and sustainable communities from John of the Eco-Village, or—as in the case of the group I have joined this week—Lily may come and share about organic gardening and working with nature. The group will also visit the pottery, the weaving studio, the Living Machine and other areas of the community, to learn about their work.

The major spiritual discipline at Findhorn is meditation, both alone and as a group, and the new guests will meditate together, as well as participate in many community meditations throughout the week. For those who have not been exposed to this before, there will be help in learning how to move into the silence and to hear their inner voice.

The Experience Week is not only extremely busy, but often a time of intense emotional change and transformation. So it's no surprise that on their free afternoon guests tend to make their way to the Phoenix store for a bar of chocolate, followed by a quiet, solitary walk on the beach!

I vividly remember my own Experience Week in 1975. I remember the people who shared it with me, and the two members who focalised the week and took care of us. I can recall where I worked, how I felt, how it totally changed the way I felt about myself and about what I wanted to do for the rest of my life. This sounds like a huge transformation in one short week, but it was very true for me. Now, twenty-seven years later, I want to observe and share this time again, and hope to connect with someone from the group who will be willing for me to 'shadow' them for a few days. And, I wonder, will Findhorn work its "magic" on me a second time?

So now I join the dozen participants and two focalisers for the Inner Life sharing. This is a time when someone (in this case, me) comes into the group to share about some area of their inner life and their spiritual experiences. The participants share as much as they feel able about their inner being—their connection to spirit, God, the Universe, Love, Angels, whatever this means to them. There are twelve members of this particular group, plus their two focalisers. I begin by sharing some stories and experiences from my life, and then ask them to do the same. Slowly, carefully, people begin to feel safe enough to speak. Many of the stories are somehow connected with the death of loved ones. At the end of the evening I ask if there is one person who would be willing to share their experiences during the week with me. With no hesitation at all, a young woman called Anja volunteers.

Anja is a pretty woman with shining, chestnut hair and a shy smile. She tells me she is a social worker with children in Holland, and she is here with her husband Jan. Before I sit down with her for our first interview, I thank the group, and ask if I might touch back in with them during the week. They all agree. I already feel connected with them—that magic which seems to happen when we make ourselves vulnerable and share ourselves, when we come together in a graceful and loving way.

I only have a short time with Anja this evening, so our 'getting to know each other session' is brief. I feel amazed that this woman is going to allow me to share her experience here. She seems to have a quiet, grounded strength and yet be open to whatever spirit has to offer her.

I ask her how she first heard about Findhorn.

"I have this book at home, it's in Dutch of course, I don't know what it is called in English, but there is a daily lesson I read every day. It's by Eileen Caddy."

"That must be *Opening Doors Within*," I tell her, feeling proud that once again it was one of our Findhorn Press books which has guided someone here.

"Yes, that must be it," she says. "I also have some other books about Findhorn, and I always wanted to visit. I wanted to meet Eileen Caddy, and wondered what the community was like."

"Where will you be working tomorrow?" I ask, wondering if it may be in the kitchen—my own favourite place.

Anja looks very happy about her choice when she tells me. "When our focalisers told us we would all be working part of the day, I felt very strongly that I wanted to be in the garden. I love being outside."

"Even now, in this freezing January weather?" I ask incredulously, shivering at the thought.

"Yes," she laughs. "Even now. I'll be working in Cullerne Gardens."

I ask her if she hopes to feel the nature spirits there.

Anja is thoughtful. "I think anyone can communicate with nature on some level, with plants, animals, and of course humans. It's a question of how sensitive I can be. I love being out in nature, that's important, important for the plants to feel that."

I realise I am getting to know a very special lady who will be willing to go deep during her stay here.

Time now for me to go home to my cosy bed in Sunflower, time for Anja and the group to get a good night's sleep before the next intense and exciting day.

Anja and I decide to meet in the Main Sanctuary at The Park for the morning meditation tomorrow and I offer to take her to Cullerne Gardens afterwards. She suggests lunch too, and I can tell that I'm going to enjoy getting to know her.

I call a taxi for my return trip to The Park, and soon I'm back in my B & B, tired from such a long and busy day. But tired in happy kind of way after so many wonderful experiences, all in one day.

BLESSINGS
AND SURPRISES

MICHAEL AND THE ANGELS

I wake up after a night of vivid dreams—no doubt my mind is trying to process all the many experiences of yesterday. Questions were running around my head all night. So many wonderful people here, so many things happening, so much to do, to see, and how will I be able to tell what is the real magic? Is just feeling good about being here magic? Is finding loving, open people magic? Surely there must be more to it than that! I tell myself that there is still plenty of time, so much more to do, so many more people to see, surely I will get there somehow.

A hot shower and breakfast bring me into the day. It still surprises me how little daylight there is here in January, though I'm pleased to see it's dry outside and that the sun is trying to emerge from behind the clouds.

I check my schedule and see that my first meeting is with Michael in the Medway Building, but first I have the meditation with Anja in the Sanctuary. It's still dark as I walk across the Runway. The first bus from Cluny has just arrived, bringing over Anja and other guests for their morning's work in Cullerne Gardens and other Park-side departments. I catch up with her on our way to the Sanctuary. The anteroom is very crowded this morning, and I have some trouble finding a hook for my coat.

I add my pair of blue suede boots to the shoe racks already filled with winter boots and trainers.

Anja and I, accompanied by Wayne, another member of the Experience Week group, find seats and join the dozens of meditators in the silence. I still have my eyes open, looking for old friends who might come into the Sanctuary. Margo is leading the meditation this morning, and when she sees that everyone is settled, she switches on the light outside the door to alert stragglers that it is too late to come in. The light also tells people walking past to do so in silence.

Margo taps a brass bowl with a small wooden hammer. A soft tone resonates around the room, the sound spreading out like ripples on a lake. She taps the bowl again and quietly speaks a few words to lead us into silence.

I have often felt that this time of communion with a group of spiritual seekers is one of the most intimate moments I can spend with my fellow men and women. I feel so utterly open and vulnerable, knowing that the person next to me, and everyone around the room, is engaged just as I am. We are all tuning in to a higher energy that will feel different for each one of us. At the same time, our group consciousness is creating a chalice to hold these energies, and later release them into the world.

I know that the period of meditation is around twenty minutes, but I enter into timelessness that is broken by the rippling echoes of two more light taps on the brass bowl. Margo then taps a third time, louder than the others, to bring us back to the present moment. One by one, people open their eyes, get up from their chairs, and silently leave the Sanctuary. Maintaining the silence, we find our boots and coats, and with renewed spirit move into our day.

Anja and Wayne are both working at Cullerne, so the three of us make our way along the road that leads to Findhorn Village, and in just a few minutes we arrive at the large iron gates that lead into Cullerne House and Gardens. Cullerne House has until very recently been accommodation for members, but is now the home of the Findhorn Flower Essences. Marion, a member from the 1970's who returned some years ago, has created the flower essences and, after several years in The Park, has now moved her business to Cullerne.

Walking up the long drive we can see the large fields and long rows of greenhouses that produce many of the organic vegetables we eat daily in the Community Centre. I point out the very large, steaming compost heap and smilingly recall the Seaweed Shovelling Song that Waterboys lead singer Mike Scott wrote when he was working in the gardens during one of his earlier times here. I'm looking forward to speaking to Mike later in the week.

Anja and Wayne are eager to join their group and get their hands into the soil. I'm grateful that my next task will allow me to remain in a warm office, so I leave them by the greenhouse and head back to The Park to meet Michael.

The Medway building houses numerous small offices. The accounts offices are at one end and various other departments at the other. Michael is waiting for me in his tiny office.

"Good morning, Karin. Let me just make sure we won't be disturbed." He closes the door and arranges his seat so that he can't see people in the other offices and be tempted to talk to them. I notice that his desk and chair are facing the window, and he tells me that's because his work is with the outside world, and he wants to face in that direction, rather than look inwards with his back to the window.

However, he is a man who also looks inwards. He asks for a moment now to go within and attune, to make himself present before beginning our interview.

He closes his eyes and sits quietly for some minutes. Around him there are telephones ringing, people talking, but Michael is finding the still point within himself from where he will answer my questions. Attunement, he tells me, is also a bridge that brings him from one activity to another.

Michael is a gentle man, softly spoken and deeply thoughtful. He opens his eyes. "OK, Karin, I'm here," he says, smiling.

"Michael, you know why I am here. I am trying to discover if there is any magic. Is there something unique at Findhorn? And, if so, what is it?"

His face lights up. "For me, this whole place is magic. There is magic in so many ways. You can see it in the guests after just a week, you can see the difference in them. They have spent a week in the kitchen or the gardens, it's so visible, so open. There is a never ending fundamental magic here."

OK, I think to myself, but what is it?

Michael continues, "Part of my work is accompanying journalists around here—hard-headed people who have never seen a place like this, who maybe come with some prejudices about what we do, or expect that we might appear flighty and airy fairy. But even they seem to end up by saying that there is a special atmosphere here."

"What is it that makes it special, Michael?" I really want to know.

"Perhaps it is because we put God first, and that intense focus brings the Divine closer. We have a close connection with the invisible realms. The community originally began with co-operation and communion with these realms. For me, that's still a magical place to tune into, these invisible realms that are so very real to us—to me."

Michael closes his eyes again for a moment.

"For many people, the word 'Findhorn' is synonymous with the beauty and wonder of these realms, especially the Angelic realm. It invokes an 'Ah Ha.' It's not that Angels and Nature Spirits are just for kids, they're a reality, and they are powerful beings. It makes very good sense to invite them into our lives. Look at what has happened around here, this place was a derelict rubbish dump, now it supports all kinds of bushes, trees and vegetation, because we work with the Nature Spirits."

"Is this how guests and new people in the community experience the magic?" I wonder.

"The real magic is love. Findhorn is permeated—it is shot through with love. That's what people feel when they come here. You can see it in the gardens, in the care of these old caravans and houses; the work is approached with this love. It's not difficult or esoteric, it's just having a good, loving approach."

I have heard similar words from many others. I wonder what brought Michael here in the first place, so I ask him to tell me the story of 'his journey to Findhorn'.

"I first came here in 1990. I was a workaholic public relations officer, raised as an orthodox Catholic, and regularly went to Mass. The spiritual life was important to me, but I did not feel my needs were being met. So I would go to Taizé in France to drink from that spiritual well, which gave me the nourishment I needed. Then I heard about Findhorn, and while I was on holiday in Wales I called and asked to participate in the Experience Week the following week. To my surprise they told me they were full. I was uncharacteristically angry about this, and called again the next day. They told me there had just been a cancellation and I could come."

He smiles, remembering his first experience of Findhorn "magic."

"To tell the truth, when I arrived here I didn't know the difference between Sai Baba and Ali Baba and I was very shy about sharing anything about myself. I knew nothing about Peter and Eileen Caddy or giant vegetables, it was all completely new to me. I found the whole experience very challenging, especially talking about myself."

I'm relieved that he seems to have got over that and is now willing to tell me his story.

"What was particularly important to me was that I found a planetary perspective here. I was a member of Greenpeace at that time and very keen on restoring the earth. That I could relate to, but things like the Cosmic Christ were totally foreign and strange to me. I kept wanting to know, why Jesus wasn't mentioned?"

Michael laughs in his shy and quiet way. He has changed a lot since those early days here. "I knew I wanted to come back sooner rather than later. Then I came for a Carolyn Myss workshop, which was amazing, and after that I was certain I wanted to come for a longer time. But life first had some challenges ahead for me."

Although I have known Michael for a number of years, I know very little about his life and am surprised by the next part of his story.

"I discovered I had testicular cancer and had to have my left testicle removed. Chemotherapy followed, because there was secondary spreading above my left kidney. Throughout that challenging time I wanted to come back here. When I was having the chemo, I would imagine myself walking along the beach here, and that helped. Later, when the chemo was finished, I was encouraged to go to a convalescent home, but Findhorn was where I really wanted to be."

"So you came here then?" I ask, amazed at his courage and persistence.

"Yes, one cold November day in 1990 I literally staggered into Cluny Hill College, still completely bald. It was really rather funny. There was a group gathering in the front hall preparing to go to India, and I was directed to them."

"I take it you did not next find yourself in India?" I laugh, admiring him for being able to see the humour in such a difficult situation.

"No, I did a few departmental guest weeks, that's a week that many guests take after the very intense Experience Week— it's a time for some integration and reflection. I think I hold the record for doing the most DG weeks ever! I participated in seven, because I was not strong enough to do anything else. When I was eventually well enough to join a long-term programme, I worked in the garden and there I discovered first-hand the healing power of nature."

"And then you decided to stay here?"

"No, not yet. After a while I went back to my job in public relations, but found it very difficult, That's when I had my dark night of the soul. I felt totally bereft. Then a miracle happened; my employer gave me early retirement, at my young age of 40. So I could start a new life."

"So your employer and the universe got together to help you come here?"

"Yes, this time I came here and stayed!"

I am deeply touched by his wonderful story. "And now you have this wonderful job—I know how much love and care you put into everything you do."

"Thank you" he replies, and pauses. "Yes, I can connect with people all around the world who are friends and supporters of the community, through the Network News magazine and through correspondence with the Friends and Stewards network, keeping people in touch with what is happening here."

"But that's not all you do, is it Michael?" I ask him "Didn't you focalise a wonderful conference on Angels a couple of years ago?"

"Yes!" he replies, recalling the excitement of that time. "That was the conference I ran with William Bloom. It was immediately clear that this subject struck a chord in so many people. It sold out six months before it took place. There was a waiting list for the waiting list! It showed me that there is a hunger for the spiritual, for the divine, and a hunger to learn how to connect with these realms."

"Yes," I say. "That's the vision a lot of people 'out there' have of Findhorn. As somewhere where people connect with Angels and unseen realms. Do you think that some parts of the community are now resistant to admitting this? Some people seem to think that we are moving on to 'more important' things, trying to get corporate sponsorship and grants from business, so that talking and listening to Angels is not appropriate any more."

"Yes, I think you are right, some people only pay lip service to the notion of angelic realms, and generally the idea of connecting with these realms has, Avalon-like, disappeared. However there has been a renaissance of interest over the past couple of years." He pauses, and continues, "There is an embarrassment in some areas of the community, and a reluctance to talk about things like that. However, we need to remember that we have spent forty years working with these realms and with God, to inspire people with this work in a very grounded way, and this is as relevant now as it ever was. Our Angelic heritage is very important."

I can see someone outside the door, anxious to talk to Michael. They open the door and give him a letter. Then the telephone rings. Michael answers it briefly and then gets back to me.

"What do you think are the major challenges in living here?" I ask him. He doesn't have to think long.

"First of all there are the pressures of living in a transformative energy field. And financially we're not doing well. I feel we have a very rich lifestyle, but money, or the lack of it, is often talked about here. Sustainability is a problem, and this pressure cooker atmosphere. We are all training to be leaders here and are all taught to express ourselves and be ourselves, and that can lead to long, endless meetings. It's all a necessary part of the mix. And just having all my meals every day with hundreds of other people is one of my biggest challenges. However rewarding it all is, living with so many different people, constantly meeting new people, is not always easy. I sometimes feel I am living in a multicultural United Nations, not in the north of Scotland!"

Then he beams at me, and I know that all the challenges, all the problems, are something he accepts gladly. He adds, "Really, I think I have won the spiritual lottery, living here. When I think of how much people benefit from spending just one week here, and here I am, privileged to live here for years."

That's just how I used to feel when I lived here, and still feel every time I visit.

I begin to collect my things and get ready to leave, but before I go Michael brings out a bowl of blessing cards and offers them to me. These cards, like the Angel Cards, are from the Game of Transformation and each one bears the name of a blessing. I pick three cards. I feel I need some blessings on my way today and find I have picked 'Openness', 'Well-Being' and 'Exuberance'. I'm not going to argue with those.

"Thank you, Michael, and thank you for your blessings." I check my schedule, so many meetings still. Huh oh, where have I heard that one before?

COFFEE AND BICKIES WITH KATHERINE

As I leave the Medway building, I am met by a blast of cold wind. I need a hot drink to warm me up. Luckily I have great hopes for that with the lady I am about to visit. I walk up the Runway to the last bungalow on the right and knock on the door. As I walk in, I am grateful to see that Katherine has already put the kettle on. I also notice that she's opened her biscuit tin and arranged some very scrumptious chocolate 'bickies' on a pretty china plate. We wander into the living room with our goodies and make ourselves comfortable for our chat.

"I hear you recently celebrated your 80th birthday, Katherine," I begin. "Many Happy Returns! Did your family come to celebrate with you?"

"Yes, they were all here. Of course Mary, my daughter, lives right next door to me now. And my family from South Africa also managed to come over, it was wonderful having them all here."

Katherine does not look anywhere near her eighty years. There must be something in the air here that keeps everyone looking and feeling young.

I ask about her first time at Findhorn.

"In 1972, I came to visit Barbara D'Arcy Thompson. Shortly afterwards, my daughter Mary came and decided to stay. I visited several times over the next few years, but continued to live in South Africa and organised Findhorn tours and workshops over there."

Katherine offers me another chocolate biscuit, which, of course, I can't refuse.

"And then one day my work over there was finished, and I came over here to live. Findhorn has been the centre of my life for thirty years now."

"I suppose you have decided to stay here permanently?" I wonder.

She fills up my coffee cup. The chocolate and the coffee taste wonderful together.

"As far as I know. There is a time to come and a time to leave. You have to listen to know when that is," she tells me thoughtfully.

"What do you think, Katherine? Is the magic still here?"

"Oh yes, particularly in the Experience Week. People seem to have this opening, something that changes them," she replies.

"What allows that opening to happen?"

"I think it is in the loving, accepting atmosphere. Of course it could be more so! It gives people the ability to let go and trust. They can just be who they are, they don't have to try to be anything else. And there are no rules here, we don't have to believe anything, yet we each in our own way acknowledge that there is something higher present."

I love the simplicity and straightforwardness of her answers.

"What about challenges, Katherine? Surely there are problems and challenges in living here. I know they exist?"

Again, her answer is simple and to the point. "Yes, we could always do things better. And unfortunately we do sometimes criticise and complain."

"And, what about growing older here?"

She smiles her gracious and genuine smile. "It is very graceful getting older here, and it's made so easy. As I have grown older I have gradually reduced my activities, and there is total support to grow old in my own way.

But I'm glad the younger people still appreciate our wisdom, and what experience has taught us. It's good to know I can still contribute something."

Katherine does not have to do anything to contribute; she just has to be her delightful, humorous and gentle self.

I see that it is nearly time for lunch. Not that I am hungry after all those bickies. However, I am meeting Anja and will soon find out about her experience in the gardens this morning.

LUNCH WITH ANJA

The dining room is already full when I arrive. All I need is a good bowl of hot soup and today I have a choice between Cream of Spinach and a Winter Vegetable soup. I choose the Spinach and pick up a crusty slice of whole-wheat bread. Anja, Wayne and several other members of their group are already sitting at one of the larger tables and I carefully manoeuvre my way through the crowded dining room to join them.

Both Anja and Wayne are glowing and hungry after their work outside.

"How was your first morning ?" I ask Anja. "Was it very cold?"

"No, it was wonderful," she replies, "I enjoyed it so much. We were preparing the soil, and helping with the compost heap."

"It has been such a lovely morning," she tells me. "First on the bus coming over here, then meditating in the Sanctuary, and of course working with the land at Cullerne. I just love doing that."

While I admire the sentiment, I can't say I would want to join her on such a chilly day.

Anja looks around the dining room at the many groups of people talking animatedly and listens to the laughter.

"You know, Karin, I really love watching the people here, and how they are with each other. I see and hear people from all over the world, all so very different, and yet all being so caring and loving together."

Others around the table nod in agreement.

"How are things in your group now?" I ask.

"Even since Saturday, when we all arrived, I feel it is already different. We seem to be more open with each other. I can see it by the expressions in everyone's face."

I look around the table—at Michael and Cynthia from the USA, Andrew from Sheffield in England, and of course Anja from the

Netherlands and Wayne, who hails from Minnesota. Everyone nods in agreement over their bowls of soup.

"Bus to Cluny! Bus to Cluny!"

Barnaby's familiar cheery voice interrupts our conversation, and all too soon my new friends have to leave.

"The whole group is coming over to The Park on Wednesday for a group project. Come and join us then," Anja calls out as they hurry to catch the bus.

"I'm looking forward to it," I call after them.

People are slowly beginning to depart from the Community Centre, leaving just the KP crew to wash the dishes, wipe the tables and vacuum the floor. There is music coming out of the kitchen, and people are singing together as they make sure that everything is sparkling clean for the afternoon crew who will cook dinner. Maybe learning to enjoy the sweeping and mopping and dishwashing is also part of the magic of this place. . .

As Anja and her Experience Week friends start boarding the bus, I spot Dürten walking into the dining area, obviously looking for me. She's the next person on my list of people to interview, and we make our way up the stairs into the lounge above the dining room. There are several other people already there, talking quietly and drinking coffee or tea, and we find a corner with two comfortable armchairs.

NO TEABREAK FOR DÜRTEN

Dürten arrived in Findhorn from Germany in 1992. As soon as she arrived it was obvious she was going to do things her way and not necessarily follow the rules. Most people who join the Foundation first go through the guest programme and later student membership, but Dürten preferred to follow her own star.

From the beginning, she was always in a position of responsibility. She is the kind of person I would totally rely on to complete any task. She is also an extremely compassionate and loving woman and has been involved in the Holistic Health Department for many years.

I'm glad that she can take a little time out of her busy day to talk to me, so I don't waste any time asking why she came here—though I think I know the answer—that she came here to serve.

"What are you doing these days?" I begin.

"I am working with the 'Living in Community' programme," she tells me. "It's designed for our long-term guests—people who stay for a few weeks or even longer."

"Are you enjoying it? " I ask her

"Yes, very much. A while ago, somebody new joined me in the department and had a very different way of working. I even considered leaving my job. Then I realised how much it meant to me, how many wonderful people I have got to know, so I decided to stay, and resolved the problem with the other person. I decided to do what Eileen has always told me she does. I held her in my thoughts and said to myself 'I love you, I bless you, I see the divinity in you.' After a while I found I could really do that."

Dürten continues to talk about her work.

"It's such a joy to be with people when they are at that moment of openness and change. These people really want to come and help, to make a difference. They want to be used. They don't just like arriving at 9:00 a.m., having a long tea break, then a long lunch break. I think we need to look at how we use our time more efficiently."

Ah, yes, I realise I am definitely speaking with an efficient and hard-working German lady.

We pause for a moment to sip our coffee and I look around me at this lovely room. This Community Centre extension was built a number of years ago. It is a round building with a copper roof. Below is an additional, circular dining area, and up here is a cosy lounge with a large, open fireplace. There is a balcony around the entire upper portion and the view is spectacular—across the Findhorn Bay to the snow covered mountains beyond the Black Isle. A multicoloured, stained glass picture hangs from the ceiling.

I bring my attention back to Dürten. "What happens to people when they come here?" I ask.

"So many people come here thinking it is just for one week, and then find it very hard to leave. Often, they want to come back as soon as possible. They almost immediately contact their potential for change. It touches something so deep that all their priorities change—whatever gave them security at home is now no longer important," she replies.

"How does that happen? What allows people to change like that?"

"For me, it is the people here: the openness, the goodwill, the openness to God. They are able to step out of their heads and into a different reality. They then seem able to find a different way, to learn what is truth for them."

"You say it is the people here, Dürten. How are they different?"

"I think it's the way we interact, the honesty, directness and integrity. The willingness to do our best. When people come here they seem to find their place very quickly, and within a few weeks are willing and able to step into a position of responsibility."

"Do many people return, or stay when they come here?" I want to know.

"Yes, it is very touching and moving to see people reconsider their whole lives. Some seem to know immediately, others go home and then come back. It's a huge privilege to work with them, to listen to their stories, to see each one open and change."

"What is the work of the Foundation?" I ask her, liking her direct and efficient answers.

"It is translating values into action, the values this place is built on. To find ways of loving where I am, loving what I am doing and loving whom I am with. When I use this as a mantra, that's all I need. The more I can do that, the more peace I find in my heart, and the more effectively I can work. I want to commit myself to living that fully.

"I hate 'process', but I know there are ways of dealing with challenges. It has a lot to do with appreciation and keeping my heart open. I use Eileen as an example, to bring her messages and guidance into my daily life. When I was first here I was touched by her guidance, but later I would just smile about it all and often forget it. But now I have come back to realising how deeply true it is and—despite its simplicity—how incredibly challenging it is."

Dürten needs to get back to her work, and we walk downstairs together.

"Karin, it is about translating values into our daily action, that's really what it's all about."

THE PARK BUILDING

As Dürten walks quickly down the street, I wonder what I should do next. I have no more appointments this afternoon, so I could choose to return to Sunflower and relax. Or perhaps there is something I could be doing to further my quest. An idea, or perhaps it's an intuition, pops into my head to visit the library in the Park Building. Plus, there are several other interesting things I could do there.

Pauline Tawse donated the grey stone house we call the Park Building, and the grounds around it, to the community in 1971. That was way before I arrived on the scene, and I never actually met Pauline in person. However, I did get to know her quite well many years later, in the early '90's, when one day she telephoned Findhorn Press to order some books. I recognised her name and we struck up a conversation about her early days in the community. By then she must have been quite elderly and not in good health, but over the next few months she often called me to ask what was happening in the community, particularly enquiring about certain trees and shrubs in and around the Park and Cluny Hill. She had not been close to the community for many years, but I do know that through our long chats on the telephone, her interest was rekindled. Not long after this, I heard that she had died. I'm glad I had the opportunity to know her a little.

I walk through the front door of The Park into cosy warmth, and a familiar smell of old books, candles, herb tea and incense. Here in this building are housed a library, the conference office, a meeting room and a sanctuary. Upstairs there are several bedrooms now used by guests, but many years ago Peter and Eileen lived up there for a short time, and I remember several very traditional English tea parties hosted by Eileen, replete with cucumber sandwiches, hot-buttered crumpets, and warm currant scones straight from the oven.

I open the door to the conference office and peek inside. I am looking for my friend, India. One of the little quirks about living at Findhorn is that people here like to change their names—which can get very confusing at times. India used to be called Maggie and she and I have sons of the same age, both born here, both now twenty-six and living their lives on different continents. It's often a challenge to actually find India; she is always intensely into something and moves from here to there at an extremely rapid pace. I've been trying to find her since I arrived and I pop my head around the door. She's not there, but I do find Clive who tells me that India is over at Cluny Hill College.

However, since I happen to be here in the conference office, I decide to have a look around, see what's happening and ask Clive what conferences are coming up. As far back as I can remember, Findhorn has hosted two international conferences every year—one around Easter time and another in the Autumn. Participants come from all over the world, and the speakers and presenters are usually some of the wisest and most interesting experts in their fields. A few years ago, so many people wanted to come to the conference on Angels that there were people on the waiting list for the waiting list. There must be something about Angels: we are born knowing them, and then spend our lives looking for them.

I recall another conference, many years before, that was called "Earth Sings." Musicians and performers of every description came to share their talents. I remember listening to Paul Winter and his wonderful recordings of whale sounds. And I recall the annual World Wilderness Congress being held here: that year, we had to erect huge marquees to house and feed the hundreds of participants.

I look at the brochure of events and conferences in 2002. The topics look as vital and interesting as ever. The Easter Conference is called "Restore the Earth," and in May an event is planned on "Conflict and Transformation." In midsummer there will be a Festival of Sacred Dance, Music and Song (wish I could be there), and then I see our old friend Caroline Myss is returning for a presentation in August. The Autumn conference promises to be on "The Spirit of Trees." I'm intrigued that both major conferences this year are about our relationship with nature.

Leaving the conference office, I walk over to the Lecture Room, which is a bright, spacious room where smaller workshops are held. Since I arrived I have been hearing about a fascinating group of women from around the world who have gathered here for the Winter School of Eco-Feminism. I have already met one of them, Mair, at the Taizé singing earlier in the week, and as I approach the door, Mair spots me. She waves at me to come and join her and the other women during their break.

She introduces me to Adriana who comes from the Netherlands, and to Jane who is from England and now lives in Findhorn village; then to Sam from Australia and Prema from India. Prema tells me that she is setting up eco-friendly projects for poor women in India to help them earn an independent living. I also meet Dido from New Zealand and Marilza from Brazil, who has decided to build a house in the Field of Dreams.

I can sense the strength and wisdom in this group, and they are eager to tell me a few of the wonderful experiences they are all having together. With many superlatives, they speak of the joy and love they have created in their circle, and how they are bringing together the spiritual and political aspects of their lives and work. However, their workshop session is about to begin again, and I leave them, feeling privileged to have spent a moment or two in their company.

There are three sanctuaries in this portion of the community that we call the Park—the Main Sanctuary, the Nature Sanctuary in Pineridge, and the one right here in The Park Building, which is known as the Universal Sanctuary. I notice a row of coats and a neat pile of boots, and realise that a group must be meditating there now. So perhaps I'll go next door to the library first.

The library is a wonderful resource for both guests and members, with books on virtually anything one might want to know about the spiritual life, nature and ecology. Many of the books look old and well handled, and some have leather covers and gold titles. The shelves are labelled Spiritual Growth, Psychic Studies, Health and Wholeness, Philosophy, Meditation and Management. Management? Why is there a book on management here, I wonder. I step backwards in surprise, and a small, hardback book falls from a shelf behind me. Ah ha! I think to myself, this must surely be

guidance! Perhaps this will tell me where next to go to find the answer to my quest.

I remember that when I was much younger and life was often full of confusing choices, I would go to the Bible, let it fall open at a random page and read the top left hand verse, hoping it might give me some guidance. Sometimes this would work—more often it just caused more confusion. It seemed to work once when I asked whether to go and visit some friends in the USA. It fell open at Mark 13:18, where my eyes fell on, "And pray ye that your flight be not in the winter." Another time, when I 'asked' whether I should take a certain job or not, the answer came from Proverbs 7:17. "I have perfumed my bed with myrrh, aloes and cinnamon." I could never figure that one out!

Later, when I came to Findhorn, I would do the same with Eileen's book of guidance *The Living Word*. This seemed to work for me far more often, like the time I felt so unloved in a difficult relationship and 'received' the answer, "My love is infinite, My love never fails, I will never fail you or forsake you." And on my 50th birthday, when I asked for some guidance about growing older, I opened the book to "Raise your consciousness and realise that you are ageless, you are as young as time and as old as eternity."

So now it is with anticipation and excitement that I pick up the book that has fallen from the shelf. I smile broadly when I read the title and know immediately what it means. I don't even need to actually open it. The book is Neale Donald Walsh's *Conversations with God*.

I hear a low rumble of voices and a clatter of shoes outside the Universal Sanctuary across the hall, and without hesitation I follow my 'instant' guidance and enter the Sanctuary.

CONVERSATION WITH GOD

The Universal Sanctuary is the smallest of the three sanctuaries here at the Park, with just six chairs in soft green velvet that seems to glow with colour. The walls are painted a delicate pale lilac. I light the candle and sit down, crossing my legs. Glad I can still just manage to do that, even at my age!

I wonder what to do? Should I just be silent, and meditate, and listen? But that's not what the book cover says—it says, "Conversations with God." Surely that means I have to talk as well as listen? But who starts this conversation? Me or God? I can't just begin with the usual question I've been asking everyone. Or can I? Nothing ventured, nothing gained! I plunge into the unknown.

"So, what brought You to Findhorn in the first place, and how long have You been here?" I ask undaunted.

"Love. Eternity." was the instant reply.

Not a propitious start, this may be a very short conversation. However, I did get a response, so I try putting it another way, to see what happens.

"I know You must always have been here. As far as I know You are always everywhere. But what brought your presence here so strongly, to this particular place at this time?"

"I didn't. It was the people who came here, who brought their love for Me, their willingness to listen, their willingness to act, and their obedience. They listened and acted with love. I find that irresistible, so of course I came with them."

"And what has kept You here all this time?" I press God a little further.

"I will be here as long as I am needed. Or wanted. I came here to serve. I love the people, they are all so different, very amusing and interesting, and often very good company."

"So You enjoy being here?" I ask, very alert by this time.

"Yes, a lot of the time I do. Luckily, I am not affected by the weather, or living in a small, cramped caravan. I mainly concentrate on all that is beautiful here, the trees and flowers, the mountains and the sea, the stars at night. But it can get lonely at times."

"You? Lonely?"

This really is the strangest conversation.

"Oh yes, when people forget I am here, when they are so busy that they forget that their relationship with Me has to be nurtured just as much as any other relationship they have."

"I have never thought of it quite like that," I reply. "I always thought You were just there, waiting for us to call You."

"That's true, but there are often long periods of loneliness for Me. It can get quite boring having nothing to do, when you are all trying to do things on your own and forget I'm only waiting to be asked to join you."

"What about the meetings, all those meetings I have heard about, surely You don't go to all of them?"

"Yes, I do. I hang around at all the meetings, waiting to be included, waiting to be asked for my advice. Sometimes they do, sometimes they don't, that's just the way it is."

"Couldn't You just jump in and make yourself heard?"

"That's hard to do when people are talking, arguing and not even listening to each other, never mind Me. All they need to do is just what you're doing right now, be still and listen. It's so simple."

"I'd like to ask You a question that I have been asking a number of people. How do I know where 'guidance' is coming from? How do I know who is answering my questions now? Am I just talking to myself, or is there really someone listening and answering me?"

"That seems like several questions to Me. Which one shall I answer first?"

I think about that for a minute, and move my left leg, which is beginning to get cramps, before continuing.

"Am I just talking to myself, and giving myself some interesting and amusing answers?"

"Yes, you are. Think about it. If there is a part of Me in each one of you, and if that is the part you are communicating with, and if you believe that you and I are really one, then yes, in a way you are speaking to yourself."

I need to think about this some more later.

"So guidance always comes from that part of me that is You?"

"Not necessarily, although of course in the end it is all Me. But sometimes you let your desires and wishes for instant gratification speak to you. Not really a good idea. A little patience can be a good thing."

"How do I know the difference?" I really want to know—and this is my golden opportunity.

The answer again is short and to the point.

"Practice!"

I'm aware that my mind is beginning to question what I'm hearing.

"God? Er . . . ."

"Yes, go on."

I can't help thinking that He/She/It knows what's coming next. I even start to fret about whether or not I should actually put all this in the book.

"I have read Eileen's guidance, as well as many other books of 'messages' from God, Spirit, Higher Self, whatever. But this conversation seems very different, it feels so ordinary, not like guidance at all."

"I speak to everyone in such a way that they can actually hear Me. With you, I use a little humour, I know that gets your attention. And I've learned never to try and tell you what to do, you don't seem to like that at all! So here we are having this little chat. I know you like that, and later you will think about it."

Whoever it is I am talking to seems to know me very well. I realise that I am now sitting bolt upright in my chair; perhaps it was the surprise that has made me do that. I relax again and then remember what it is I really want to know. I take a leap of faith and ask my $64,000 question.

"Is there a 'Magic of Findhorn'?" I ask, getting straight to the point.

"Yes."

Looks like we are back to the short and sweet answers.

"Will You tell me what it is?" I try again.

"You don't really need or want Me to tell you that, do you? You are having so much fun doing it yourself. And if I were to tell you, you'd like it about as much as you like being told what to do."

That's true.

"But a little bit of help would be nice. I am hearing so many different things." I'm still hoping for some help here.

"Aren't you enjoying meeting and talking to all these people? And remembering stories and experiences from the past? You're even enjoying the food in the CC, aren't you?"

If I could believe what I am feeling, I would say we are smiling at each other.

"But what if I don't find the answer?" I ask. "I'm committed to writing this book, and I really want to be able to share the essence of the magic with the people around the world who want to hear it."

"I'll tell you something. You continue what you are doing. You're doing just fine as far as I can see. Then you go home and write your book. If, when you have finished, you really still need Me, then we'll have another little chat. How does that sound?"

"I think that sounds great. I have a feeling You are with me on this project anyway, and perhaps You might give me the odd little nudge in the right direction. So okay, I'll get back to You when I've done everything I can do, and see if You agree with me then."

"Anything else you need now?"

I think for a minute and look out of the window at the darkening clouds.

"Yes, I wouldn't mind a little snow before I leave."

"I'll see what I can do."

I continue sitting in my chair for a while, not really thinking, just letting everything wash through me. Then I blow out the candle and leave the Sanctuary. Back outside, I look up at the clouds, hoping for instant gratification. Doesn't look much like snow. Perhaps I need to learn some patience.

I suddenly realise I have forgotten something. I return to the library and replace *Conversations with God* on the shelf. Who knows? It may fall down for someone else one day.

As I leave, I whisper, "Thank You, I enjoyed our little chat."

"You're welcome," says God, and adds, "Come back any time. In fact, I recommend it."

I don't think I can add anything more significant to my day. Time to go back to Sunflower and do some thinking.

ORGANISATION OR ORGANISM?

THE NEW AGE CAVALIER

I slept well last night. It seems that chatting with my good friend in Sanctuary yesterday had a calming effect on me. It slowed me down and gave me time to just 'be'. I feel tempted to continue doing more of the same, but then remember all the interesting people I still want to talk to, and all the fun things I want to do while I am here. So I check my schedule and see that my first appointment is with Alex in his office in Pineridge. A few minutes later I am knocking on his door.

∞∞∞∞

When Alex first arrived in the community in 1982, he was a fresh-faced young man of twenty-three. Perhaps the fresh-faced bit is not quite correct—his face was in reality almost totally covered by a black, curly beard and moustache. His dark, wavy hair hung down to his shoulders, and he looked like a new age Cavalier! He was, and still is, one of the few 'real' Scots in the community, although over the years I have noticed that his original strong Scottish accent has been mildly diluted by many years of living in an international community.

I remember Alex as one of the youngest members of that time, an intelligent, hard-working man who laughed easily. He was also a very welcome addition for the young women in the community; there always seemed to be more women than men around. This handsome, young Scot brought a breath of fresh air into a vaguely middle-aged community.

Now, twenty years later, Alex is one of the stalwarts of the community. Twelve years ago he married Pauline, and they have an eleven-year-old son Craig, as well as Barney, now twenty-two, Pauline's very handsome son from a previous relationship. Alex worked for many years in the Accounts and Finance offices of the Foundation, which later led him to become the Managing Director of New Findhorn Directions Ltd (NFD). Nowadays, Alex is an independent, self-employed management consultant working both for the Foundation and the wider community. He lives with his family in Findhorn Village, a mile down the road from the Findhorn Community at the Park.

I knew that Alex was one of the people I had to talk to. I have always found him very articulate and willing to speak his mind. He has a very wide experience and knowledge of the community, is grounded and not inclined to be 'wishy-washy' in his opinions. I was also curious to see how he would react to my questions, and to find out whether the magic had got to him too, and in what way. After all, I wonder, what makes an intelligent businessman want to spend his life in the dreary weather of the North of Scotland?

The building I am about to enter is what used to be the Family House. Alex has worked here for as long as I can remember. As I walk into his little office I also remember a time many years ago when I actually worked with him for a while, and he did his best—with little success—to teach me how to reconcile bank statements. Many years later my husband is still trying to do the same thing—I think I have almost got it!

Alex welcomes me into his office. I notice a few more grey hairs, an odd wrinkle or two. The dashing young Scottish hero is now a mature family man, a solid citizen of our community. I'm very grateful that he has taken some time off from his very busy schedule so I get down to the business in hand immediately.

"What made you come here in the first place, Alex, how were you drawn here?"

Alex grins.

"Curiosity mainly. Funnily enough, I had heard about the community through reading the original *Magic of Findhorn*. I was interested in many things, like community lifestyle, and perhaps psychic experiences rather than spiritual ones. I really had no conscious spirituality at all at that time. So, living just a few hours away, I decided to come up and visit."

I glance at his greying hair and say. "I believe you were the youngest member here at one time?"

"Yes, perhaps. I was twenty-three then. I was one of the few very young people at the time."

"Did you find the 'Magic' described in the book?" I ask.

The phone rings and Alex switches on the answering machine.

"I decided it was a good place. I liked it, found myself interested and fascinated. But I also asked myself why this group of likeable, interesting people chose to invent this absurd spirituality as an excuse to live together. It just didn't make sense to me then."

I smile, remembering how young he was then.

"So what happened then?" I ask.

"Oh, I came back for a few casual visits, but it took me a couple of years to realise that this spirituality was the glue that made everything here work, and that if I wanted to have anything more to do with it, I needed some of it in my life too. But it was a long process, it took a long time to get involved in the spiritual side."

'Well, you're still here after twenty years. Were you hooked?" I wonder how he will answer.

"'Yes,' is the short answer, but I did not really feel that way for quite a time. I found the first year very challenging and thought seriously about leaving. I decided to stick it out and to stay for probably a couple of years, to learn something interesting and then move on. But somehow I never did! I suppose I never found anything even remotely as interesting to move on to."

I can totally understand what he means. I have moved on, and found a lot of interesting and wonderful places, certainly much better weather. However, there is something here—and what that certain something is, that's what I'm here to find out.

"How have things changed Alex, is the 'certain something' different now?"

" It is inevitably different, just as when I first came here it was different from the early '70's or '60's. It's different but I think it's still here. I think it is very difficult for people who live here to experience it in the same way that someone visiting for the first time or, like you, coming back after a long time, because there are humdrum aspects to life here just as there are everywhere, the routine, the ordinary. Here, the humdrum is happening in the midst of the extraordinary, and life would be difficult and very different if we lost sight of that."

Of course I can remember what it was like, living here for so many years.

"So the magic, the Factor X, it just becomes part of your life here after a while, just routine?" I ask.

"I wouldn't say it becomes routine, but when you are first here it's all new, there is so much to discover, and after a period of time that's less true. I find, somewhat to my chagrin, that I get called on quite a lot to be a kind of walking filing cabinet of historic events, because I have a long history of Foundation management matters. That feels odd because I still feel that things are new. Within a year or two of my arriving here there was this very exciting new project—the ecological village—that we were embarking on."

Alex looks out of his office window, over to the Field of Dreams where we can see all the new houses, and more being built.

"Eighteen years later it still feels as though it is just beginning. I constantly need to discipline myself to look to the future rather than dwell on the past, although of course it's also nice to reminisce."

I still find myself gazing at all the new houses; I'm even staying in one of them. So much has happened over the past few years.

"So you think the village is still only at the beginning?"

I can see that Alex is very excited about this project.

"Absolutely. There are now ten dwellings complete out of the forty planned on the field. Then there are another ten or fifteen buildings already in Pineridge, out of the thirty or forty being built there."

I lived in Pineridge for many years, in a small trailer set among many others. I know that Alex also lived there, and started his family there before any of the new buildings went up.

"Of course, there is also the central area. I know there will be a lot more buildings going up there over time. And then there is Dunelands, sixteen more acres, which will double the area available for development. There is still an enormous amount of work to be done."

"You were a member of the Foundation for many years, Alex, but now you are part of the greater community?"

This is always a hard question to ask, and to answer. Years ago, "the Findhorn community" and "The Findhorn Foundation" were one and the same. Now the community encompasses so many areas, and the Foundation or original community, where it all began, is just one aspect of the whole. I want to find out how important the Foundation is to the community, or at least I want to have Alex's opinion about this.

"Yes," he replies, "I am a community member, but I also do some work for the Foundation."

I remember that when I was still a member of the Foundation, some ten years ago, there was a lot of resistance to the growth of the wider community, with the Foundation still wanting to be in control of who came here and what was happening. So I ask Alex: "How do community people relate to the Foundation now?"

"Because there is a large turnover of people coming and going, perceptions of the institutions now change relatively quickly," he begins. "Five—certainly ten years ago—there was a lot of tension between the Foundation and the community, because the people living in the Foundation suddenly saw that people were coming to live around them and they questioned whether they were the appropriate ones. Now of course, when people join the Foundation, it is evident that they are surrounded by this much larger community, it's part of the landscape already and they don't question whether it's appropriate. They may want to tinker with the process, change this or that, but nobody would suggest that the relationship is wrong. It's just somehow part of the landscape. About a third of the Foundation workers change every two years. So it follows that a new generation very soon takes things for granted just as they are. So the answer is, yes, things are less difficult now than they were in those initial years. But of course, the whole thing is also much more complicated."

Now for the big question.

"But the magic, Alex, where does that come from now, is it still mainly in the Foundation?"

Now he laughs and replies, "That would be a very controversial statement!"

"That's why I am asking it!"

"A lot of community members would say that is nonsense. I don't think they would deny that it exists within the Foundation, but you want to know to what extent it exists beyond that. Like everything here in the community, it's difficult to generalise. There are plenty of people living within the community who have very little to do with the Foundation at all. Not that they have any resistance to it, but it just does not play a large part in their lives. They may shop in the Phoenix store at times, but that's the extent of it. However, if you were to ask them, were they inspired to be here, they would probably answer, yes, why else would they be here! Whether that has anything to do with magic, I don't know."

"What about the Steiner school, does that play a big part in the community?"

"Yes, very much so", Alex replies "Education for their children is another important reason why people come here. The Steiner school is a very significant part of community life, and it is possible to go to a Steiner event where you may get 100 to 150 people, very few of whom have any connection with the Foundation. Yet they are here because of the original impulse of the school, which of course came out of the Foundation."

"Would these parents consider themselves part of the community, or just parents who send their children to the Steiner school."

"I think the school seeks to be a legitimate part of the local environment, seeking to attract a wide cross-section of people into the school, but the fact is that most of the parents with children in the school would probably experience themselves as part of the community."

My own son Michael, now twenty-six, started his education in the Steiner school here, but quickly found he preferred to go to the local primary school in Kinloss where many of his friends went. I wonder how Alex's son is getting on at the Steiner school.

"Your son Craig, is he happy there?"

"Well, of course he grumbles about school, like any child would. We did think about moving away some time ago, and at that point he realised he did really want to stay in the Steiner school. He is a particular kind of child who has responded to the Steiner system very well."

I remember my son and Alex's older boy, Barney. Both found they were happier in the state system.

"Some children seem to blossom in the Steiner school, and others seem to be happier in the local state school."

"Yes, Barney started off in the Steiner school, and it did not suit him at all. He then went into the state system, which also had its challenges, but ultimately it was good for him. They are just different children. It's good to be able to choose the best system of education for each child."

I would agree with that, having brought up two children in the community. I have also seen dozens of other children born and raised here, and now living their young adulthood all over the world.

"I have noticed that children brought up here—born here—are special," I continue. " Of course, all children everywhere are special, but perhaps because children here have the special advantage of being loved and respected by so many people, that seems to do something for their spirit. I particularly remember all the children I have seen grow up here and who are now out in the world, they seem very successful in their lives, they love learning and want new experiences. Would you agree that there is something special and magical here in the way children grow up?"

I wonder if Alex's experience is similar to mine.

"There is clearly something unusual about their childhood, it's not run of the mill at all, and in my experience it's been very positive. How the youngsters themselves would describe it, I don't know. Though I believe that they also have noticed something about it; many are now living close by, in Edinburgh and Glasgow."

"This amazing experience of growing up in a loving and supportive community, do you think it is still working for the children and young people today?" I ask him.

"Well, I don't have a teenager at home myself, but I do pick up a sense that it's no longer as good as it was in the 'old days', with some teenagers running a bit wild. But perhaps that's just part of the teenage experience. In my younger son, Craig, I notice a similar pattern as happened with Barney; he is developing some very close relationships with his school friends."

It's nearly time for me to go, for I need to start making my way down to the Community Centre area. But I want to ask Alex one last question.

"So Alex, what, in your great wisdom have you learned here? What is the magic for you?"

He grins, trying to deny the "great wisdom."

"Something that is true for me is that whatever the magic is, it is a process of continual effort, not just the day-to-day work but also of spiritual learning, however you choose to define that. You don't find some cosy plateau where you can dispense your wisdom to the cheering crowds, you always find another challenge, a new edge to the world that you can explore.

"I started off as someone with no conscious interest in spiritual matters at all, and I am astonished at how far down the road I've gone, it's a long way from where I started and that continues to be exciting! This is also a very challenging and not infrequently extremely frustrating place. One needs to ask oneself, why is that so? For me the answer is that it is part of the curriculum. I am living and working in a very intense environment which, quite apart from any esoteric reasons, is very important in the day to day life. If you don't seek to engage positively in those challenges, it can get very difficult. There is always more to learn, something new. I have struggled with that frustration and sense of angst, but . . . there comes a point where you can see that it actually works out."

I have a final question.

"Has it all been worthwhile? Are you glad you came here?"

Alex doesn't have to think very long before answering.

"I think it has been worthwhile. It's extremely hard from this perspective to be able to say, with any sense of clarity, how else might it have been. I have spent practically the whole of my adult life here, and there are some aspects of that which I do regret, not least the weather!"

I can certainly agree with that.

"Yet, on the whole, yes. After all, there is nothing that's stopping me from leaving, and I'm still here!"

And, I am still here too, but realise I must soon be somewhere else. I am visiting Eileen next, so I thank Alex for his help and quickly make my way down to the central area where I will find Eileen's new house.

ThE LADY IN BLUE

I enter the small porch, carefully wipe my shoes on the doormat, and knock at the door. All this is very familiar to me. Whenever I come to Findhorn for a visit, I always pop in to see Eileen. As her publisher, I like to come and let her know how her books are selling, how many new foreign language editions are out, and about the grateful letters we receive from people all over the world who are inspired by her books. As a friend, I also like to see how she's doing. This time, I especially want to hear her thoughts and feelings about what is happening now.

A quiet, gentle voice calls, "Come in."

As always, Eileen is dressed beautifully. Today she is wearing an outfit of royal blue. Her make up is immaculate and her white hair looks freshly styled. I notice that she looks frailer than the last time I saw her, and walks more slowly, but the smile on her face is just as welcoming and bright as always. We sit in her living room on the same chairs as usual, overlooking her small patio now, in mid-January, bare of flowers.

I don't know how to describe Eileen, it seems that everything that can be said has already been written a hundred times. So all I can do is speak about my personal experience of her, how I have felt about her for more than a quarter of a century. From the day I first met her, I have not only totally trusted her but also trusted what the Findhorn Community was. I knew that if Findhorn was based on the words coming from this woman, it was a place that I wanted to live in and be associated with.

What has always amazed me about Eileen is her very ordinariness. This is what makes the very existence of Findhorn so very extraordinary. That God would have chosen this women to be a channel might once have surprised me, but as I have got to know Eileen over the years, I can't think of anyone better suited to be a messenger for Spirit. Eileen has had to learn to be strong, tenacious and outgoing. I know how difficult this has often been for her. Since, fifty years ago, she committed herself to obeying that still small voice within, unquestioningly and with total faith, God has tested her and pulled and pushed her every day.

I have just re-read her autobiography, *Flight Into Freedom*, as Findhorn Press is re-publishing it with a new, additonal chapter later this year. I still find myself utterly amazed that this charming, gracious, elderly woman—who could be anybody's mother and grandmother—has been through so much and at the age of nearly eighty-five is still willing to do more.

Eileen and I spend some time catching up on our news and she is thrilled to hear of the new French and Czech editions of one of her books. Her books of guidance, particularly *Opening Doors Within*, have been translated and published in over twenty-five languages. She is always so very grateful to know that people all over the world are reading the same guidance every day, just as she does.

"So, Karin," she asks me, "What is it that you want me to tell you, what do you need for your book?"

"I really don't know what I need from you, Eileen," I reply honestly. "I think that I can get most of the information I need about the community from all the other people I am talking to. And as far as your life and work is concerned, I pretty much know all about that, and anyway, it can be found in any number of books."

"That's true. Books and books, so many books," Eileen says, smiling at me.

"So perhaps we can just enjoy our little chat and talk about what's important in our lives right now. Tell me, do you still get up before dawn and go to Sanctuary to meditate every day, just as you did when you came here forty years ago?"

"Oh yes, I do," she answers immediately. "However, now I have to get up even earlier than I used to, in order to have a hot bath to warm up these old bones of mine. So I get up at around four o'clock because it takes me so long to get ready. Then I go to Sanctuary at six o'clock."

I know how cold it is at that time of the morning, and am in awe of anyone willing to do this every day. Eileen's face lights up as she continues telling me.

"But something wonderful has happened lately. Every morning, when I arrive in Sanctuary, I find a small Japanese lady who has risen even earlier than me. She has opened the curtains, aired the room, and lit the candle. She speaks very little English, so when I thank her she goes to her little book and finds a phrase she can use to reply to me. She is always dressed in white, always smiling, and it makes such a difference for me not to be alone at that time of the morning."

Eileen's gratitude shines from her eyes.

"I think her name is Junka. I invited her for tea the other day, and because she does not speak much English, she brought a small instrument with her—it was like a lyre—and when we could not communicate with words, she played and sang for me. I call her my little Angel."

This is so obviously something that has touched Eileen's heart.

"When she left, she spoke a little phrase which she must have practiced beforehand. In her sweet voice she said, "It was very lovely to have tea with you." And I said to her, "It was very lovely to hear you sing and play.""

Eileen, who is celebrated and loved all over the world, is utterly moved and touched by this woman who is willing to give her what she really needs, a friend and companion in her early morning meditation.

"And then, at 6.30 a.m., others often come and join me in my meditation. Today there were perhaps nine others who came. I can't tell you how much that means to me, not to be doing this alone any more. I have done this on my own for so many years."

Eileen leans back in her chair, and I can sense a tiredness in her body. Yet her spirit is still so strong, as is her commitment to serving God and this community. She will continue to give of herself for as long as is needed.

"In the morning," she speaks very softly, "I always ask for a blessing on the day. But these days I don't always manage to get to the evening Sanctuary, I am often too tired. Although I do like to always say a little 'thank you' for another day.

"You know, Karin, sometimes I am tempted to get stuck and not do anything anymore. After all, I am nearly 85. But then I shake myself and just get on with it. Some years ago I had to stop giving workshops, I just couldn't do it anymore. But holding the energy in Sanctuary, that's something I can continue to do. I feel as if I am an anchor here, an anchor holding the Christ energy."

"Do you ever go over to the Community Centre for your meals these days?" I wonder.

"No, I can't manage it very often, although when Dorothy Maclean is here she tries to persuade me to come over. I do go on special occasions like Christmas, just to let people see I am still alive! Otherwise people only see me in Sanctuary, or wandering about. I do want them to know I'm still here," she says with a smile.

Eileen, like any mother and grandmother, now brings out some photographs of her family and we look through them together. She is mother to eight children, a grandmother to twenty-one, and now has several great-grandchildren. She points to one picture.

"That's my eldest daughter, Jennifer. I did not hear from her for forty-four years after I had left them so long ago. And then one day I had a letter from her asking me if she could come here to celebrate her 60th birthday with me. You can imagine how thrilled I was. She really wanted to come and see me. This was another instance when I realised that God does everything in perfect timing. I don't need to worry, everything will always be very, very well."

"All is very, very well" is a phrase Eileen first received in guidance half a century ago—it is a saying we use a lot here—and it has proven true time and time again, even though the rational mind might not believe it.

"That's what I want people to see," she reminds me. "That I have been through so much, but it's all been worth it. Forgiveness is so important. That's the answer—love and forgiveness. I don't want to die and leave any muddy relationships behind, I want them all to be clear."

"So that you don't have to come back and do it all again?" I ask her.

"Yes," she laughs. "You know, I have also been lucky enough to completely heal my relationship with Peter. Peter and his little son Daniel used to come to Findhorn during the summer for a number of years, and they would stay somewhere in the community. One year, there was no accommodation so I offered to have them here in my house. So for eight weeks he lived upstairs with Daniel. I was able to resist any temptation to do his cooking or washing for him, I was able to break all those old patterns from when we were married. After all, he had already been married twice after he left me!

"We had a wonderful time. It was so good to just be together, to talk, to clear everything up between us."

Eileen is quiet for moment before she tells the rest of this story.

"I then rang him up that Christmas to wish him 'Happy Christmas', and the next thing I knew he was dead."

Peter was killed in a car accident in February, 1994.

"So I said, 'Thank you God,' for the wonderful gift of last summer so we could sort out everything between us. Then he was gone. I did not need to grieve for him, I knew he was now free."

We both sit quietly for a moment, remembering Peter. I sometimes wonder if he isn't watching us all from somewhere, probably impatiently waiting for us to DO something.

"Eileen, I have one last question for you. I know you have told me this several times, but I always seem to forget. I know there is something you do when you have difficulty with a person. I sometimes find myself just not able to like somebody, and wish I knew how to deal with that in a creative and loving way."

"Oh yes," Eileen replies, "that's simple. What I do is to picture this person in my mind and then say, 'I love you, I bless you, I see the divinity in you.' You may have to do it more than once, but eventually it will work. You will begin to see this person in a different light and the difficulties will fade away."

"I love you, I bless you, I see the divinity in you." I try saying it now. I don't want to forget it again.

"Now I have a question for you, Karin," says Eileen.

"Of course, what is it?"

"What's the difference between an organisation and an organism?" she asks.

This is not what I expected, so I take a moment to think and hope I can answer correctly.

"As far as I know, an organisation is man-made, male-structured and mind-led. It is an organised body or society like the army or a political party. On the other hand, an organism is an organic structure that acts like a unified whole. It is led more by female intuition, and grows and contracts organically . . . Something like that."

I hope I have got it right.

"Why do you want to know?" I ask her.

"There's this new Global Membership they are now talking about in Management, and they want to call it the Global Membership Organisation. It just feels wrong to me, this word organisation. We are more of an organism, aren't we?"

"Well, I would say that the Foundation is becoming more of an organisation these days, but the community is definitely an organism. It is growing and changing in a very organic way," I reply.

There is a knock on the door, and Katherine comes in.

"I'll come back later," she says.

"No, don't go," I say. "I think we're done here."

We walk to the door and I make my farewells. Eileen points to a piece of land opposite her house.

"That's where the caravan was that I used to live in, they've towed it away. I'm so grateful to have this warm, dry house now. That caravan had a leaky roof, it was time for it to go."

Time for me to go too.

ROBIN'S DREAM

Just a few steps lead me into the Community Centre again, where the now very familiar parsnips, potatoes and rice await me once more. No problem, I can handle parsnips ten days in a row, knowing I won't be able to find them back home in France.

After a noisy, friendly lunch I make my way over to Sunflower, where the logs are already in the fireplace, ready for me to light to welcome my visitor this afternoon. I am expecting a man whom I know has been part of the community since 1995, and is a recent addition to the Foundation's Board of Trustees. Although I often saw him around the place when I lived in the community, I don't ever remember speaking to him. However, it was hard not to know who he was because he immediately became a very visible and well known member of the management team, and eventually co-focaliser of the Foundation.

So I am extremely glad to be meeting him at last, and learn more about him.

At precisely 3.45 p.m., the time of our appointment, Robin walks through the door, removes his shoes and jacket, and sits down expectantly in front of me. He is a tallish man with dark hair and intense brown eyes and has a very strong, masculine energy. Hard not to be just a little intimidated by him, so I think it best to get right down to the business in hand, with no small talk. This is not a man who wants me to waste his time.

"Why did you come here initially, Robin?" I ask him.

"I first came here ten years ago for the Experience Week because my homeopathic doctor had given me a leaflet and suggested I go to Findhorn. Sometime earlier, friends had been here and came back with amazing stories of this place. I was happy for them, but I could not imagine wanting to come here myself, all this group stuff, and paying money to clean out the toilets, it was not my thing at all."

Put like that it does sound rather strange.

"Then suddenly, this leaflet was put into my hand, and out of nowhere I made the decision to go. I remember phoning my friends just before I came, asking them what on earth this place really was. Wisely they told me nothing, except to suggest that I be open, and not cynical. I know I can be cynical and doubting and suspicious, but I thought I'd just go and throw myself into it and see what would happen."

"And what did happen?"

"On the Wednesday night of Experience Week I had one of 'those' experiences. I looked around the group, there were sixteen of us, and I felt that I loved everybody. I felt there was something in every single member that I could connect with, that was beyond the personality, beyond the façade, beyond all the things that separate, I just loved everyone. It was an amazing experience. I wrote in my journal that evening, 'Life will never be the same, I want to live in a place and in a way that I can continue to give and receive unconditional love.'"

Robin has the look of a tough businessman, so this must have been a very dramatic experience for him at that time.

"But you did not stay here then?"

"No, I went back to London, back to my work, but started to do different things, like Tai Chi, co-counselling, and generally opening up. Then six months later I came back and decided to go on a trip to India with Angela."

Angela was a long-time member involved in education, and also led many spiritual pilgrimages to India.

Robin looks at me intensely: "That is where I found faith."

"I was so confused while we were in India, I was in a rage, smashing things, singing violent Rolling Stones songs. And then I had this transformative conversation with Angela."

He pauses for a long while, and I wait quietly.

"Angela told me that what I was going through was just my attachment to drama, the drama that I had experienced in my work in London as a criminal justice social worker, working with offenders in prison. If I wanted to deepen my spiritual path, I had to be willing to let go of all the attachments to that which I thought I was. I had to ask myself if I was willing to be who I really am.

"She asked me to make a list of all the things I thought I was. And then to let them go. So I made a long list of all the things I was attached to, like my sexuality, being a man, Judaism, humour, my salary, jealousy, my car, my flat, my friends and family. Could I let go of all of them?"

Robin is reliving this deep experience and I continue to listen in silence as he continues.

"I came back to Angela and told her I was willing to do that. I cried, and she cried, it was a very transformative moment. When I came back to London, the first thing I did was type out my resignation. I didn't know what I would do, but I knew I had to do something else. I had complete faith and certainty that I was doing the right thing."

The fire is beginning to die down so I add some more logs. The flames immediately grab the dry wood and I can feel the warmth reach me.

"So then you decided to come and live here. How has that changed you?" I ask.

"It has changed me beyond recognition. I had this desire and longing to bring more of myself to my work, to all of my life. In London, I would go to work and I would be this little part of me—rational, linear, cool and collected. Then I would go home and be this other person, the poet, the singer, the dancer, with emotions, instincts, intuitions. Being here at Findhorn allows me to bring all of that into my work. I can start a meeting with a song or share a poem. I can cry in a management meeting. There is a huge integration of all the aspects of myself that is allowed and enabled and facilitated and encouraged. That is extraordinary."

Robin's dark eyes flash intensely as he shares his feelings with me.

"I used to dream about meditating together before starting work. I had this dream, this vision back in London, and now it is real for me. There is magic in that, to come together on a deep inner level, and then do the work from that place. It is very profound and very simple, it enables all sorts of experiences to happen, relationships to deepen, and all sort of things to occur during our work."

He looks out of the window where the sunset is beginning to paint the edges of the clouds with pink and violet.

"I also live in a place of phenomenal beauty, so very different from London. I am constantly bathed in the beauty of Findhorn Bay and, like now, the beauty of the sunset."

His voice has softened and become somehow gentler. He then takes a deep breath and continues speaking. "Last weekend, I hosted a group of people from the Social Venture Network. Seventeen business people who had no idea what Findhorn was. They were here for just two days. They did all the 'Experience Findhorn' stuff—dancing, trust and leadership games, the tour around the place, a talk from David Hoyle [manager of the Phoenix store] about spiritual economy. We went to the Taizé celebration, took a trip to the river, all the things we usually do with our guests.

"They were all blown away, and I thought, that's the magic here."

I'm listening deeply, I just have to hear the word "magic" and I'm there!

"They told me that they felt there is a way we talk here that is very, very real. We make eye contact and say what we believe. They found that extraordinary. They noticed that the level of authenticity here is very profound. And I believe that is true, I think that there are less and less layers here between us and true reality. We don't defend ourselves, because we don't need to do so.

"Someone also asked us about the shadow side of community, and I talked about all the difficult things here. When I had finished, he said, 'All day you've been telling us about the positive things about living here and now you share about the shadow side without any change of body language. You are not ashamed of it, nor did you avoid it.'"

Changing the subject I ask Robin about his work in the community.

"My main job now is focalising the consultancy programme. That means taking the Findhorn impulse into businesses."

"Tell me more."

"Well, what they want is some of the 'magic' that we have in the workplaces here. So we take it out to them. We do all the same things when we go out to visit businesses as we do here. Afterwards, they tell us that it was like no other training they have ever had."

"What is so different?" I ask.

"They tell us that they love what we do, the funky exercises. But what really amazes them is the quality of our presence, how easy the trainers seem to be with themselves, the peace we bring with us. They feel we really care and want to connect with them. Which, of course, is true."

Robin pauses for moment and then continues.

"It's hard to notice all this when you're in it, but I must have learned and embodied some of the magic of this place so I can share it with the outside world. Yes, we share ourselves on a form level, but there is something beyond that too. People experience it here and also when we take it out. It's just magical. That's what keeps me here too. I can't imagine working in London again—I'm still learning and transforming."

"What about challenges? I know that it is not all sweetness and light here."

"There are huge challenges," he replies. "As a leader in the community, I have sometimes felt we were processing endlessly and I find that really difficult. I once stood up in a community meeting, feeling extremely frustrated, and said, 'I've spent six months working on this, we've had ten meetings, and we still have not decided anything. It's driving me nuts.' And this woman turned to me and said, 'Maybe that's what you have come to learn.' I told her that if I've come to learn that, then I've put an enormous amount of effort into things which go nowhere at all, and that's not what I want to learn.

"Of course, to some extent, I do need to learn that the 'how' is just as important as the 'what.' The process is important, not just the content."

I remember similar challenges in getting the balance right between accepting the process and wanting to have results. Perhaps this is sometimes out of balance at Findhorn—too much process and not enough results.

"On a personal level there are also challenges," Robin continues. "On a good day something can be an opportunity, and on a bad day it's a challenge. There are times when I want to hide and not show myself, not have anyone notice what I'm feeling. Then the transparency and authenticity seem really difficult.

"But on a good day it feels like such a gift that I can show all of myself to the community. It is an amazing gift to be totally open and vulnerable. It's an incredible healing journey for me to feel I can accept all parts of myself. I particularly get this through my men's group. They are a group of men who are strong and compassionate. We meet every week and tell our stories. It is very healing to be mirrored in other men, to discover that we all have similar experiences and feel the same."

I remember the support and friendship I had from all my women friends when I lived here, and voice my thought that men may have a harder time being here than women.

"Why do you feel that?" he asks.

"Women seem to change much more gracefully and quickly than men,"

I reply. "Women here seem to find it much easier to be vulnerable and find their strength in that. Men seem to struggle with it more. And there are also usually more women than men living here."

"I think it's actually very hard to be a powerful man in the community," Robin says, "because you can be accused of trampling over others' sensitivities. We are suspicious of leadership and have anti-authority issues. Mari, the current Foundation Focaliser, can exhibit more direct authority than I ever could as a man. It's hard for male leaders to be powerful. The ghost of Peter Caddy is very strong. While there is a kind of love and reverence for him, there is also the attitude that 'we don't do that any more'. This is the time of the group—we don't want charismatic leaders."

He paused to reflect, and I recognize a familiar theme, though his next observation surprises me.

"We don't want a leader, but really we do want a leader. But not a leadership that will tell us what to do," he says firmly.

"A leader with responsibility but no power?" I wonder.

"Exactly, we don't want a leader who will call us to account or tell us what to do."

"It's always been like that," I remember. Except for Peter Caddy, and that was because he was the founder.

I ask Robin, "Considering all our challenges, though, we have still achieved a lot here, don't you think?"

"Yes," he replies. "We have achieved an enormous amount of progress towards a sustainable community, towards building a human settlement that is sustainable not only economically, environmentally and ecologically but also spiritually, socially and culturally. The phenomenal thing is, that though we may have our struggles—especially financial—to have achieved as much as we have is pretty impressive."

"But the financial struggles are mainly in the Foundation," I reply. "Look around you here, at the new houses, people are coming to live here who must somehow have the income to do so."

Robin disagrees with me.

"The financial problems are also in the community; this is not an affluent community."

I remind him that, during my years of living in the community, we certainly did not have much money but had an amazingly rich lifestyle.

"When I was in London," he responded, "I earned enough money, but lived amidst violence, dirt and noise. Here I don't earn anything, but I feel like a millionaire. I feel it is my community, it's all mine. My fear is that when we move into greater financial responsibility and accountability, this will start to change."

I ask him about being a Trustee of the Foundation.

"I feel very privileged and honoured to be a Trustee, and for me personally it's a real learning curve to be part of the advisory board, and having to find my way in."

I ask him if it feels as though he has joined the Trustees at a difficult and vulnerable time.

"No," he says, "I don't feel like that. I have no doubt we will move through this, I have total faith. I don't feel any fear. I am curious how it will all work out, but know that it will. I think it will change us hugely, but I think we will probably become more effective. Perhaps we will become a leaner, meaner machine, but I am sure we will move through it."

Leaner perhaps, but meaner? Never!

While I am thinking about "leaner," I remember that I have been invited to have dinner this evening with my old friends Mary and George. Luckily, they live right next door to where I'm staying, so I don't have far to go. Mary is another of the pioneers of the Field of Dreams, and I am looking forward to seeing her new house. I also know I will have a delicious meal there, but more than that, we will enjoy telling stories and sharing memories. Perhaps I won't even take my tape recorder tonight, so we can relax and be totally outrageous.

I glance at my watch, and find that the three quarters of an hour booked for our interview is just over. I am once more amazed at how quickly I can get to know someone, particularly here at Findhorn, where someone like Robin is willing to share about his life, feelings and thoughts with me in such an open and honest way. I'm so glad to have had the chance to get to know him, and hear his story. I thank him warmly and say my goodbyes.

WORK AND PLAY

IN THE WHITE HOUSE

I am finding myself waking up very early now. Perhaps this is because it is the only time of the day I am able to have quiet thinking time, when I am neither talking nor listening to others. Moments to reflect and allow all my experiences to land. Time to take everything into the blessed silence of meditation. It is still very dark outside, and although lights are beginning to come on in the houses around me, there are no sounds of cars or other noises—not even the birds have woken up yet.

And then it is time to move into the day, more wonderful people to see, more great experiences to have. Not far to go for the first one.

I have caught several glimpses of Kay Kay over the last few days. Her house is right next door to my B&B, and when I wake up in the morning and look out of my bedroom window, I often see her in her kitchen making breakfast. This morning I will be visiting her. I am looking forward both to visiting Kay and seeing the interior of another of the new houses on the Field of Dreams.

It hardly seems worth my while to put my shoes on, especially as most houses here are "shoe free." There is a place in the front hall for leaving shoes, and often a selection of warm slippers for visitors to choose from. However, I do have to walk several metres over the damp ground first, so I compromise, don't tie my shoelaces, and leave my coat behind.

A quick hop and a jump, and I am in the house next door where a smiling, welcoming Kay Kay is waiting for me. Kay is a pretty woman with curly blond hair, sparkling, intelligent eyes and a charming smile. She is also a strong woman who looks like the kind of person who will speak her mind and have strong opinions. She comes from the north of England and speaks with an attractive accent that reflects her very proud working-class background.

Everything around me looks very new, and there is a smell of new wood and fresh paint. Of course I ask for a tour of the house. While the outside is painted grey and is an interesting and unusual shape, the inside is all very pale wood and white decor. White curtains, white bed linen, white cushions, white everywhere. Kay tells me that she is "painting" her house, that first she is filling the house with light and everything is white, and later, when she feels moved to do so, she will add touches of colour. I look forward to visiting again in a few years to see how it has all evolved.

For once, I actually refuse the offered cup of tea, having just had my breakfast next door. So we walk up the short staircase into the living room upstairs. It seems that a number of houses here on the Field have the bedrooms downstairs and the living area upstairs, in order to benefit from the glorious view across Findhorn Bay and the distant, snow-capped mountains. We make ourselves comfortable on the couch (white, of course), and I ask Kay how her book, *Growing People*, is doing. I have seen it on display in the Phoenix store. I know Kay is sad that Findhorn Press did not publish her book, and I assure her that this is purely on the grounds that, as a small publisher with limited resources, we cannot publish everything we might like to.

This little challenge out of the way, I ask her how she first came to Findhorn and what drew her here.

"Oh, the usual kind of story," she begins. "I had already been doing quite a lot of personal development beforehand, and then suddenly the Findhorn Catalogue fell off a shelf. I don't actually remember ever putting it there!

"At first, it wasn't a particularly heart-opening experience. I had done a lot of group work before this—in the seventies—like 'est' and other workshops. So it was not a surprise, or a first opportunity to blossom, as it is for many others. But it was delightful all the same. I only came for a week and then was due to return to London."

A small smile lifts the corner of her lips as she remembers.

"But my car would not start, so I stayed another week as a working guest. Then at the end of this second week, I found my car still would not start and the garage could not discover what was the matter with it. So I went for a while to Minton House, the large pink house opposite the Park that was then run as a retreat and workshop centre, and there discovered that a wider community was emerging around the Foundation. It was this broader community that inspired me, and where I felt I might fit in."

"So you decided to stay?" I ask her.

"Not yet. I decided to return to London to talk to my partner about coming to live here. And at that point my car started again, although the garage still could not tell me what was wrong with it. That's part of the magic of Findhorn—that there is an essence, a kind of knowing, a something—that if you are willing to go with the flow of it, your life is embellished."

That's very true. It is this essence, this something, that I am trying to find here. Kay continues her story.

"To cut a long story short, I went away, came back, and was very clearly guided to start Friends of Findhorn. This was the first attempt at a global network, to connect people who had been here and also people who are aligned with the principles of this place, even if they had never been here. Initially, there was fierce resistance by almost everyone in the Foundation, but I did it anyway."

It's difficult to imagine anyone trying to stop Kay doing something she really believes in.

"Three years later, of course, it was adopted by the Foundation, which was always my intention, and it became the Stewards of the Foundation, which is much more of a fundraising activity than the mutual support and exchange of information that I had envisaged. However, they also resurrected the Friends of Findhorn later, and now there are discussions about opening it up to something like I have always imagined it to be— something like Greenpeace, which is a group about saving whales; and of course Findhorn is a group about awakening consciousness. That was always my vision, and now, eleven years later, it may come to fruition."

I'm looking forward to hearing more about this and hope Kay will explain her vision to me.

"Over the next few years, I was sometimes here, doing some voluntary work, and then off on my travels again. But somehow Findhorn always felt like home from the day I arrived. Then, about three years ago, I returned from a trip and discovered that there were negotiations going on to create a new form of community that would include everyone—that would break down the barriers of 'them and us,' of being 'in' or 'out,' Foundation or non-Foundation—something inclusive. I was asked to stand for the role of Listener/Convenor, a new role created to be one of two people to be the ears of the community, to have a finger on the pulse and to know what was happening. At the time, I was not ready to do that, I had become sick. When I was healed and the opportunity came up again, I decided I could do it, and was elected. I have now held this role for two years."

"You were elected?" I ask in surprise. "Surely we don't have elections here?"

"Yes we do," Kay answers. "You're right, we had not held elections before, but the New Findhorn Association is a democracy, an association of all the organisations that go to make up this place. Some of them are charities like the Foundation, which is the biggest one. Others are businesses like the shop, and there are also groups of like-minded individuals or collective practices, like the therapy groups, the arts and crafts people, and the residents on the Field. Every aspect of life here is covered. It gives people a gateway into the community."

"Who makes the decisions about who will come into the community?" I now ask.

"We don't need gatekeepers as such. The feeling was that this was an association that everybody could identify with, no need for gatekeeping. We have organisational members, like the businesses who make some financial contribution, and members also join as individuals and pay a subscription on a sliding scale, so everybody can feel included. There are now two Listeners/Convenors, myself and Rory."

Kay speaks very fast and it's a challenge to keep up with her. She has so many ideas and thoughts that she wants to share with me.

"There is still a lot to be done to ground this community, to make it financially sustainable. People need to start more little businesses, so that we are not so dependent on the one large organisation—the Foundation—for bringing in the money. At the moment, some people need to go away for a while to earn the money to live here. We need to look at how we can be both economically and ecologically sustainable. My role is a fascinating one, one of the best jobs on the planet, and my peculiar life experiences have equipped me very well for it."

"Peculiar?" I ask, wondering what she specifically means.

"Marketing, sales, being a mother, a coach, a counsellor, a project developer, a designer, I have organised things, raised money for charities, it was all very varied. I come from northeast England, from good, working-class stock. My family were miners and steel men, so I have a very strong sense of community. I grew up in a mining town where everybody looked after everybody else, all the time. I suppose I want to recreate that here in this setting. I am always inclusive, always want to say yes, find a way to make it work, and look to see where is the common ground between people. I like to help folk find co-operative ways to move forward rather than say, 'it's never been done like this,' or 'we don't think this will work, so let's not try.' I sometimes feel I am going against the stream of the culture here, but it is changing!"

So it seems, and it looks as if Kay is right in the middle of the changes.

"Yes," she agrees. "Everything is changing. It's very exciting. We are more willing as a community to look for exciting and risky new ways of doing things. The Foundation is also being forced into it at the moment because of its financial situation. As a species, we rarely seem to do things unless we have to. We talk about change but we are incredibly resistant to it. It's a bit like tightening the bow or stretching the elastic band, we resist and resist until we actually have to do it and then, if we are lined up at that time, we can go straight to where we need to go."

Kay looks out across the Bay, to the high hills.

"I see a lot of tightening of elastic bands at the moment. To mix my metaphors, I think our arrows will shoot true soon," she says confidently.

"But back to the New Findhorn Association," she continues. "It's a most unfortunate name, I feel. It was chosen by the steering committee as a name that would not offend anybody, not the Foundation, not the local Findhorn Village who sometimes resent us using their name, but in the end it was a compromise that doesn't really mean anything."

"What would you like to call it?" I wonder.

Kay's face glows at my question.

"I would like to see it spread out to be global, so I would probably call it 'The Findhorn Global Community.' That way, absolutely everyone who wants to can feel included."

"I've been hearing something about this global membership lately, is that what people are talking about?" I ask her. "You are involved in this?"

"Yes, this is the idea, and I will be involved. I'm very excited about this, it ties in with what we are already doing and what we could do."

"Can anybody join, even if they have never been here?" It feels so far beyond anything that has been done before.

"Yes, for my part they could, why would we restrict ourselves? Why would we say someone isn't good enough? I could see a global membership that people could join—just like Greenpeace. I could also see something like an associate membership of people who had actually been here. And a residential membership for people who are keeping the core running here."

"This all sounds very exciting and new, Kay, but tell me, why here— why at Findhorn?"

"I have been to many communities. There has been an enormous amount of work done here, mainly in the '70's I think, with some extraordinary pioneers who are now off doing pioneering work somewhere else. Like all pioneers, they did what they had to do here and then moved on. There is a strong ethos here that work is love in action, where Spirit is manifested in daily life. This was all grounded here in the early days. For me, it makes perfect sense to use all of these extra dimensions that have not been traditionally part of western life. To make them everyday. To bring ethics into the forefront of decision making."

"But this is not the only place where it is happening, is it?" I ask.

"Absolutely not," Kay replies. "Nor would I say we have already got it. But we are aspiring to it. For me that's good enough. I have more respect for people who aspire than for those who say they've 'got it.'"

I hope she knows that right now I am aspiring to discover "the magic of Findhorn."

"Here, there is an aspiration to put all the ethics and the ethos of our common ground statement into daily practice: that I will treat my fellow people with respect and high regard; I will bring spirituality into my daily work; I will commit myself to my evolution as a spiritual being. All these kind of things can be done in very practical ways. And you demonstrate them by not raping the planet, by eating local foods if you can, by helping others, by being inclusive and open to new ideas, by being guided by intuition, by looking for new ways of doing things. All this is already grounded here to some degree and you can find it all over the place. You don't have to recreate it, but you can build on it. There is a very strong Foundation here and it can only get better."

"Do you ever think that perhaps the original community, or the Foundation, may no longer be important?" I ask her. It's a question I have asked many people, with different answers. Now I wonder what Kay will have to say to it. She is thoughtful for a moment, and then answers.

"Yes, I sometimes wonder if we have outlived our purpose, whether we have done what we were supposed to do, if we are still of value to the world." She pauses for a moment, smiles at me and then nods vigorously. "I'm pretty sure that we are still of value," she says with conviction.

"And the Foundation, what is the role of the Foundation within the community?"

"I think it's very necessary, and its role is spiritual education. It's what they do better than anywhere else I've ever been. The more simply it is provided, the more effective it is. The simple way in which the Experience Week is run is a wonderful gift to the planet. The Foundation also holds the spiritual core. Of course, it is also in the rest of the community. But I think the Foundation could be much smaller and more efficiently run and still provide the same level of service that it does now."

"The community has now been here for nearly forty years. Do you think there was a power in this land before we came? Or has it evolved since we have been here?"

"There is a spirit in this land, there was something here long before Peter, Dorothy and Eileen arrived. Perhaps it has been added to, but perhaps also diminished by fear. Added to by courage, leading lives with spirit rather than just talking about it. The spirit of this place attracts people from all over the planet. That gives us all a wonderful opportunity to act globally on a local level. I interact with every nationality, with many different cultures. I have the daily opportunity to do global things right here locally. I think that is real planetary service. My belief is that what we do on an individual level has an impact in the world. I can aspire to be the change I want to see in the world."

"Do you have a spiritual practice, Kay?"

"Yes, my own spiritual practice is Transcendental Meditation, but my real spiritual practice is how I am in relationship to others, and I have opportunities to practice that every day."

She laughs happily. "And it's such a joy!"

It is time for Kay to get back to what she enjoys doing most, to her spiritual practice with her fellow community members. I find my shoes downstairs; this time I do tie the shoelaces, and I make my way out into the chilly morning light.

I suddenly remember that this is the day when Anja told me that all the Experience Week group would be over here at the Park, so I walk quickly to the Community Centre where I know they will be working. Or possibly even having a tea break!

HIDE AND SEEK

I arrive in the Community Centre and find that the group are neither working nor drinking tea. In fact they are not there at all! I ask the person busy polishing the floor if there has been any sighting of the Experience Week, and am told that they have been there and they have been working. In fact, they have been working so hard that they have already finished their project, mailing leaflets and catalogues. And then they all disappeared!

Somewhat disappointed, I try to think where they may have gone. It does not take me long to realise where that could be. Chocolate and books. Those are what Experience Week members long for when they have any free time.

As I approach the Phoenix and look into its windows, I can already see some of my new friends wandering through the narrow aisles, browsing among the books, buying souvenirs to take home—and eating some of the many irresistible chocolate bars.

"So this is where you all are," I call to them. "I thought you were busy working. I was coming to help you."

"Too late," someone replies. "It's all done. We've been let out to play!"

They do almost look like a group of school children given time off from their studies. There is an innocent childlikeness in their fun and laughter. It's hard to believe these are the same strangers who met for the first time just a few days ago. They already look like a family. A very loving family.

"I'll leave you to your fun," I tell them. "Can I join you all for your last dinner on Friday night?"

"Sure," they agree. "Come over to Cluny, you're very welcome to join us."

I thank them, and before I leave the shop I choose a bar of caramel-filled chocolate. That will also be my last dinner, my last night here. My quest is almost coming to an end. But there are still some very important things to do, besides eat very delicious chocolate. For now I need to make my way to Bag End at the end of Pineridge, where all the new houses have been built. I am meeting Hanna, the Park Focaliser.

LADY OF THE DANCE

Hanna greets me at the door of her house, one of the earlier ecological buildings, built to house several single members. There are a number of large bedrooms and a shared kitchen and living room. This is my first time visiting the house, and after a tour, we make our way to the living room—with cups of tea in hand of course.

Hanna is a tall, graceful German woman with chestnut hair. She lived in Berlin before she came here, and while I have seen her around the Park for a long time, this is our first real conversation together. I am looking forward to getting to know her better.

We make ourselves comfortable and I ask her when and how she first came here.

"It was one of those little miracles! I was living in Berlin and one day I found a note offering an afternoon of Findhorn Sacred Dances. As I was not busy that day I decided to go and was instantly intrigued. I had never danced like that before and wanted more. That afternoon completely changed my life.

"At the time I was a political feminist and was very much into personal growth and therapy. Through the dances I experienced so much joy and happiness and contentment, it opened up my spiritual path which had been dormant for a long time. Accessing spirit suddenly seemed so easy, so I wanted to come to Findhorn. Then, Anna Barton, who focalised Sacred Dance in the community, came to Berlin, and after I had danced with her I was convinced I had to visit Findhorn."

"What happened then?" I ask.

"I booked for a Sacred Dance week," Hanna continues, " but was told I had to do an Experience Week first."

"Yes, that's true," I comment. "All guests are asked to participate in an Experience Week before they join one of the workshops. So what did you do?"

Hanna bursts into delighted laughter. "Well, I grumbled a bit, but then decided I would do it. In the end of course, the Experience Week was a much more important experience than the Sacred Dance. It was a big heart opening experience for me."

She laughs again as she recalls her experience. "Like many have said a hundred times, people come from all over the world, you don't know one another, and then suddenly, half way through the week, you love them all! Total, unconditional love and acceptance, and being loved and cared for.

What an amazing experience. I knew immediately that I wanted to come and live here, even then."

"Did you return to Berlin?"

"Yes, I went back home and I talked and talked to my friends about Findhorn until they got quite bored with me and eventually said, 'Why don't you just go there for a while?'"

Hanna picks up her cup and holds it tightly. "That's when I realised that yes, of course I could do that. I decided to come in winter, to see what that would be like, because in Berlin the winter is so awful, the air is bad and it's very cold."

I look outside and it looks pretty cold here, too.

"I came at the end of January and it was beautiful. It was crispy and the sun was shining."

I think to myself that this probably has something to do with the outer world reflecting how she felt inside.

"Then one day I realised, 'I have to come and live here.' It was a very strong impulse. I didn't know about guidance then, it was just an inner knowing."

Hanna's voice is filled with the amazement she felt in those early days.

"It was not all easy coming here. I had to leave all my friends in Berlin as well as my work—it was quite hard. But the pull to come here was stronger than anything else."

"So what happened when you came here?" I ask her.

"I began to work in the Park Kitchen."

There is something akin to awe in her voice when she says that. "The kitchen became my life, my school, my classroom. I worked there for five years. I began to feel that there is no life after the Park Kitchen. For me, it was the heart of the community."

I am listening very intently now. This is an experience I can completely relate to. This is just how I felt when I worked in the kitchen. Hanna continues to share her experiences.

"We always had the hatch open, everybody walked through the kitchen."

Then Hanna's voice changes, and a small smile plays around her mouth. "You probably know that I am a very impulsive person and have a very hot temper. So while I was opening my heart, I also learned a lot through conflict. The kitchen was the perfect place for that, it was like a pressure cooker. It was so small (before the extension was built), with lots of people working there, all strong characters. I loved cooking—still do— and I felt so appreciated there. I learned to bake bread and make tofu.

Funnily enough, I never learned how to bake just one loaf; I learned how to make 80 loaves, or tofu for 150 people."

My own memories are racing through my head, everything that Hanna says feels so familiar.

"It was so hard to leave the kitchen—I was Hanna, the queen of the kitchen."

And twenty-five years ago, that's just how I felt.

"A lot of people thought my time in the kitchen was over, and then I had a big conflict there. I was so upset, I wanted to leave, but could not remember how to say, 'I resign,' so one day I said, very loudly, 'I fire myself!'"

Hanna is a very fiery lady.

"People then said maybe it was just the right time for me to leave my kitchen." Her voice still sounds very sad as she remembers this. "And then suddenly the conflict was gone, and I realised it really was just my time to leave."

Even that part of her story reflects exactly what happened with me.

"And shortly after this I had a strong pull to focalise the programme for the new members."

She laughs loudly, and I wonder why.

"Half the people in personnel thought it was a great idea, but the other half said, 'Hanna? Never!' They knew me well."

"So did you do it?" I ask, intrigued.

"Oh, yes, in fact I did two, the first one went so well that I also focalised the next one. The universe always seems to provide me with challenges, but challenges I can grow into. Not overwhelming ones. Just big enough so I developed into them."

"And . . . ? " I wait as Hanna falls silent for a few moments.

"Then I was diagnosed with cervical cancer, which was another amazing experience. I decided to go for the operation as it was still in the very early stages. Strangely enough I can't regret that this ever happened. The level of support I got was amazing. I am not a patient person, but during this time I somehow became very patient. All that waiting around in hospitals. I was even becoming nice to everybody."

She laughs at herself. She is a strong woman learning to become soft and vulnerable. She reminds me so much of myself.

"Have you ever thought of leaving the Foundation, Hanna, or will you be here for ever?"

"I had a crisis about two years ago, when I thought I did not belong here anymore. I thought my time here was over. I wanted to leave and had even decided on the date—I was all set to leave."

She is quiet again before continuing. "Then people began offering me some very interesting jobs, like working with long term guests, or becoming Park Focaliser—that, especially, was the last thing I wanted to do. Everybody wants something from you, and you're responsible for everything all the time. No, the last job I wanted to do was Park Focaliser."

She laughs again, and her eyes sparkle. "Then, of course, it happened again—that feeling, the strong inner knowing. 'How about becoming the Park Focaliser?' it said, and suddenly it felt like the best job ever. I had so many ideas of what this job could be and how I would do it. I could give my best, all the things I have learned over the years, how I know this place so well, what I would like to see different. How we have to change. This excited me totally and it all became very attractive. So that's what I am still doing now."

"Hanna," I ask, "what is the feeling, the strong inner knowing, that told you to do this?"

There is silence while she thinks about her answer.

"Karin, that's a good question. How to answer? You know, I suppose that even if I think I don't get guidance, I do!" She laughs again. "I think it has something to do with the vibrations here. Certain jobs or functions have a certain vibration and when I vibrate at the same wavelength, then it all comes together, because there is an alignment with the energy field of a particular task. I could call it the angel or unseen beings, but it's very strong and tangible here. My vibrations at this time are totally aligned with the job of Park Focaliser, and my enthusiasm and energy are part of it. As are my struggles and challenges, as well as my doubts."

"Do you think there is there a 'Factor X' here, something special, something magical?"

"Yes, there is something here. I think it is possible to find it everywhere, but somehow it is much stronger here, more focussed. Generations of people have built up the energy, and it is easy just to slip into it. There is definitely something."

"And by the end of the week—before I leave in two days' time—I have to know what it is," I add desperately.

We both laugh!

"It's beyond words, Karin," she says, kindly.

"But that's just what I need, I need to put it into words to share it," I continue hopefully.

"Yes," Hanna replies, "but the Tao that can be spoken is not the Tao. You are trying to describe something that is not describable."

I suppose she is meaning something like the paintings by Magritte, showing the picture of a pipe which says, "This is not a pipe." If I try to say, "This is the magic," the words will actually only describe the magic and not be the magic itself. I can feel myself becoming quite confused.

"I can sometimes convey it by making eye contact with another person, just looking into their eyes," she says, trying to help me.

I will find it difficult to make eye contact with every reader of this book, I think, pondering.

Then she tries just once more. "I can tell you how I experience it, Karin. For me, it can happen through dance, through song, through certain rituals, and through working at something I love."

I remember that tomorrow afternoon I will be cooking in the Park Kitchen. If I can find the "Factor X" anywhere, surely that will be the place!

I slowly make my way back down towards the field of dreams, wondering why I seem to feel so weak and sluggish. Breathing in the cold air is becoming quite painful, and by the time I reach the haven of Sunflower I am sneezing and coughing, and my head is aching. Looks like the North of Scotland has got to me in the form of a cold. Now what? There is still so much to do in the next couple of days. I don't have time to be ill.

Back inside the warmth of the house, I put the kettle on for a hot drink. Then I remember that upstairs I have the perfect cure for my problem, a bottle of Malt Whisky I was going to take back to France with me. I carry the cup of hot water, lemon juice and honey upstairs and then open the Whisky and pour a generous portion into my cup. I curl up in bed and sip my potent drink until I fall into a deep and healing sleep.

CONQUERING MY DRAGON

A good night's sleep and a morning in bed, plus the magic of the "hot toddy" seem to have done their work. I am feeling much better today and ready for more adventures. Just as well, because the afternoon I have been waiting for has arrived—today, I am cooking dinner in the Park Kitchen. Since the day I arrived at Findhorn, some twenty-seven years ago, I have loved this place above all others. I immediately felt totally at home in there. Not that I was an expert cook; in fact, because of my background in

hotel management, my opportunities for cooking anything had been few—
I was more used to eating in restaurants. But for some reason, when I
walked into this particular kitchen, it immediately welcomed me.

That first day, in spite of my advancing pregnancy, I insisted that the
kitchen was the place where I wanted to work. Eric from Personnel,
noticing my growing bulge, tried to persuade me to work somewhere quiet,
like the Accounts Department. However, after one week juggling with
figures, I knew for sure that I much preferred juggling with pots and pans.

So my unborn baby and I spent the next three months learning how to
cook vegetarian meals for two hundred people. I coped happily with
enormous pans of food and managed to take large trays of vegetables out of
the ovens. I learned how to do a hundred different things with potatoes,
how to make leftovers look completely new and exciting, and how to make
a different soup every day for a month. I also learned how to cook with
some strange and quite new foods like tofu and miso. I particularly enjoyed
seeing the fresh vegetables arrive from our gardens every morning, and
making delicious dishes with them.

Not that everything always went smoothly: I still remember with horror
the day I burned three huge pots of vegetable stew—every single one of
them tasted awful. I tried adding different herbs but they only made it
worse. As a last resort, I added several spoonfuls of hot curry powder, but
even this could not disguise the burnt taste. I escaped from the kitchen in
tears and let my fellow cooks serve the meal. I never asked them how the
meal was received, and I'm glad to say that nobody ever told me!

It was not until I went into labour that my fellow workers could drag
me out of the kitchen and into the local hospital in Inverness. Then,
within a few weeks of giving birth to Michael, I was back at the stove with
a newborn in my arms! The place had an irresistible draw for me.

Over the next twenty years, my relationship with the kitchen grew
from better to wonderful. While my baby was still young, I only cooked two
or three meals a week, but as soon as he was old enough to go to nursery
school I applied for the position of kitchen focaliser and to my great delight
I was accepted. Of course by then I had become a pretty good cook, and had
lost my tendency to burn the stew! I enjoyed myself to my heart's content
in the kitchen. As well as the daily meals, I cooked Christmas Dinners,
made wedding cakes and birthday cakes, and catered for numerous other
special occasions.

Best of all, I could create the most amazing cheese soufflés—for two
hundred people! I loved the sensual, tactile experience of separating the

eggs by hand, and delicately folding the stiffly whipped egg whites into the rest of the soufflé mixture—again all by hand. I would not allow anyone to help me. The best part of all came when the perfectly risen soufflé was ready to come out of the oven and the waiting, hungry community would "Oooh" and "Ahhh" with appreciation and admiration at the elegant, velvety, cheesy concoction. These days, the only person I impress with my soufflés is my husband, but he certainly enjoys them.

So, here I am, once more in the Park Kitchen. I have not cooked here for many years, and since then it has been completely remodelled. Even so, I feel sure that this must be the one place in the community where I will definitely find my magic. It is now much larger, and the ovens and most of the equipment look new. The people I will be cooking with this afternoon don't know me at all, nor do they have any knowledge of my love affair with this wonderful kitchen.

I notice that even the aprons have changed. In the past we would wear coloured, floral aprons made from old curtains. Now there are white aprons and overalls that would be at home in any restaurant kitchen. I accept that this is progress, and perhaps more hygienic, but nothing will ever match the memory of Joanie bringing over the new aprons and the cooks fighting amicably over who would wear the one with the large red poppies. Luckily, I often lost this fight.

This afternoon, I will be cooking with three other women. The one who is obviously the focaliser is a very attractive and vivacious woman. I watched her make some energetic and meaningful contributions at the Internal Conference a few days ago. She invites us to sit at the table in the corner of the kitchen, another new addition that had not been there in my days. She introduces herself as Lydia, an inter-faith minister from New York. She tells us that she has been here for three years and is currently acting kitchen focaliser.

The next person to introduce herself is a dark haired young woman called Mohini. She tells us she is from London and has been working here as a volunteer for some months. She is also a professional cook, which augurs well for the afternoon's cooking.

Anita, the third of my three fellow cooks, is from Columbia, and I discover she is now married to an old friend of mine with whom I once shared many days cooking. She also tells us that she is pregnant, so I immediately have a feeling of sisterhood with her, remembering my early days in this very kitchen.

Then I introduce myself, but feel reluctant to talk about my past relationship with this kitchen. I suddenly feel quite shy and think it's best to just be in this moment and let things develop as they will.

We hold hands and close our eyes while Lydia speaks a few words welcoming us into this space, inviting us to connect with the Angel of the kitchen, to open our hearts and minds to each other, and to put our love into the meal we are about to create.

After a few more minutes of silence we bring our attention back to the kitchen and talk about the task ahead of us. Lydia tells us we will be cooking Pasta Primavera, with leeks and kale fresh from the garden. She will also be making some foccacia bread, and the Phoenix store has sent up a hunk or two of delicious Parmesan cheese to grate and sprinkle over the pasta.

I wonder what part I will be playing in cooking this meal and am not left to wonder for long. Lydia asks me to join Mohini in cleaning and preparing several enormous bins of very muddy leeks at the two sinks in the corner.

Soon after the leek-washing marathon begins, my sink is awash with dark brown mud. A second rinsing makes little difference and it takes a third sink full of clean water to make an impact on the soil-encrusted vegetables. At least there can be no doubt that these leeks are freshly dug from the gardens. A long hour later—well past my love affair with leeks— we have prepared enough for the meal. I notice that there are another two large bins of these tasty, but pesky, onion cousins in the corner of the kitchen and am relieved that I don't have to wash them. However, their presence has not been lost on Lydia, and—as if she can read my thoughts— she has us washing them all for leek and potato soup tomorrow!

I am just beginning to dry my hands, noticing that my once clean, white apron is now a soggy, muddy mess, when I am given my next task. This time, it is several even larger bins of curly, dark green kale. There is obviously a lesson here for me to learn, but right now I am too busy washing and chopping, and hoping that I am enjoying myself.

At last it is teatime. I am relieved that this tradition is still going strong—a break in the middle of a work shift when everything stops for a cup of tea. In the dining room we find an urn of boiling water and various teas and hot drinks. We all make our drinks and sit down together for a comfortable chat, sharing how we are doing and getting to know each other more. Normally, we would also be working with some new guests, and this is a time for asking questions and discovering more about the community. Today there are no guests, so it's just the four of us sharing a quiet moment, with me sitting in a tired little heap wondering what I will be doing next.

I don't have to wait long to find out. We drop our dirty cups in the dishwashing area and return to the kitchen. Time to grate the Parmesan, which is a very hard cheese. I look hopefully across the kitchen at Hobart, the wonderful machine that can grate, chop, mix or whip anything. But because the pieces are so small, we use hand held graters instead—the kind that I use at home and which can take the skin off my knuckles. I'm really struggling until Mohini notices my problem and offers to take over my task.

At last, I am given a job that I'm sure I will enjoy. I find a couple of the very large cast iron frying pans to sauté the leeks and kale in fragrant olive oil with plenty of garlic. From the ovens I can smell the aroma of bread baking, and beside me are several pans of bubbling pasta. It looks as if it is all beginning to come together. However, there is one more task for me to do this afternoon. And this is the job I always used to avoid at all costs. In fact, I would choose to cook dinner on my own for the whole community on a Sunday afternoon, rather than have to do this—the pot wash— affectionately known as Left Hand Sink!

Perhaps the Angel of the kitchen has been waiting all these years for me to do this. I should have realised I could not avoid it forever, no matter how hard I tried. So here I am in front of the left hand sink. At 1.57metres (5' 2"), I can only just reach over the edge of this enormous sink, and there is certainly no way that I can reach its deep and mysterious bottom. All around me are huge cauldrons with burnt-on food, pots so big I can't even get my arms around them. A desperate glance at the clock tells me I have at least another half hour before our cooking shift comes to an end. With no hope for release, I plug the sink, begin to run the hot water, squirt in the dishwashing liquid and pick up a very large scouring pad.

Half an hour later, I proudly survey my sparkling clean pots and pans. I've made it. I have faced one of my dragons that I avoided for so many years. The dreaded Left Hand Sink has been conquered. Harry Potter conquered his enormous dragon, and I have conquered mine.

It's six o'clock. The dinner smells and looks delicious and has been placed on the buffet tables in the dining room. The hungry diners are beginning to arrive with happy smiles and appreciative appetites. Now I can relax and think about my experiences of the afternoon, to discover what I have learned and to find the magic in that discovery.

I slowly allow the realisation to come to me that my relationship with the kitchen has changed. We are no longer in love. The fantasy that everything would always be the same is over. The Angel of the kitchen has moved on to other things, and onto other people, and so have I. The magic that I experienced for so long is still there, but a whole generation of young, enthusiastic people have now picked it up and are doing things in new and different ways. I know I will always remember my joyful days in the kitchen with deep gratitude, but like many relationships, we have both changed and grown and our time together is past.

Lydia and Mohini are doing a fantastic job, bringing their skills and love into what they are doing, just as I did many years ago. Feeding such a big family is an important and valuable task. I am grateful that the kitchen is in such good hands.

I collect my coat from the cloakroom and make my way out into the cold night. I feel a little sad; my experience today was not what I had expected it to be. But there is also some relief, a sense of release. Standing out here in the dark, I look back into the brightly lit kitchen and see someone washing pots in the left hand sink. I smile; it wasn't really that bad, scrubbing all those big pots. But, with a little bit of luck, I won't ever have to do it again.

THIS PERFECT DAY

LET IT SNOW, LET IT SNOW. . .

I wake up this morning sensing that something feels different. The quiet of early morning on the Field seems even more profound than usual. I wrap my duvet around me and stay in bed for a few more minutes, thinking about the day ahead of me, which I have reserved as my 'serendipity' day. Instead of meetings and interviews, I will let the magic come to me. A whole day of no appointments and nothing scheduled.

I think about staying in bed and drifting back to sleep, but nature calls me to leave the warmth of my cosy bed and walk down the corridor to the bathroom. I still sense something special in the unusual silence, and then, from the bathroom window, I see what it is and what has happened during the night—my own very special gift from the universe—snow!

Having lived in Florida and the South of France for the past four years, I have not seen snow for a long time. To me, snow spells magic that allows me to become a child again. I love to roll around in it, take handfuls and rub it into my face, have snowball fights with friends and make a snowman, preferably with some children.

I get into the shower and start singing. It feels as though this is going to be a very joyful day and I know just where I want to go first. A quick breakfast and then I am ready for my special day. I wrap my red coat around me—red seems perfect for the snow—and step outside. I turn my face towards the clouds, sticking out my tongue to catch the snowflakes, feeling others gently melting on my cheeks and sticking to my eyelashes. Mine are the first footsteps in the virgin snow, and I take each step very deliberately, appreciating every soft and crunchy footfall. The field is already covered in a blanket of pristine white, with the wooden houses looking like something out of a classic children's storybook.

I find other footprints when I arrive in Pineridge and walk through the Quiet Garden. This small garden in the centre of Pineridge was created more than thirty years ago as a place where people could sit or walk silently in meditation. In the centre of this garden is the Nature Sanctuary.

Since Ian Turnbull built this unique and quaint little Sanctuary in the mid eighties, this has been one of my favourite places. Now, with the turf roof covered in snow, and the pine trees and bushes around it glistening, it looks like something the fairies would have created. A real fairyland, right here in the centre of Pineridge. The three small windows, each a different shape, are lit by the lone flickering candle inside. I open the creaking wooden door, bending low to enter the ante room inside where I join several people who are removing their dripping shoes and coats. Then I walk through the curtain into the circular, inner room.

In the middle of the Sanctuary is a candle placed on a polished stone, surrounded, even in midwinter, by fresh flowers. The floor is carved and painted in many colours, and built against the walls is a round, curved bench made from old whisky barrels. Ian built this Sanctuary on a shoestring, and used whatever materials he could find at little or no cost in order to create his dream. On the bench are bright pink cushions, made with the old fabric from the ring beam in the Hall. Sitting there now are about a dozen people, including a smiling Ian.

I choose a cushion and join the others in the circle, crossing my legs underneath me; the uncarpeted stone floor is cold this morning. The candle illuminates our faces and, looking around the room, I see several old friends.

Earlier in the week, at the Taizé singing in the Universal Hall, Ian had told me about the daily "Singing Sanctuary" in Pineridge, and today is so clearly the perfect day for me to be here. This tiny Sanctuary creates a more intimate environment for our chants, and led by Ian, we begin the melody and then gradually add harmonies. We sing the chants over and over again, letting them fill us and become one with us. Then gradually as the first song fades, another song begins.

Ian had told me that, "We sing three songs, then God arrives, and then we sing one more song just to give thanks."

I am so utterly absorbed in singing that I don't know when God arrives—or perhaps She/He is here all the time. Our voices fill this Sanctuary with joy and peace and grace—the same qualities that emanate from the very fabric of this building created with such love and reverence.

As the last song fades, I feel as if I am bursting with joy and can only think of one way to make my early morning even better—a big cup of hot chocolate in the Café. Wrapping myself back up in my red coat and blue boots, I step outside the Nature Sanctuary to find that it is no longer snowing. The clouds are clearing, and a sunrise of gold and coral and turquoise is unfolding over the sparkling white Field of Dreams. Somebody up there must really love me!

Just a short while later and I am joining several other people in the café, all ready for their cappuccino, tea, or, as in my case, hot chocolate.

"With whipped cream on top?" the young man behind the counter asks me.

On a day like today I feel that even this is allowed and watch him spoon the white, frothy cream into my cup, looking rather like the snow on the tables outside. I notice Kate sitting at one of the round green tables and join her with my drink.

Kate has been in and around the community for nearly twenty years, and I know her best from her singing and performing in the Hall and for leading the choir. To the background sounds of the cappuccino machine and some Scottish fiddle music, we take time to share some stories of the Hall. Kate is currently working here, taking bookings for concerts and co-ordinating people who want to use the various Hall facilities.

She is passionate about bringing the arts to a more prominent position in the community, and to share the Hall with everyone in the local area.

"Mike Scott is giving two benefit concerts here next week," she tells me. "Both were sold out as soon as the tickets were printed."

"Benefit for what?" I ask her.

"For the Steinway piano. It needs tuning and some other work doing to it. Mike calls it his 'friend in the Hall' and is helping us raise the money to pay for the repairs."

That sounds like a very generous thing to do. More than ever I am looking forward to meeting him tonight when he returns from his trip down south.

I'm just taking another sip of my hot chocolate and licking the cream from my upper lips when I hear a loud sound behind me.

"Tarataratarat. It's me! You've been looking for me?"

I turn around in surprise and see a laughing young man with short brown hair and sparkling, mischievous eyes that look straight into mine.

"It's me, Nitzan!"

SURPRISED BY JOY

It's true, I have been waiting to speak to Nitzan ever since Geoffrey told me about him. Although it seems that over the past week I have actually seen him without realising it.

Several times, I have come across a young man who always seemed to be right there when I needed help. On the day I arrived, I was carrying my suitcase over an icy road when he appeared out of nowhere, took my case from me, deposited it in the doorway of Sunflower and before I could thank him, he was gone. Working in the kitchen, I had to lift some very heavy garbage bins, and this same charming young man took them from me and disappeared with them. Another day, I was trying to help a tourist who only spoke Spanish, and while I do speak and understand un poco, I was struggling. It was hardly a surprise that once more the mysterious young man arrived, began chatting to the tourist in effortless Spanish and, with a friendly wave to me, took him wherever he needed to go. I was beginning to wonder if this young man was real, or an Angel who could materialise whenever I needed help.

He looks very real to me now, and I offer to buy him a cappuccino—an extra large, double espresso cappuccino!

"I'm so glad to really meet you at last, Nitzan," I tell him. "But how did you know I was looking for you?"

"I heard you were looking for the magic of Findhorn, and of course that's exactly what I am. So you need to talk to me!" He grins from ear to proverbial ear.

I take my little tape recorder out of my bag, click it on and try to be serious, but it only lasts a moment. Nitzan's smile is very infectious and I can feel myself twinkling in its presence. Besides, this is my day off, I'm not supposed to be doing any interviews . . . but I clearly can't miss this opportunity.

"A number of people have told me I should definitely speak to you if I am looking for the magic of Findhorn. So, tell me, why do you think that is so?"

"Because it's true!" Nitzan tells me, full of confidence and still smiling.

Oh dear, I think, this may in fact be a rather strange interview, but then, whoever said it had to be easy and straightforward?

"OK, Nitzan, let's talk, where do you come from?"

"I was born in Israel," he replies. "But later I was brought up in Texas, before returning to Israel as a teenager. At the age of twenty-two I embarked on my conscious spiritual path. That's when I first heard about Findhorn—in a book—but it took me another thirteen years before I actually managed to get here."

"Why did you decide to come here?" I ask him. My glass of hot chocolate is empty, and I'm seriously wondering whether to order another one. I need something while I listen to this energetic and very enthusiastic young man.

"I just had a sense that I would come here. And then a friend called me, she had bought a ticket to come here and could not make it. I did not have the money to buy it from her so I gave her some Reiki healing in exchange for the ticket."

I've decided I really do need the second hot chocolate and wave hopefully across at the serving counter while Nitzan continues his story.

"From the first moment I came here I just knew I was Findhorn, but it took me a while to come out of the closet."

"Explain yourself," I ask, almost desperately.

"Because I am very energetic, very creative, very expressive, outgoing and self-assured. I enjoy communicating, frolicking, putting on festivities and doing it all in as heartfelt and joyous a manner as possible. I particularly enjoy communicating in very deep, frolicking ways. I already started madly frolicking when I was in my mother's womb. My mother said she couldn't stop laughing and that it was the happiest time of her life"

I might be tempted to forego my second hot chocolate and escape into the beckoning snow outside were it not for his totally genuine manner, his warm, caring voice and the fact that he is very real. I decide to try and understand this free and joyful spirit in front of me.

"What did you find here, Nitzan?"

"It began in my Experience Week when someone gave me a flower. I was confused at the time about whether I wanted to stay or leave. Then someone gave me a flower and this flower told me all I needed to know, and that I should stay here for a while."

If I were anywhere else, this might be the point where he lost me. But then I remember my own story of how I came here, why I stayed here, and all the other weird and wonderful experiences that I have had, and so I continue listening.

"I found a deeper connection to the many selves that make up Nitzan, to the underlying self. I found my manhood. I found magic. I found an extraterrestrial connection. I found a greater sense of esteem. I found humanity trying to do the best they can. I found many opportunities to be expressive and to infuse with that Nitzan energy and make things lighter."

He takes a quick sip of his coffee and then continues, "I found a greater sense of empowerment and of peace. I found many challenges. Sometimes it felt like stepping onto an obstacle course where I myself had laid out the obstacles, and meeting them face on and pretty much getting through most of the course."

I'm hanging onto my glass, trying to keep up with him and rather wishing I'd bought him a decaf cappuccino!

"I also had some opportunities to heal my sexuality. I communed with some exquisite women. I got to know some wonderful men and was able to learn more about myself from them."

"But, Nitzan, you've only been here a few weeks, how did you find time to do all that?"

He smiles his warm smile, knowing I am doing my best to keep up with him.

"It was only yesterday that I was finally able to slow down. I looked at a little plot of soil and marvelled at the quantity of different kinds of flowers there were in that tiny patch of land. For me Findhorn has not been the place for me to come and seek peace—not the calm kind of peace. It is just a tremendous, intense creative vortex of opportunity to heal and transform and become aware. If you choose to step into that, that's what Findhorn is, but of course you always have the choice. But that is my path."

"And you'll be leaving here soon, what happens next?"

"My vision is to create family entertainment that uplifts and inspires, and connects people to their hearts and souls in as creative and troubadouresque and playful a way as I can. I envision a cross between Hans Christian Andersen and Danny Kay and Robin Williams and Charlie

Chaplin . . . I guess!"

My mind tries to get around how that would manifest itself.

"It's taken me many years to ground myself. I carry with me a tremendous sensitivity that has tapped into a lot of pain and into the trauma of being human. It wasn't until my twenties that I could really sift through that and allow myself to experience and ground all this creative, vibrant energy, so that it doesn't always come out as sparkles but as a graceful flow."

Nitzan's mischievous grin makes me think that the sparkles are still there.

"On the physical level, I will be going to Glastonbury, another magic spot. I feel that I am on a very conscious quest and the Grail beckons. I believe in the old ways of knights, and chivalry, and questing and initiations . . . and of course the magic. I believe in magic."

I'm very glad to hear that!

"Merlin whispers in my ears, Lao Tsu whispers in my ears, St. Francis whispers in my ears, Beings from other dimensions whisper in my ears—the fairies and elves. I want to find my creative family, make magic manifest. I also believe not just in the magic but in the practical ability to manifest, to create magic by adhering to universal principles. I am a visionary, I can have creative mind-storming sessions that last for hours. I am ready for it now to ground and take root and bear tangible fruit."

I take a sip of my hot chocolate and realise it has got cold. I forgot to drink it.

"So, what else do you want to know?"

I'm not sure that I dare answer that. "Perhaps I have got enough for now, Nitzan," I reply.

"Ah, come on, Karin, I was just getting started," he teases.

"No, really, I need to go and think about it all," I insist.

"In that case, why not tell me all about you, what's your story?"

An hour later, now on our third round of hot drinks, we are still sharing stories about our lives in this amazing community. I notice that it has begun to snow again and I really can't resist the temptation to go out and play.

"Here is my camera," I tell Nitzan. "Please come out and take a picture of me. I don't want to forget this day."

Back outside, I let the snowflakes caress my face. Some brave birds looking for food are leaving tiny footprints in the white carpet around me, and the branches of the pine trees are bending under the weight of the snow. No, I don't think I will forget this day.

BURNS NIGHT

I'm feeling very excited about this evening at Cluny—everything seems to be coming together for me tonight. Soon, I will be having the final celebration dinner with the Experience Week group, and afterwards I will get together with Mike Scott who at this moment is driving through the highland mountains in a blizzard. It is also Burns Night tonight—the evening when the famous Scottish poet 'Rabbie' Burns is celebrated all across Scotland, and indeed everywhere in the world where Scots gather together for the occasion.

I arrive at Cluny a little early, which gives me time to have a last look around and visit the Cluny Sanctuary. There are no other shoes in the anteroom, so I know I will be alone. When the community bought Cluny Hill Hotel in 1975, this room was the snooker room with an enormous old wooden snooker table filling almost the entire space. For twenty-six years now this lovely room with its large bay windows has been a Sanctuary where guests and members come together for meditations. I pick up a yellow, cotton blanket by the door and make myself comfortable on one of the golden velvet chairs, wrapping the cosy blanket around me. Closing my eyes, I try to release my thoughts, my memories, of the past ten days here at Findhorn and the anticipation of leaving tomorrow. A difficult task when so much is running around in my head. As my mind stills, I silently thank all the beings—both seen and unseen—who have welcomed me here. My experiences have turned out to be beyond my wildest expectations. Everybody has been happy to share their stories with me, and I smile as I remember that there is even snow outside!

As I leave the Sanctuary, I hear a commotion going on downstairs in the reception area. As I approach the group of people, I realise it is the Experience Week group, laughing, crying, and hugging each other. Two of their members are leaving before dinner to catch a train—Michael and Cynthia need to catch a plane back to the USA. Everybody waits to give them huge hugs, smiling with love and gratitude, tears of joy welling in their eyes—as well as a few tears of regret at the parting. As I watch them from the stairs, it looks like a family wishing bon voyage to loved ones— hard to believe that these people have only known one another for seven days.

The taxi takes them down the drive—everybody is waving until there is nothing left to wave at, just the swirling snow that reflects the lights from the windows. We make our way through the lounge into the dining room.

There is a gap in the group, but there is still much to celebrate.

Friday evening dinner at Cluny—as at the Park—is always a special event. It is the end of the working week, and often the end of workshops and Experience Weeks. Tonight, instead of the many small tables that usually fill this dining room, there are just three large tables laid festively for the various groups dining here. Our table is just on our right as we enter. Janette and Susie, the focalisers of the Week, have decorated our table with red candles, fresh flowers and brightly coloured napkins. There are also a few bottles of wine waiting to be opened.

I greet Anja who is beautifully dressed up for the occasion, having on a long wool dress, so different from the mud stained gardening clothes she wore during the week. Everybody is laughing and chatting as we find our seats and wait for dinner to arrive.

Suddenly, I hear a strange, loud wailing noise and it takes me a moment to recognise the unique drone of bagpipes. I look around the room, expecting to see the Master Piper, and realise with a little disappointment that it is only a recording. I have experienced many Burns Nights, and know that the haggis is traditionally brought in to the sound of the pipes. The kitchen door opens wide and five clapping, cheering cooks appear, the first one bearing a tray on which lies the famous Scottish haggis. Slowly the cooks walk around the dining room, presenting the haggis to the appreciative crowd. One of the cooks, Stewart, is wearing his tartan kilt for the occasion. By now, we are all clapping to the music and cheering on the cooks.

Stewart puts the haggis on a table and, wielding a large knife, ceremoniously cuts it open to reveal the spicy meat and tenderly cooked grains. Burns Night is one of the two days of the year that the 'vegetarian only' rule is broken in the Foundation dining rooms. The other is at Christmas when organically raised turkey is offered, as well as a special vegetarian alternative like roast chestnut pie. Even on this night there is a vegetarian haggis alternative. The traditional haggis is made from minced organ meats and barley, spiced with lots of black pepper and garlic. In my opinion, both the real haggis and the veggie concoction are eminently missable! After Stewart cuts open the haggis, the cooks each pick up a glass of pure malt Scotch that has been thoughtfully poured for them, and with a loud cheer from the waiting diners, they down the fiery liquid.

Before we can eat, there is one more Burns Night tradition called 'saluting the haggis', which includes reciting some of Robbie Burns' most famous poetry. Stewart, wearing his green kilt, is making sure we don't miss anything. As he completes the last stanza, the waiters serve our meal. I have asked for the 'real' haggis and it arrives complete with 'tatties and neeps' (mashed potatoes and bright orange mashed turnips). I look bravely at my plate—the only way I have ever been able to eat haggis is with a liberal amount of ketchup, but I see none around anywhere. Reluctantly, I take a forkful of the grey soggy mixture, and then—surprise—I find it's not as bad as I feared. Another mouthful, this time with a sip of red wine, and I almost find myself enjoying it.

I look around the table and see that my fellow diners, after a cautious start, are also enjoying this unusual fare. There is a lot of animated talk around our table, some people drinking wine, others sipping fruit juices. Some are discussing their experiences during the week, others are exchanging addresses and phone numbers. Janette and Susie look a little tired—focalising the Experience Week is always an intense and emotional experience and tomorrow they will see most of their new friends depart. It is a difficult moment for everyone, to allow the feeling of connection and love to flow while knowing that the next day they must release it again. It is like falling in love and saying goodbye.

A deep and emotional experience has brought these people together; some of them have come to the point of making big changes in their lives. They have opened their hearts to each other and shared deep feelings, fears and joys together.

My path over the past ten days has been more solitary. I have listened to many people and had some very special evenings with friends. I have walked around the community I love, and I have touched in with this group of very special people with whom I am sitting tonight. But nevertheless, I am not quite an insider here; at this table I am a welcome guest. My role is to observe and listen.

"Dessert!" calls someone from the other end of the table.

The main course has been cleared away, and now trays of chocolate mousse with whipped cream have arrived. I may have found the haggis reasonably edible, but this is something I really enjoy.

After finishing dessert, people begin to drift slowly back into the lounge, picking up cups of tea and coffee to take with them. Our group pull up extra chairs around the open fire and make themselves comfortable for an evening of cosy talk and relaxation.

Anja and I find a couple of chairs in the corner and have our final conversation.

"You seem to be enjoying yourself tonight, Anja," I begin. "How does it feel, now that the week is over?"

"Of course, I am a bit sad it's all over and that we will be leaving tomorrow, but that's part of life. And I think I need some time to let it all sink in," she replies.

"What would you say have been the highlights of this week for you?"

"There have been so many things. Perhaps the best has been getting together with this group of people here, they are all so different and all so wonderful, it has been an amazing experience getting to know them all."

We look over at the rest of the group, sitting around the fire and talking quietly together. Then Anja continues, "For me, every person in our group seems surrounded by light now. They all feel happier, brighter and more open. Every day this has got better and better. At our final sharing this afternoon I saw it all again, everybody shining and open. I felt so very happy."

"What do you think did that, Anja?"

It's not easy for her to express herself. I wish I could speak Dutch so she could talk in her native language. But she does her best.

"The spirit of Findhorn. There is a very high energy here, and I think it works on hearts, and love, and opens people up. I think it comes from the universe, and that there are people here who can connect others to this energy. Throughout the week, it felt as if we were being prepared to receive some of this energy."

Anja's English also seems to have improved over the week, she is expressing herself very well.

"Do you think it was important to do this in the Experience Week, or could you have done it on your own?"

"Oh no, I don't think I would have had the same experience if I had just come on my own for a few days. I feel I was led into it. There was no force to get involved in anything, just all my own choice, and I could take as much of it as I could deal with at the moment, I felt this during the whole week. I met a lot of people—on the bus, in Sacred Dance, in the dining room—like you, Karin." We smile at each other. "Every time, something more opened. I feel so very at home here. This afternoon I told the group that for the first time in my life I could be just who I am. That was such a very good feeling. The spirit and energy of this place allowed that to happen, I don't know what it is, but it developed more and more during the week."

She stops for a moment. There is burst of laughter from the people sitting next to us.

"I think that when a group of people are together and you all focus on something, it becomes more—bigger. Like love, like trust."

I think Anja is right, and this is part of the magic here, that most tasks and experiences are created by groups.

"We also are just human beings," she continues, "with all our feelings and problems and emotions. But by sharing these with others, I somehow feel more, better, and the energy seems to go up. Synergy, that's what I experienced here."

"Is there anything else you want to tell me?" I ask.

"You know, Karin, I had not expected the community to be so big. I thought it would be a small group of people living in little wooden huts. And here I am in this big building that used to be a luxury hotel. That was a big surprise for me. There is also no expectation for everyone to behave in the same way, there's a lot of individuality here, so people can express themselves and be who they are."

A woman enters the room and comes over to us. She gives Anja a hug and wishes her well for her departure tomorrow. It seems Anja has also made new friends outside her group.

"I also wanted to tell you how wonderful it was working in the garden, and how much I learned from the group there."

"What did you learn?" I wonder.

"I learned that life in community is based on values. I learned that it is not always happiness and joy but also stress, not feeling well, having doubts, wondering whether to stay or not. There are problems with money. There is anger and frustration, just as anywhere else. It's like, we are all human, just like out there, but what makes it different here is an extra dimension."

Ah, I think to myself, the elusive magic.

"And that's what I want more of in my life. I want to know how to bring that into my life at home. I'd like to share what I have learned with friends there, and perhaps come back some time. So much has happened this week, it all has to sink in. I'm like a battery that has been recharged with energy. Now I want to relax and be happy."

Anja and I give each other a warm hug. I hope I will see her and Jan again one day. I know we will keep in touch. I have her e-mail address, which makes that easy.

I now have one more very important thing to do, just one more person to talk to, someone I have been looking forward to all week. I notice it is already nine o'clock and I wonder when he will arrive. And then at last the door to the lounge opens and, shaking the snow from his clothes, he enters the room.

LOVE & ThUNÐERBOLTS

Into the room walks a slender man wearing a long, black wool coat and hat, his long, dark wavy locks still windblown and wet from the blizzard outside. The room suddenly falls silent as everyone becomes aware of the intensity of energy that has just entered.

He removes his coat, the shoulders still covered with a sprinkling of snow. His red waistcoat and striped trousers testify to an impeccable and creative dress sense. High, fine cheekbones confirm undeniably that here is an artist. The award-winning, accomplished musician and rock star Mike Scott.

Like the passionate words that clothe his music, Mike Scott, the Scottish-born inspirational driving force behind the internationally acclaimed rock/folk band The Waterboys, has a lyrical bearing. This is my first meeting with Mike, although I feel as if I have got to know him through his music. I remember the very last Winter Gathering that I ever focalised in the Universal Hall a number of years ago. This Gathering is a yearly Christmas gift from the Findhorn community to the people of the local area, and I had been producing and presenting it for many years. This particular year we screened a film of Mike singing one of his new songs, "Building A City of Light." I remember the stunned silence in the audience when it was over. Perhaps for the first time some of them realised the immensity of what we were trying to achieve here—Building A City of Light. For me, too, the experience was intense. I could feel Mike's music in my solar plexus, the vibration of the sound and the intensity of the words. And yet over the years I have always missed him when he was in the community—until tonight.

I already know that Mike was born in Edinburgh in 1958, and has also lived in Ireland and New York. He is married to Janette, an ex-member of the Foundation, who happens to be focalising the current Experience Week which I have been following. They now live in London, but also tour all over the world with The Waterboys, whose albums include *This is the Sea, Fisherman's Blues* and *A Rock In The Weary Land*. The album *Bring 'Em All In* was actually recorded in the Universal Hall recording studio.

I also know that Mike is a Findhorn Fellow and has many times given very generously of his time and talent to the community. I am curious how Mike came to be involved here and what his experiences have been. He is sitting in one of the big, comfy armchairs in the Cluny Lounge, beginning to relax after his hazardous drive through the snow and wind. He looks at me expectantly, willing to answer my questions. I take a deep breath. After all the interviews I have held with old and new friends, this one feels very different.

"When did you first hear about Findhorn, Mike?" I begin.

He takes a moment to think, and then in his soft, quiet voice replies, "I remember hearing about the Findhorn Community in the early '80's, reading something about Peter and Eileen. I was immediately impressed. I felt instinctively that these people were authentic, and I sensed a power of love working through them. But I was young at the time, busy with rock and roll, and it didn't occur to me then to come to Findhorn myself."

I am trying to imagine the life of a young rock and roll player; and yet, looking at him now, I see in his clear, watchful eyes that this is no wasted rock star but an intelligent and compassionate man.

"Ten years later, I saw Eileen's video "Opening Doors Within." It hit my life like a thunderbolt. Everything Eileen said about gratitude and unconditional love was what I needed to hear. By the end of the video I knew I would come to Findhorn to live."

"So that is when you first came here?" I ask.

"Yes, two months later I visited the community, staying at Minton House for a few days. Someone took me to Sacred Dance in the Universal Hall on my first night, and I had a love for the Hall from the beginning. For those first few days however, I had a lonely experience—I wasn't in a workshop, I didn't have a role, and the people I saw around the community were absorbed in their own business. I could feel the power of the place, but didn't feel part of it.

"Then, just before I left for Inverness Airport, I went to the Friday lunch-time Sanctuary. The theme was "Network of Light," and a woman led the meditation. With my eyes closed, I heard her invoke the linking up of Findhorn with Iona and Glastonbury and the spreading of the spiritual Light around the world. I'd been doing 'light-visualising' to the world in my prayers for years—probably not very effectively—yet here in this magical

Findhorn Community, people were doing it for real in their lunch hour!"

I sense what is almost a smile crossing his usually serious face, and quietly wait for him to continue.

"I later described this sanctuary experience in a song as "shuddering in the power like a seedling in a storm," and that's exactly what it was like. Wave upon wave of inspiration passed through me. I knew I had come home."

I hear the passion and intensity that the remembrance of this experience has aroused in him.

"How long before you came back?" I ask him.

"Six weeks," he tells me. "I returned for an Experience Week. It was another thunderbolt—or rather a series of thunderbolts. The sharings, the Group Discovery games, the experience of working in the Community, all affected me deeply. During that week, my heart opened. For the first time I knew what those well worn words, 'an open heart,' really mean. I could feel a great living fire inside my chest, centred in my heart, at once familiar, awesome and full of a loving power. It was like all the loves of my life rolled into one. It felt like love was breathing in and out of me through my heart. And it felt absolutely, beautifully right—like how being alive is meant to feel."

His poetic way of telling his story reminds me again that he is an artist with both words and music. He closes his eyes for some moments, recalling the feelings and then speaks again.

"This lasted 8 or 9 days. I wrote a song about the week and sang it during the final sharing. I was surprised and moved to see that the entire group were weeping as I sang it. I'll never forget the atmosphere of love and power in that room. I'd done something with my song I'd never intended. Or rather, 'Someone' had done something with my song—it's called the Experience Week Song—now it is played on CD at the end of each Week. I feel very honoured to have given something back to this workshop that changed my life."

The Experience Week has changed many thousands of lives over the years, and it seems it also happened for Mike. I have heard his song on many occasions, always with shivers going up and down my spine, and know that it reflects the experience of many, many others who have trodden this path.

"I've lost count of the blessings I've received from my connection with the Findhorn Community," he continues. "And they also include the surrounding area with which I've come to be so familiar. Morayshire is a beautiful part of Scotland and Forres is a terrific, no-nonsense town. I love the beauty and neighbourliness of Findhorn Village too, where, regardless of my 'day job' as a rock musician, I've always been welcomed in a normal and undistorted way."

"So how has all this affected your life?" I have the question ready, but almost feel it is unnecessary to ask it now. However, Mike is still willing to continue describing his relationship with the community and the lessons he has learned here.

"The greatest thing I've learned at Findhorn is to turn inside for my answers and life decisions, and in my moment to moment actions. After my Experience Week, I realised I'd been using the principle of 'Guidance' in my music for years—intuitively sensing where to take a melody line or a lyric, for example. I could tell if something in the music was right or not. I just 'knew.' After Findhorn, I started learning to apply this to the other parts of my life. I'm still learning it. I've found that my inner instruction usually comes in the form of intuitive promptings—what I call a 'go feeling,' a kind of unmistakable green light of the gut that has a sense of peace and potency in it."

Janette is sitting at the other end of the room, still talking with those members of her Experience Week group who have managed to stay awake after this energetic and emotional final evening. Her sparkling eyes and smiling face don't show that she, too, probably soon needs to "switch off" from the intensity of it all. Mike follows my glance over to his wife.

"How did you meet Janette, Mike? It was here at Cluny, wasn't it?"

A slow, warm smile lights up his face. I know that Mike is a very private person and hope he will be willing to share some of this love story with me.

"Janette was a Foundation Member living at Cluny when I was a "Living in Community Guest." We didn't know each other personally, but she'd led a Sacred Dance evening I'd attended, and I started to like her a whole lot. I felt she might be my life partner and co-worker. I remember wondering if it was all a projection or illusion on my part, so I decided to offer it up to God. I sat down in my little room at Cluny and said inwardly, 'I give all these feelings of love for Janette to you, God.' At that exact moment I heard her talking to someone right outside my door!"

The smile continues as he recalls his surprise. "I figured God gave that one back to me pretty fast so there must be something in it! So I left her a note on the Cluny message board asking to have a chat, and remember a mystified Janette coming into the kitchen next morning to ask if the note was from me."

"Was she surprised, or did she know what you were about to say?" I ask him.

"She had no idea what it was about—in fact she wondered if she'd unwittingly offended this man she didn't know, and that perhaps he wanted to give her some feedback! Anyway, she graciously agreed to have a chat and we went for a drink at the Ramnee Hotel in Forres that evening, and I declared myself. She was completely surprised and told me she hadn't thought of me in that way."

Now it's my turn to smile as I think of the surprise and shock that Janette must have felt. Then Mike tells me the rest of the story.

"But a few days later she stopped me in the Cluny corridor and suggested we meet again. The rest is a tale of love and fabulous magic. I was right—Janette became my wife, best friend and spiritual partner. I've understood so much from her and from being with her. I couldn't do what I do in my musical work or be where I am in myself without her love and influence."

Just a few steps away, still giving and sharing herself with her group, is the beautiful lady in person. I know that Mike, too, has been giving much of himself to this place, so I ask him about it.

"You give a lot of yourself—your time and your talent —to the community. Why do you do this?" As always, he listens carefully and intently to my question, then thinks deeply before he answers.

"I love the Findhorn Community. I see it as a high and great endeavour of the human spirit, a birthing ground for a new way of living, so new that the mainstream world still has no frame of reference for it. I'm committed to the Community. And I'm in love with it!"

I nod my head in agreement. Mike takes another moment to reflect on my question before continuing. "I feel that when the Beatles and other movers and shakers of the Sixties were navigating their way through fame and illusion, Peter, Eileen, Dorothy and the builders of the Findhorn Community were quietly and obscurely living and grounding the New Age ideals that everyone else just talked about. I believe theirs was actually the greatest adventure of those times. And it continues right now. I feel it falls to those of us who share or have been inspired by their vision to carry on building what they began. Anything I can give here, I will."

We are all beginning to feel very tired: Mike, after his long drive up here in the snow; Janette at the end of her week with a group of new guests; and myself too. I realise with a shock that in just a few hours I will be leaving here. This is my last night at Findhorn, and Mike is the last person I am interviewing—I'm sure this is no coincidence. I have just one more question for him.

"Is everything wonderful here, Mike, or do you still have some challenges in this spiritual life you are living?"

"Yes, it is a challenge to remember to turn within and live from my place of peace and potency. That's a minute-to-minute challenge for me. It means to be open and vulnerable when that's what needs to happen, to speak my truth when that needs to happen, and not to retreat into my 'little man' ways; an old habit of mine is to lessen myself by not being all that I can be, by not speaking what I know or feel. And on the other hand, it's also a challenge to be the 'Big Me' without getting carried away by power or momentum. I need to find the balance. I desire to be all that I can be— lightly. To maintain and protect my open heart—especially when I am out of the Community—without closing it down under a defensive wall."

He brushes his long hair out of his eyes and continues slowly and thoughtfully, "Part of my role is to walk between the worlds—the new world of the Findhorn Community and the mainstream world outside— helping direct the energies of each appropriately to the other. And to learn that, in God's eyes, both are one, that there is truly no separation, and to manifest this in action."

The flames in the fireplace have died down to a flicker and the lounge is becoming quiet as the last few people make their way sleepily to their beds. It has been another amazing day, filled with many miraculous moments. I watch Mike and Janette, their hands touching lightly as they leave to go home in the snow.

I call a taxi to take me back to the Park. The driver drops me on the Runway a few paces from my B & B, but before starting to walk across the snowy Field of Dreams I hear the strains of bagpipes coming from the Community Centre. Peering in at the window, I see that there is a Ceilidh — a very typical Scottish celebration of music, poetry and dance. I watch the dancing for a few minutes—the men in their swirling kilts and the ladies dressed in their finest—I think it must be Jonathan Caddy calling the dances as usual. I recognise the familiar tunes of The Gay Gordons, Strip the Willow, Mairi's Wedding and The Piper O'Dundee. This is the community at play.

I leave the energetic dancers and return to my little home in Sunflower. The snow has stopped falling, and the stars lighting my way over the slippery paths seem brighter than ever. Going home tomorrow. Or is that leaving home? Perhaps a bit of both.

Leaving home,
going home

Early one morning

The woman quietly rises from her bed and checks the clock—it is 4:00 a.m. She does not need an alarm—after so many years, her inner clock automatically wakes her at four in the morning. Outside, the snow is a white, icy blanket, reflecting the light of the moon, but inside, the house is warm—the heating has been on all night.

In the bathroom, she fills the bath with hot water until steam fogs up the mirrors and window. She slides carefully into the bath, letting the heat warm her body. Getting up so early never seems to get any easier, and now in her mid eighties it takes more time for her to move into the day.

She dresses warmly, and even at this early hour her clothes are co-ordinated and attractive—a royal blue silk blouse with lighter blue trousers, and a navy wool jacket to keep her warm. She sits at her dressing table, applying make-up and styling her hair while waiting for the kettle to boil. She pours herself a cup of hot tea and eats a light breakfast—that's all she needs before leaving the house. She glances at the clock—it is 6:00 a.m.

Wrapping herself in a warm coat, she walks the few yards to the Sanctuary. Hers are the first footsteps in the newly fallen snow and everything around her is totally silent. The Community Centre opposite her house is empty, and she seems

to be the only person about at this time on a winter's morning. On the way to the
Sanctuary she passes the caravan she lived in forty years earlier—the caravan she
used to leave at the same time every morning for the same purpose as today—to
listen to her still small voice, the voice she recognises as God's words.

Even at this early hour she is not the first one in the Sanctuary. Her "little
angel," a small, smiling Japanese woman, has opened the curtains, turned up the
heating and lit the candle in the centre, which casts soft light into the room. The
two women smile at each other—they are very grateful for one another's presence.

∞∞∞∞

For the next half hour these two women sit with their eyes closed in
silent meditation, each with her own intimate, inner experience. And then
there are small sounds from outside, more footsteps in the snow, the
creaking of floorboards, and a soft cough. One by one, other people are
arriving to join the meditation.

For Eileen, this has been a daily ritual for forty years. For me, it is the
first time I have joined in this very early morning time of silent
contemplation. The only sound comes from the breath of the dozen people
now in this room. I slide softly into nothingness and for a while there are
no thoughts and no feelings.

Perhaps an hour later, I become aware once more of my body sitting
heavily on the chair. I feel wet tears rolling down my cheeks; from where
they came, I don't know. I feel only an inner peace.

And then I am back outside, in the deep velvet darkness of the hour
before dawn, making my way back to my home, to Sunflower. Time to go
and pack, to get ready to leave, to say all my farewells. Time to reflect on
my experiences, to search through my memories and discover if I have
fulfilled my quest. I'll have plenty of time to do that on my flight back to
France. Now I want to enjoy my last few hours here. I notice that the snow
is already beginning to melt. What a wonderful gift the snow has been—
just enough to have fun with but not enough to make my return trip a
problem.

The next few hours are a blur of goodbyes and "see you again soons."
Of warm hugs, a few tears, and many last-minute photographs. And then
my dear friend Judi arrives to take me to the airport. We drive in the
opposite direction along the same route we travelled ten days earlier, and
this time there is grey, shovelled snow banked along the sides of the road.
We pass through the small towns of Forres and Nairn and then, on the

outskirts of Inverness, we turn right towards the airport. The sea looks just as grey as the day I arrived, but the fields surrounding the tiny airport are now white. The flight back should be beautiful, over the Highlands in the snow.

I give Judi a big hug, hoping she'll come and see us in France soon.

"So, did it happen?" she asks. "Did you find the magic?"

"What do you think?" I reply with a secret smile. Then I walk through the security gate and board my flight, finding a seat by myself to sit quietly and begin the task of remembering.

Tbe way bome

I close my eyes, and see all the faces I have just left behind—friends I have known for many years and others whom I have just met. I am filled by the many moving and sublime experiences I have had—both those on the inner and on the outer. How can I possibly describe in words something so indescribable?

I recall someone's words, though I don't remember who said them: "Findhorn is an incredible awakening to just how beautiful it is to exist, the intensity of wonder and discovery."

That is how I feel now—this time at Findhorn has re-awakened wonder in me. After the initial amazing explosion of experience and discovery when I first came to Findhorn twenty-seven years ago, I actually got used to living like that. It is only since leaving that I have realised the gift of grace that was my life there.

I hear again: "The true value is in what it has done for my experience of reality and the wonderful quality it has added to my life." I see again the faces of the people at the Internal Conference, the intense listening, the trust in each other, the willingness to change, the tangible feeling of love in the room. I wonder if these people even realised what they were creating that afternoon? They thought they were trying to create a balanced budget, to find ways to reduce their debt. What I saw was a room full of people wanting to serve God and Humanity. I saw that in Mari who is willing to risk taking on the mantle of the Foundation at this time, and I saw it in a very new member who stood up and offered to work longer hours and take fewer holidays. And I felt it again when we all held hands and sang together, realising that what really mattered was the love we were sharing at that moment.

I emerge from my thoughts to see that Priscilla from the Experience Week and Dido from the Eco-Women's Gathering are sitting across the aisle from me. They are talking animatedly, sharing their experiences of the past week. They invite me to join their conversation but I choose to stay with my own thoughts and put on my earphones to listen to the Taizé CD I bought in the Phoenix earlier this morning.

The music takes me back to Sunday morning in the Universal Hall when Geoffrey was leading us in the singing. I try to remember some of the things that he told me later: "I tend to be more with the people who are new here, because that's often where the joy is." Looking across at the two women near me who are sharing what being at Findhorn has meant to them, I understand what he meant. Geoffrey also managed to find the same joy in washing dishes, preparing financial reports and taking young people sailing. He is a special kind of person.

Of course! I suddenly remember! That's what everybody told me—"It's the people." But surely not just the new people? Everybody was new at some point, and the magic, the specialness, it doesn't leave them when they stay longer, does it? Surely it includes the people who have been there a long time; people like Alan, and Judy, and Rosie and Geoffrey . . . and Eileen. They are all very special.

I pause for a moment, as something else occurs to me.

They are all ordinary. Just ordinary people. That's what is so special about them, they are ordinary people who are willing to do extraordinary work. And every one of them—like me—arrived because in some way they were 'called'. Each one called in a way that they could hear. I was called to have my son there. Thierry, my husband, was called through the Game of Transformation. He has told me that if he had read *The Findhorn Garden*, he would never have come, it was just not his thing.

Brian was called by a Ouija board—and then found out that he was even expected. Merv was called by a book that fell at his feet. Javier was called by the beauty of the landscape, and John was called by the British Consul who told him he was actually British as well as American. Robin was given a leaflet by his homeopath, and Kay Kay had a catalogue, which she didn't know she had, fall off her desk.

Even Peter and Eileen originally came to the Findhorn Bay Caravan Park with their little green caravan, not because they had—at that time— a great vision of a community or a City of Light, but because they were out of work and had nowhere else to live. They were the first to listen to the call to come to Findhorn and they have been followed by thousands upon thousands of others. Each called in a way that allowed, or in some cases forced them, to listen.

I take some moments to let this land in me. The flight attendant is bringing around tea and coffee and some limp looking sandwiches. Perhaps I'll pass on those, though of course I welcome the hot tea.

I relax into my thoughts again and try to remember what all these people found when they arrived in Findhorn, how they experienced the magic.

Brian found his magic in discovering just how beautiful life really was, and in his first communications with the nature spirits. For Margo, it was finding a place where the spiritual values she yearned for were practised daily. John found his dream of building an eco-village, while Geoffrey saw a very diverse community where all beliefs and spiritual practices were accepted. Alex found a group of pleasant, interesting people who seemed to have invented an absurd spirituality as an excuse to live together, and Joycelin was happy to find a place where it was not only all right to talk about God and spirit, but was encouraged and expected to be part of daily life.

Lyle came to build the Universal Hall in three months and found it took more than ten years, and Karl and Deborah found that Findhorn was exactly the right home for them and their young family, even though they'd resisted the idea and looked everywhere else instead. Anja found a garden where she could experience the joy of getting her hands in the soil, and Michael made friends with a whole host of Angels and even learned the difference between Sai Baba and Ali Baba!

But what I heard over and over again, and what was also my experience, was the feeling of "coming home." Almost everyone I spoke to felt like that. There is a moment, usually in the first few days after arriving, when each person is enfolded by an intense feeling of having found their spiritual home. For many it also becomes their physical home, but it's true even for the hundreds of thousands who have visited Findhorn for only a week or a month, that almost all take that feeling away with them. Here, on a windswept peninsula in the north of Scotland, there is a small community that has changed their lives, and will, on some level, always feel like home.

The drone of the aeroplane engines and a message coming over the loudspeaker brings my attention back to my surroundings: "This is a non-smoking flight, and anyone caught smoking in the toilets will be asked to leave the plane immediately," I hear Deborah, the flight attendant, tell us.

There is a ripple of laughter from the passengers, and then I resume my contemplations.

Another word I have often heard these last few days is 'service'. Almost everyone I spoke to has told me at one point that they had come here to serve. I remember Judy telling me many years ago, "If you come here to serve yourself, to transform yourself, it may or may not happen, but if you come to serve God and the Planet, then your own transformation is guaranteed." I believe that people who come to Findhorn only to serve themselves don't stay very long, the intensity of the energy there is too strong for them.

I think about my heroes and heroines, the people who have given themselves to serve the planet, humanity and God. Of course the first person who comes into my mind is Eileen, who continues to hold the spiritual anchor of the community, who for fifty years has been obedient to her still small voice within. Eileen's first commitment has always been to Spirit, love, God, and seeing the highest in everyone she meets.

I also think of Alan, who made his commitment to heal the planet and whose resolve nothing has shaken. He has persevered in making his dream come true and his enormous love is in every tree that he has planted. And there is the other Alan, who loves Findhorn and reached out to Nepal to share his gifts with less fortunate people. I must include Karl and Deborah in my special list of world servers. Without complaint they changed their mind and decided to build a house, not just for themselves, but as a model of what is possible for the planet.

And John, whose perseverance built first a windmill and then, as his vision grew, created an eco-village. Shin who came to Findhorn from Japan, played his music for us, and then took the magic of Findhorn back to his homeland. Anna, living in her little wooden bungalow in Pineridge, who brought the transforming energy of Sacred Dance into the community. And in any list of heroines I must include Mo, the woman who likes to say, "Yes."

There are also other, less visible people who are my heroes. Like Klaas who has been faithfully caring for and driving our buses for longer than I care to remember, and Rosie who takes the Findhorn energy out into the world, where people tell her that Findhorn is a beacon of hope for the Earth.

So many heroes and heroines have been part of the evolution of Findhorn and so many are there now, holding the energy and building on the magic. So is it the people who are the magic, or is the magic something that happens to them when they come here?

Another little 'Ah ha' has me searching for my notes, which are in my luggage in the locker above my head. These lockers are surely built for people over 6 feet tall, not short 5' 2" people like me. I manage to drag my bag down and find the pages I am looking for.

"There was something here long before we arrived, an energy in the land," I read and, "I think the veils are very thin here," says someone else. "The power and magic were here before us, it's what drew us here," says another. I remember that Marko Pogačnik describes how that may have been seeded in his book *The Daughter of Gaia*. It appears that a lot of people feel that the magic has been here for a long time, and it was this that drew the people here originally. People, whose vibratory levels fit in with the energy here, were called and are still called to come here to transform the planet and themselves.

I sift quickly through my notes, and begin to notice a thread running through each conversation: "The people meditate, and serve, and transform and hold this vibratory level, which in turn allows others to hear the call and come to Findhorn to do the same work." And then I find a quote of Judi's who said, ". . . Then they think of a lot of good reasons why they are here, but the reason they are really here, why they fit in, is because their vibrations harmonise with it."

One of my pages has fallen into the aisle and, as I pick it up, I see it is a page from Julia's interview. "I think people are transformed by the energy and the atmosphere of this place. Something happens to them when they come here. It's part of the willingness that people themselves bring, wanting something to happen, and here the terrain is propitious, so then it happens."

So according to Julia, the energy is already here, and the people bring their willingness to be transformed by it. Then I see something else she said. "It definitely doesn't have anything to do with us, it must be something above and beyond what we do or say."

All these thoughts and questions are running around in my mind. I am hoping to find one clear and sure answer, but the more I think, the less I seem to be sure of anything.

Deborah, the flight attendant, is still amusing the passengers with witty chat and telling us that we will be landing in Carcassone in twenty minutes. I better start thinking again, fast.

I remember something else. Almost everyone I spoke to said, "I can be who I really am," or "I have found a place where I can be myself." Robin told me about his experience in India, when he made a list of all the things he thought he was, and then released them. And yes, I too feel I could be who I really am at Findhorn. I could be the sometimes outrageous and extrovert personality that I play with, and I could also freely talk about and live the spiritual being that I know I really am. There are no limits to who I really am, and I know that this is just as true of everybody else. Not just in Findhorn, but everywhere. However, at Findhorn it is accepted, spoken about, trusted and encouraged. Out there in the world I am about to return to, it's more challenging, and much easier to forget who I really am.

"Please fasten your seat belts. If you don't, the captain will be very cross with you." Deborah is still making everyone laugh. I look out of the window to see the old city of Carcassone below me.

I just have time to quickly reflect once more about the amazing, complex, wonderful and challenging place I have left behind. How did the people I spoke to describe living there? "It's like winning the spiritual lottery!" said Michael. Alex describes it differently. "Whatever the magic of Findhorn is, it is a process of continual effort, not just the day-to-day work, but also of spiritual learning."

As the plane comes in to land, I think of Julia, that dear lady oozing love and enthusiasm. "When things get tough, I always need to remind myself that here I get to live in Paradise—with all the difficulties and challenges of Paradise—but nevertheless, Paradise."

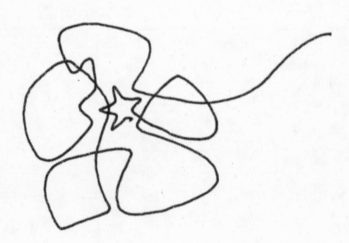

The Magic Finds Me

Another Conversation with God

It is spring in the south of France. The yellow daffodils have come and gone and there are now more exotic flowers in the Friday morning flower market. The leaves are already a pale green halo on the trees and the longer days are returning. I can feel the warm sun through the window as I sit in front of the computer. My computer, a pure white iMac called "Peace," and I have become very close over these past few months since I returned from Findhorn. Together we have shared the story of this book, and slowly but surely have seen it come together. For me, there have been laughter and tears, and frustration and tiredness, and even a few sleepless nights. For "Peace," it has been an endless daily ritual of "save," "new document," and "spelling and grammar check."

Today it feels almost over. The champagne is on ice; I am ready to send the manuscript over to Carly in Santa Fe to weave her special magic before Tony begins the final edit. I feel there is one more thing I need to do. Just one more conversation with the special Friend who sent me the snow. This time, it won't take place in the Universal Sanctuary in The Park, and it is unlikely that another book will fall at my feet telling me exactly what to do. Today, I make myself comfortable in the room I call my 'boudoir', my own special room in our home, and wonder if it will happen again.

Once more, the most difficult part is knowing how to begin this conversation.

"So, what do You think? Have I done it?" I ask tentatively.

I hold my breath, hoping for something—anything—to happen.

"Of course, you've worked really hard."

What a relief, there really is someone there.

"You listened, that was very important. And you resisted trying to interpret it all, you let people speak for themselves. That was good."

"Thank You. And thank You for the snow. That was so special, I've got some lovely photos of myself laughing and playing," I say gleefully.

"I'm glad you enjoyed the snow. Luckily it was due to come anyway."

"What do You think of the book, does it truthfully reflect my experience at Findhorn?" I ask.

"Yes, of course it does, how could it do otherwise? A different person would have seen it, and written it, very differently. You had your experience, you saw it your way and that is just perfect."

"Will it do what I set out to do—inspire people and tell them about the magic there?" I wonder.

"Wasn't it you who said, 'Those who are called will find the book and read it?' It's not something you need to worry about. You have done what you were called to do, you followed your inner voice and completed your task. Now let it be, release it to others to do what needs to be done."

"That's going to be hard, it feels like my baby. I keep thinking that if I only had a few more months with it, I could make it so much better."

"Don't you know why you had to do it all so quickly?"

"Aren't You going to tell me?" I tease God.

"To stop you thinking too much. So you had to follow your intuition and instinct, and just go for it. So you didn't lose faith in the middle. It's worked, hasn't it?" God replies, ignoring my sarcasm.

"Yes, it has," I say with grateful relief. "This morning I wrote the last chapter."

"No, you haven't!"

He/She/It's voice resonates a little like far-off thunder—sounding a bit like I imagine God sounded to Moses during the Ten Commandments episode.

I feel so stunned that for a moment I forget to breathe.

"I haven't? What do You mean? This is what this is all about, right now. I wanted to say thank You for Your help, and it's all done now," I say desperately.

I feel as if a gentle, loving mantle is enfolding me, and then I hear the words.

"Just one more little step, Karin. I've kept this for last because I didn't want you to be distracted by it. You needed all that work, all that searching in order to be ready to hear the next part. The part about the magic."

"But . . . I thought it was all done. I thought I had found all the magic already."

"You did. But there is one more piece of the puzzle I want to share with you. Searching for the magic of Findhorn is like climbing a mountain; every time you think you have got to the summit, you find there is another one waiting to be discovered."

"So what do I have to do to complete this journey?" I ask.

"Wait. It won't take long, you'll find the answer will come to you very soon. Take a day off, drink another cup of tea, enjoy the sunshine."

"Will You help me find it?" I ask hopefully.

"Remember the snow?"

I sincerely hope it will not take long for me to receive the last piece of my puzzle—the deadline for delivering the manuscript is coming up, very soon.

THE FINAL DOOR OPENS

The next few days were an exercise in trust and patience. I also had time to clean the house again, water the plants and have conversations with my husband. I hardly looked at my computer and slept well at night. Until, about a week later, I woke up in the middle of a bright and moonlit night, knowing that it had arrived.

As in a dream, I saw a huge, pulsating light. It felt like something alive and organic and I watched it grow before my eyes, getting brighter and more intense every second. I felt myself drawn as if to a magnet. For a moment I thought that I was dying, it felt so much like the many near death stories I had heard. There was no fear, just a warm, welcoming energy that drew me closer and closer. Then, with a shock, I realised that I was not approaching the light from the outside, but that I was on the inside of a doorway of light, looking out. The nearer I came to the light, the happier I became. It felt like a thousand blessings were being beamed at me.

And then the blessings became words and I knew that I could write them down. I quietly left my bed and went over to my desk. I switched on "Peace" and began writing. The words poured out of me and I had no time to think as my fingers flew over the keyboard. Here is what I read when I had finished typing:

Findhorn is not home, but it is, for the many who are called there, a doorway, a gate, a Star Portal to their home. The pulsating, enormous light that I saw is this Portal.

Our lives, in all their ordinary day-to-day-activities, are nothing less than a journey home. Shortly after I arrived at Findhorn, twenty-seven years ago, at the perfect time in my own spiritual evolution, I found my Star Portal and walked through it. I didn't know what it was at the time, I just knew that suddenly everything was different.

Now, all the things I had heard from so many people at Findhorn in January made sense—especially why people seemed to find the energy and magic at its most intense at the beginning. This is the time when they discover the Portal, when they walk into that loving, blessed light and are changed. The light is irresistible to the pilgrim and the searcher. That is why I felt it again so strongly when I was there, because I was looking for it. Because I found it again.

Living at Findhorn means living with the doorway, getting used to its brilliance and intensity and strength. It's an intense and challenging life. Findhorn has been prepared as a Star Portal since Earth was formed. For millions of years this Portal has been waiting to be activated, waiting for the Beings that will walk through it on their journey home.

Some people walk through the Portal and move on with their lives. The changes in them may even lie dormant for a while. For others, the experience is totally life changing and they move out into the world and serve the planet in very significant ways. Many others decide to stay at Findhorn and hold the energy there. These are the guardians of the Portal. Many generations of guardians and servers have kept the Portal vibrant and glowing and open.

Findhorn will continue to be a sacred place, and the Star Portal will be clear and bright as long as there are guardians willing to energise it. Some will do this through meditation and prayer, others by communicating with the nature kingdoms, and those who can will speak with Angels.

Sometimes fear stops certain individuals from going through the Portal. Sometimes it is just wrong timing. But for everyone who is called, the Portal will open, and the choice to move through it will be presented to them.

Not everyone who passes through Findhorn walks through the Portal. Some see it in the distance but choose not to enter. Some are frightened by the light. But most people who are called or drawn to Findhorn are ready to make the leap, sometimes trembling, sometimes with slow and tentative steps. But always, when it happens, they are filled with joy and peace; this is a journey of delight, into light. It takes courage and often hard work to prepare for the journey through the Star Portal. Like an astronaut, the preparation and study can take a long time. Begin with a first step and, for each one that takes the step, there is a moment of grace when everything will be made clear.

The first step may be that vulnerable moment in the Experience Week when a person first opens their heart to share themselves with a group of people. Or it may be that moment in the garden, when touching a plant suddenly feels "different," when they feel the energy behind the form. For me, it happened that moment twenty-seven years ago, sitting in the little theatre watching the audio-visual "Love Is," when the knowing, the experience, came to me. I really did know what love is. I had walked through the Star Portal into a different reality and nothing was ever the same again.

What happens after someone has walked through the Portal? For some it is immediately apparent, for others it takes longer to reveal itself. But once it has happened, there can be no going back, the Portal only goes one way. When you have moved through the Portal, everything can suddenly feel different. Fear begins to lose its power. The urge to serve becomes irresistible, and unconditional love becomes the goal.

The way to recognise people who have walked through the Portal is often by their magnetic power; others are drawn to them. They may be leaders and teachers. But often they are very ordinary, simple people, perhaps working in the garden or polishing the floor. But their energy belies their ordinariness. They seem to radiate love, acceptance, compassion and forgiveness, and they demonstrate who they are by their actions.

Many of these people are still at Findhorn, but thousands are now living and working throughout the world. I know many of these dedicated, caring and loving people in Australia, New Zealand, North and South America, Europe, South Africa, Japan and every corner of the Earth. They are consciously working to bring more love and peace into the world.

There are also many, many other Portals around the world. Findhorn is the one my vibrations harmonise with. When I want or need a glimpse of home, I go there and find my brothers and sisters.

And then what? After the exhilaration and excitement of walking through the Star Portal, what happens then?

The answer is simple. We pick up our mop and bucket and continue living. Our attitudes and values change, and our ability to love and forgive are expanded and continue to grow. Walking through the Star Portal is not an end, it is another beginning. The beginning of reality when mysteries become known and we discover who we really are. We live on the Earth, but we are not of the Earth. Our essence is of Spirit, and this is where our journey is leading us. It takes courage and commitment to follow our star, the way through our Star Portal, the portal to our soul and to God.

Beziers, April 2002.

THE ANGEL OF FINDHORN

POSTSCRIPTUM

A LETTER FROM ANJA

Middelburg, 27 February 2002.

Dear Karin

Thank you so much for your letter, I was so happy and surprised to hear from you, like a little present. My husband Jan and I have often wondered how you were doing, how the book was coming along. I found it very special to meet and speak to you, sharing my Findhorn experiences, talking about our lives, personally as well as in our experience group. Can I share with you now what has happened for me since I left Findhorn?

It was still snowing on the morning we left Cluny Hill College. As we drove through the Scottish moors and mountains everything was covered with snow, it was a beautiful sight, reflecting just what we were feeling inside. We played the tape of Findhorn music, joyfully singing along with the songs, sharing our experiences and feelings and sometimes silently thinking our own thoughts. Wales was lovely, we walked a lot and rested before driving home to Holland. And Findhorn was still close to us.

It began in Wales, but even more so when we returned to Holland. I was off balance. I began to feel homesick for Findhorn. Those days at Findhorn were intensely in my mind. I wanted to be there. It was such a shock. I had felt so good when we left, and now suddenly I felt restless and could not settle into my life. I knew that in Findhorn, for the first time in my life I felt complete. I felt totally at home.

I was so very happy that I had found somewhere a place where people lived the way I want to. I felt so lucky that I didn't mind having to leave. I thought I could take Findhorn with me. It would be within myself. And now this wonderful feeling was gone. . . I began to feel disturbed, uncertain. I didn't feel at all happy anymore. What was this all about?

I tried to face my feelings without struggling. Just face them and see what was happening. What I realised is that I want to live like that too, like people do in Findhorn. I want to be with others sharing a spiritual life and practicing it in day to day living. I want to discover and explore more. But what can I do right now? The answer is not to go to Findhorn immediately. The best thing for me at this moment is to live in the present. Not to try and rush into what I really want.

Jan and I have talked a lot, and he does not feel as I do right now. We have discussed what it would be like to live at Findhorn. What would we do there? What would that choice mean to our lives? To our relatives, friends, work and, most of all, to ourselves? And what was Findhorn all about? Was this a real feeling, just after one week? Perhaps it would be possible to develop those valuable things we touched in ourselves at Findhorn, and bring them in our lives, into our own world right here? We don't know the answers yet.

So, we have decided to return to Findhorn to experience some more. We have booked to go there for a week in July to participate in a Spiritual Practice week. We'll see how that works out.

At the moment I feel stronger again. I don't know what the future will bring. I try to live day by day. Findhorn is still very present in our lives. Jan and I tune in, we share and check in with each other. And, what is very new for us, we meditate together now and then. In everything I do, I also tune in before starting, and I try to work with attention.

I learned a lot about myself during the time we were in Findhorn, and the learning continues now in my daily life. I will write and tell you more about this and about how we are getting on as things develop.

I'm so glad that we are keeping in touch and allowing our friendship to grow. Jan managed to find some books about Findhorn in the local library, so I read them with him again. It's nice to read them now, after we have been to Findhorn, they mean even more to us now. In the books we are with Findhorn again.

Much love Anja and also from Jan.

A LETTER FROM WAYNE

Dear Karin,

Thanks for your inquiry. I had a tremendous time at Findhorn and I will try and tell you how it has settled in for me. But first, I want to say that my Findhorn experience fulfilled and surpassed every expectation I had about community. I have never lived in community, yet I've always had an innate interest in the concept. My common sense resents transporting myself all over town daily to do and see and visit all of the responsibilities and places and people that are important to me—who came up with this plan?

Walking, working, eating, politicking, volunteering, meditating and entertaining within a wide but familiar group of "people with intention" is as calming and supporting as it is exhilarating and challenging. I don't know where else on the planet there is a place so formed around spiritual values and human sensibilities (if I may separate the two for a moment)—but it should be everywhere. I feel I was in an environment completely committed to acceptance, individual freedom of thought, and spiritual exploration. I moved seamlessly into attunement and check-ins and I found the experiences sweet, vulnerable, empowering and, above all, respectful of every person. Actively extending this respect to all creatures, beings and energies—to all creation—is a sacredness I will not attempt to describe.

Now for some quick specifics:

It speaks volumes to me that when I was done with my two weeks at Findhorn, I was still glad to be there and also happy to go home. I had a strong sense of completion (not an end) of something in me that would stay with me. I felt connected to both Findhorn and home with the same deep belonging.

My spiritual practice has blossomed. I have been meditating sporadically for almost twenty years, but a circumstance exactly one year prior to my Findhorn visit stopped me meditating altogether. In recent months I had started again but only for 10 minutes a day. At Findhorn, it was suddenly easy for me to meditate. By the end of my stay, my daily meditation was over two hours and I am ecstatic to say I have been able to sustain this routine at home with the same ease and open heart. I feel that Findhorn gave me a spiritual second wind that is accelerating.

At home, I am getting a consistent and curious response from the people that know me. Instead of the typical vacation comments, "You look rested", or, "Nice tan", my friends and family have been telling me that I seem "changed." (Thankfully, they say this in a soft, curious, and pleased way.)

Synchronicity in my life is increasing. Angels have never meant anything to me, but I have been noticing a rich and unfolding realm of synchronicity around my Experience Week Angel of Communication. My study of Tarot has taken off, inspired by a book that Skye at Findhorn recommended. I am coming in contact with a lot of 'threes' at this time. I think Tarot is highlighting a synchronicity to body-mind-sprit. I was talking to someone the other day and I realized that Eileen Caddy, Peter Caddy, and Dorothy Maclean were a trinity. Eileen has a "Live in the Will of the Lord" sensibility (spirit); Peter was the communicator and theorizer around agency, Co-creation and Manifestation (mind); Dorothy was channelling the spirits of the physical world, the forces in plants and minerals and the processes that their energies govern (body).

My main grousing at Findhorn (aside from a shortage of time to do all I wanted to do) was a criticism of some organizational aspects in the Foundation and the programmes it runs. Even though Experience Week is an extraordinarily well conceived and tightly run programme, I thought Spiritual Practice did not have all the relevant information and resources compiled into a ready-to-use structure. In other areas, too, I found it difficult to get what I like to call "primary and comprehensive information." At one point, I was discussing this with someone, however, and their comment has stuck with me—they described the Findhorn environment as "Creative Chaos." The more I consider this, and the more I realize the gifts I have acquired from my Findhorn visit, the more I am grasping the value and potential of that kind of energized, loosely controlled space.

Another comment has come to me that underscores the credibility of free structures. Recently, I heard Meredith Monk speak after one of her performances—she is a composer/choreographer who is as rigorously intellectual as she is intuitively inspired. While talking about her work and the difficulties and joys of her collaboration with a visual artist, Ann Hamilton, she commented that she likes to keep things a little dangerous, artistically, so her work doesn't become static and bland. "After all", she said, "I want my work to be about life and Life energy is messy." That's the world I know, and the world Findhorn honours.

Thank you, Karin, for the opportunity to process my thoughts and reactions in this way. You may feel free to use any of my personal comments in anyway that pleases you. I have no secrets, only mystery—blessed, endless veils of discovery.

Good Luck with your book and maybe we will meet again at Findhorn someday!

Namaste   Wayne

BIBLIOGRAPHY

BOOKS BY EILEEN CADDY

Flight Into Freedom and Beyond (autobiography) (Findhorn Press 2002)
Divinely Ordinary, Divinely Human (Findhorn Press 1999)
God Spoke to Me (Findhorn Press 1971)
Opening Doors Within (Findhorn Press 1987)
The Living Word (Findhorn Press 1977)
Footprints on the Path (Findhorn Press 1976)
The Dawn of Change (Findhorn Press 1979)
The Spirit of Findhorn (Findhorn Press 1977)
Foundations of a Spiritual Community (Findhorn Press 1978)
Waves of Spirit (Findhorn Press 1996)
Choosing to Love (Findhorn Press 1993) with David Earl Platts
Bringing More Love Into Your Life (Findhorn Press 1992) with David
Earl Platts

AUDIO TAPES BY EILEEN CADDY

Loving Unconditionally
The Challenge of Change
Be Still: Meditation for the Child Within
Faith and the Power of Prayer
Why Meditate?

OTHER RELATED TITLES

The Findhorn Garden (Findhorn Press: UK, Europe &
Commonwealth; Harper Collins: rest of the world; 1975) by The Findhorn
Community
Growing People (Pilgrim Guides 2001) by Kay Kay
The Kingdom Within (Findhorn Press 1994) by Alex Walker
Nature Spirits and Elemental Beings (Findhorn Press 1996) by Marko
Pogačnik
Findhorn Flower Essences (Findhorn Press 1997) by Marion Leigh

In Perfect Timing (Findhorn Press 1996) Peter Caddy's autobiography
Simply Build Green (Findhorn Press 1993) by John Talbott
Playful Self Discovery (Findhorn Press 1996) by David Earl Platts
A Pilgrim in Aquarius (Findhorn Press 1996) by David Spangler
To Hear the Angels Sing (Anthroposophic Press) by Dorothy Maclean

OThER FINDhORN PRESS AUDIO TAPES

Communications with the Deva Kingdom (cassette tape) by Dorothy
Maclean
Conversations with Pan (cassette tape) by ROC (R. Ogilvie Crombie)
The Elemental Kingdom (cassette tape) by ROC (R. Ogilvie Crombie)

FINDhORN MUSIC

Homeland (cassette tape) by The New Troubadours
Love Is (cassette tape) by The New Troubadours
Music from the Magic Garden (CD) by Various Artists from Findhorn

*Please note: all of the books, tapes and CDs above
are available from Findhorn Press (findhornpress.com)
except* Growing People *and* To Hear the Angels Sing.

∞∞∞∞

FOR INFORMATION ABOUT MIKE SCOTT, GO TO

www.mikescottwaterboys.com

acknowledgments

karin's

I cannot pretend that this book is anything more than my subjective adventure and experiences during my visit to Findhorn in January 2002, sprinkled with memories and anecdotes. I am extremely grateful to all the people who were willing to talk to me, and I have done my best to report their stories accurately.

I lived in the Findhorn Community for nearly 23 years, from late 1975 until mid-1998. I must thank my son Michael for originally taking me there and my daughter Tamsin for. . . well, for just being the best daughter I could possibly have.

I know that there is far more happening in the community than I have been able to put into one book. To mention everything and to include all the amazing people who live and work there would probably mean several volumes bigger than this book. I can't even say that I am giving a balanced view of the community, I'm not sure that is even possible. During my quest I let myself be guided to meet whoever appeared in front of me and I tried hard not to force anything to happen. I did make some appointments with particular people, but the rest was all serendipity.

I am sorry I did not manage to spend more time with the gardeners; the cold and wind kept me inside most of the time. I regret I was not able to speak to many of the people I tentatively had on my list. Like Richard who is an artist in wood, like Randy and all the other artists who are sharing their gifts in the community, or Marion who has created the Findhorn

Flower Essences. I would have loved to get the views of people living on Erraid, and in Newbold House, and from Earthshare and the Steiner School. I tried my best to get together with May East who has taken Findhorn to the United Nations, but she was busy running the Eco-Feminist group. I wanted to participate in some Sacred Dance and I am still looking for my friend India! For anyone who gets the "taste" of Findhorn from this book, I recommend you look at the Findhorn web site, findhorn.org, where you will find all these people and many many more who are all doing amazing work, many of them quietly in the background.

I would also like to apologise to all the people who so willingly gave me their time, told me their stories and sent me material for the book. In the end I had way too much for one book, and some items have not been included. I am keeping all your contributions, and who knows, there may be other books.

I send a big thanks to Susan, who welcomed me into Sunflower and took care of me with cups of tea and open fires. To all the people who were willing to give their time to talk with me, Katherine, Brian, Julia, Judy, Judi, Javier, Margo and Karin H (almost!). Also to Roger, Geoffrey, Alan J, Joycelin, JT, Karl and Deborah, Viviane, Alex, Dürten, Robin and Kay Kay, Michael H and Hanna. For the people who cooked me meals, Carol and David, Mary and George and of course the Featherstone family, I remember every delicious mouthful. Thanks to Mike Scott for answering all my questions and sending me your music. To Janette and Susie, thank you for bending the rules and letting me come and talk to your group. And to the Experience Week group, thank you for letting me be part of your experience, with a particularly big thank you to Anja and Wayne.

Of course I send much love and thanks to Eileen. And also to Lydia, Mohini and Anita for welcoming me into the kitchen and giving me just the perfect experience I needed. Nitzan, for all your enthusiasm and always being where I needed you, and Pauline for telling me where all our sewage goes to.

I also want to thank all the dear friends from the Findhorn Worldwide Circle who came to Carly's "Gathering" and told their stories. You are all an important part of my life.

A big hug and thanks go to Tony, who edited this book, and who shared many of my adventures with me in our early days at Findhorn.

Without my friend Carly I would not even have attempted to begin writing this book. Just knowing she was by my side, holding me, advising me, and helping me, and then taking my raw material and adding her golden touch to it, was an enormous gift.

The person who probably deserves my deepest thanks is Thierry, my beloved husband and publisher. He sent me off to Findhorn for my research, he gave me the months it took to put all the material together, and trusted me enough when I asked him not to read any of it until it was finally finished. He is truly an amazing man.

No list of thanks would be complete without "my Friend who sent the snow", who was my first inspiration and my last word in this book. What a delightful, humorous, interesting, kind, generous, persistent and most of all surprising Being my Friend is! I look forward to many more conversations in the future.

CARLY'S

At three o'clock in the morning of October 18, 2001 while I was deeply asleep in New Mexico, an e-mail dropped in from an old friend in the South of France. The previous evening, at sunset, I had lit a candle in memory of my mother's birthday. In one of our very last conversations before her death in 1998 she said, "Carly, why don't you write a book, you've had such an interesting life?" Typical of my generation, I grew up hoping for my mother's approval of my many creative and unusual endeavours, rarely finding it—she definitely frowned when I joined a little-known community in the far north of Scotland! Nearly thirty years later, her words conveyed the support and understanding she truly felt, and healed a wound in my psyche.

So, that morning, I quickly checked my e-mail before leaving for the school where I work, and was intrigued by one with "Is this for you?" in the subject line from karin@findhornpress.com

> Next year is Findhorn's 40th birthday. Findhorn Press wants to publish a book (about) "The Magic of Findhorn," different of course, and not a "history of" or even a description of Findhorn, but something with feeling and magic in it. We have asked various authors . . . nobody has the time . . . but the book is still 'out there' somewhere waiting to be written and published. A couple of days ago, I had a very strong impulse that I could write the book myself. I would go to Findhorn for a few weeks in search of the magic . . . an exciting adventure, a quest for magic. Does it still exist? Where is it? And what is it?

However, I am not an author—or even a writer—although I can tell a story. What I would need is a co-writer . . . and I thought of you—someone to share the journey with from conception to launch of book. I would go to Findhorn, I would have the experience . . . I would send it all to you and you would put it together. Do you have the interest and the time? Is this for you?

Now start breathing again, and let me know what you think? And feel? Much love, Karin.

I have taken many deep breaths while working on this book with Karin. I swam under water a few times, and we've thrown life jackets to one another across the miles. Now, it's here, and I am immensely grateful to Karin for the original opportunity, for her generous heart, unflagging energy, adventurous spirit and wonderful sense of humour. At the time of writing, I haven't seen her in over twenty years—we plan to meet again on the eve of Findhorn's 40th Birthday—around the cosy fireplace in Sunflower B & B on the Field of Dreams! And I am grateful to Thierry at Findhorn Press for blindly believing in both of us, and to Tony in Florida whose editor's eye turned this inside out and back again.

I would not be here writing if it were not for the Angel of Findhorn herself who called me there in the summer of 1970. Once I heard the call, I didn't hesitate. The 'magic' has never left me and has informed my life in a myriad ways for thirty-two years. My most special thanks to Eileen, Peter and Dorothy, without whose vision and obedience to guidance you would not be reading these words. To the Beings of the Devic realms and Roc's beloved 'nature spirits,' about which I am only now beginning to truly understand. To all my many friends and "accomplices" in the early days of the community, especially Ian, Angus, Hugh, Joanna, Ricki and Linda. And to Limitless Love and Truth, which I am still integrating.

And to those of you who have gently or not so gently urged me to write: Greg, Ann, Kathleen, Cynthia, Bruce, Alma, Narayani, Barb, Diego, Ellen, Bill . . . . To the wild and wacky Findhorn Circle—my cyber lifeline. To don Miguel Ruiz and the Circle of Fire; to Starhawk for her luminous perception; to Ammachi and to the Goddess.

And to my children, Khaila and Joss—I love you.